THE ART OF

TRIATHLON TRAINING

A PROVEN GUIDE FOR YOUR TRIATHLON JOURNEY

BY DIRK BOCKEL IRONMAN® CHAMPION & OLYMPIAN.

Table of Contents

Foreword

This is the single step that starts the journey toward the finish line. We all begin here. We are mere mortals catching a glimpse of greatness out of the corner of our eye. A spark lights the fire and we are compelled to act, and ultimately jump into that fire. Doubt might creep in, but as part of the process, it fuels us forward as we construct the path to our own personal triumph.

This is the path that takes us to places where we will fulfill our destiny, bolster our confidence, find our peace, and find ourselves. We train and compete to prove that we are able, no matter the disability, no matter the aching muscles, no matter the mental stress and strain. We take our families along so our lives remain balanced and steady. Sometimes we trek solo because our story demands it. We struggle to reach the summit and amidst the struggle, our lives become enriched and expand. We come to the race with different motivations and abilities. Define your own, to fuel your journey.

What keeps bringing me around to the power and the beauty of the triathlon experience is the depth and the breadth of the experiences, the people and the stories that I witness. I meet people with new and exciting ideas on the design of this grand exploit and it fuels my own journey and strengthens my resolve to live the fullness of my experience.

The people I've met along the way range in age, ability and motivation. David Daggett is a successful lawyer, an experienced triathlete, champion for the sport and devoted family man. I see his dedication and commitment to the sport mirrored in his unwavering support for his community. Triathlon is only one of the anchors that make up the framework of his life. Balancing the four anchors of family (also social), spiritual, physical and professional (also work) has been his formula for a happy life. A good foundation for life learned by building his solid foundation in triathlon.

The practice of moving through the sport of triathlon in search of healing is witnessed in Dustin Brady's story. Triathlon was a challenge undertaken by Dustin in an attempt to transcend his grief after losing his fiancée to breast cancer. Out of shape and carrying extra weight, Dustin trained hard and finished his ironman race as a promise to her. I watched him scatter his wife's ashes, every emotion pushing through the moment. I could almost see the weight being lifted off of his shoulders. The intensity of his efforts allowed him to move through his grief and emerge just a bit more healed and whole.

Marc Herremans' powerful example is a model for perseverance. He sustained a spinal cord injury during training, shortly after an impressive 6th place finish in Hawaii at the World Championships. Most would crumble after such a hit but Marc's warrior heart propelled him to compete again, as a wheelchair athlete, only 10 months after his accident. He has competed each and every year since and it wasn't until 2006 that he finally attained his goal of finishing first as a wheelchair athlete. He has channeled this new focus into developing a foundation to serve others with spinal cord injuries. His life is enriched and ever searching for a path to walk again. Perseverance learned and executed through the test of triathlon.

This is the triathlon family that competes together, celebrates victories and never shrinks from failure. We create and navigate our own trajectory while still feeling the fullness of the triathlon community. We are focused ahead but always witnessing these moving stories just out of the corner of our eye.

From the novice and the amateur, to seasoned age-grouper and professional. My goal in creating this book is to teach and guide you based on the knowledge I have accumulated over the many years that I have trained and raced all over the world. My intentions are to share every bit of insight with you so that you can apply it directly to your own personal blueprint. You can use the information in this book to fine-tune your current plan of action or to start from scratch to form your path to success in achieving your goals. Some of my suggestions might be different from your current approach, but trust in my experience and knowledge and you will become fitter, faster, and more successful than you have ever been, not only in triathlon, but also in life.

Before you get started on the road to your personal success, you will need useful and reliable information that you can use to set realistic expectations for yourself. Of course you could simply line up at the start line and go, but if you want to avoid pitfalls and ultimately be triumphant in the most demanding one-day sports event in the world, you need solid guidance from someone who has been there and has succeeded.

Trust in the wisdom of my experience. I will provide you with draft as you stay on my wheel as we navigate the flyways and byways of triathlon training and racing. I'll share stories from my own experience that contain meaningful takeaways that will carry you to your own success. No secret will remain untold as I reveal all of the shortcuts, the roads less traveled and the wealth of my wisdom and understanding, proven by results, science, and a quarter of a century of experience in triathlon. Together we will dissect the world's toughest one-day sport and put you on the fast track to success. We will get you 100% prepared for your peak race, wringing out the value of every minute you spend training, doing things wisely and with your goal always in mind.

This book was organized as to allow you to jump to any section that you might be interested in based on your particular stage in your triathlon journey. Feel free to move back and forth between chapters as you work these strategies into your own game plan. Enjoy reading and don't forget to take notes along the way. Make use of the power of the present moment when you come across something that resonates with you and plan to implement changes as soon as possible. There is no time like the present. I'll be there along the way until you become a successful triathlete and more importantly: a happy, well-educated and well prepared one!

Please note that I have not been paid or sponsored by any company or persons to use names, products, or examples in my book. You will not find any affiliate links here, and no money or contributions have been accepted to influence the content of this book. It's just you and me, exploring all of the possibilities along the road to the adventure that is triathlon.

Any use of the word IRONMAN in this book is based on the awareness that Ironman (R) is a registered trademark of the World Ironman World Cooperation (WTC), registered in the US and other countries. The use of this word and its meaning in this book is only intended to be explanatory of the event name and its various distances. Use of the term "Ironman®" does not imply any affiliation with or endorsement by them. This publication has not been prepared, approved, or licensed in any way by Ironman®/WTC

Chapter 1: The Call to Act

"The unexamined life is not worth living."

~Socrates

My intention is to elevate your experience on your path to the finish line. You are a triathlete; the novice, the amateur, the expert, the pro. I want you to become a champion.

This is the moment when the gun goes off.

Picture, for a moment, a 9 month old boy with casts on both legs. Legs normally designed for the running and jumping of childhood, forced to sit on the sidelines due to distortions of the bone. Now imagine a man leading the triathlon race at the Olympic Games. Imagine those two are one and the same. Can you dream up the journey that boy took to get there? Who could ever write such a story? That story is mine. What will your story be?

We All Have Our Reasons

My heart was pounding through my chest as my legs singed with lactic acid. I had always been naturally athletic, and pushed myself to the limit plenty of times in my short 14 years of life, but I never had as much on the line as I did that night. That night I was running away, through the dark, away from the sirens of the German Polizei. Jumping fences, cutting through backyard gardens, and scaling walls, I would have done anything to put those blinking lights far behind me, to escape the mess I created for myself, and the life that was leading nowhere, and fast. I had gone from honor student to hoodlum in the matter of one school term, and when the police rolled up to our amateur car heist, running was the only thing I knew how to do.

During one of our gang's nightly joyrides, where we would routinely take one of our parents' cars out on the town in the middle of the night, things didn't end as they usually did, with the car back in the garage before daybreak, parents none the wiser. One of the older guys had taught me how to drive a car and so when he asked me for a special favor, I knew I had to say yes. Unfortunately, this bad judgement resulted in a big, long scratch in the right front fender of his dad's car.

As luck would have it, his parents were out of town so we had two days to fix it. Nothing to worry about, we thought, we would set off together late into the next night, and find another car in the same color and model to swap fenders with. Executing this task was pretty easy considering my buddy knew how to open a car thanks to his part time work at a local car dealership. I would employ stealth tactics to sneak out my bedroom window in service of the mission.

The plan was for us to meet up at 2:00am and drive over to the quiet residential street where the perfect donor car was parked. We would unscrew the fender and take it back home to replace the scratched one, before daybreak, when my friend's dad was returning from his weekend business trip. Unfortunately this wasn't exactly "The Fast and the Furious," and someone must have called the cops when they saw us out there with our flashlights and screwdrivers. I got away that night, thanks to my nimble abilities, but my friends weren't as lucky.

That cold fall night, back in my hometown of Schwaikheim,

proved to be a turning point in my life. One of my buddies ratted us out, and we each had to do community service to pay for our crimes. It wasn't a grave sentence by any means, but it was enough to get my mind thinking that maybe I needed to change something. My parents were upset, to say the least, but their disappointment wasn't much of an incentive for me—the willingness to change had to come from within. How in the world did things go so terribly wrong in such a short time, and how was I going to fix it? Well, I had plenty of time to think about it during the 60+ service hours I spent scrubbing the neighborhood public pool, the Winnenden Wunnebad, the very same pool where I would later find myself every morning before daybreak, torturing my body in that underwater pain cave. That pressure would transform a rebellious young terror into an Olympian and Ironman® champion.

Triathlon saved my life. It shifted my drive in a more positive direction. The path I chose has served me well. Several guys from our skateboard gang ran into serious issues down the road. Most guys were doing drugs, some turned into aggressive hooligans and a few didn't make it out alive. Somehow I escaped that downward slope I was in. I owe this sport all that I have and all I have become. That is reason enough for me to get up in the morning and keep doing what I'm doing. What is your reason? What is your motivation? Why would anyone torture themselves day in and day out to simply have the chance to torture themselves again on race day? There are many ways to put your life under a microscope and test your limits. Why do we choose triathlon?

Triathlon: The Family Tree

1978 Oahu, Hawaii

At an annual get-together, a few tough Navy guys in cutoff jeans and tie dyed t-shirts were chatting and drinking beer, trying to decide which of their athletes were the strongest. They were debating between those who completed the Waikiki Rough Water Swim, the Around-Oahu two-day bike ride and the epic Honolulu Marathon. Many beers later, they came up with the answer. It was agreed that whomever could complete all three disciplines at once, without a break, would be the king of all athletes; the Ironman®. What a crazy idea! It's ancient Greek Myth reimagined.

What is so special about triathlon racing, and what makes it so different from other sports on the planet? Triathlon is unique in that amateurs and age-group athletes toe the start line with the toughest and fastest professional triathletes in the world. Triathletes can meet their heroes on the race course, talk to them, and compete alongside them. No other sport provides this opportunity. No matter if they are young or old, an experienced athlete or a novice in the sport, everyone is treated as an equal. As a general rule, pro triathletes are very easy to approach and enjoy meeting, greeting, and hanging out. Most of the pro guys are down to earth, just doing the sport they love, trying to make a living and enjoying the lifestyle of freedom and endless summers. There is a mutual respect that everyone has for anyone who is able to lay it all on the line to reach their own personal goal. There is a reason why the Challenge Family Race Series chose their slogan: "We are family." Because we really are.

Nowadays, the international reputation of iron-distance events has given the race the official title of the most demanding one day sporting event of all time. At a young age, I had a dream that I would cross that finish line in Hawaii, and a long time ago, I put completing an iron-distance triathlon on my bucket list—it seemed crazy to me at the time. Now I have accomplished and exceeded that goal, and I'd like to give you the opportunity to do the same. Don't just dream about it, toe the line and become the best version of yourself.

Whether it's a Challenge long-distance event, an Ironman® branded event, or the World Championships in Kona, Hawaii, the distance and the accomplishment are one and the same. It is not just about how quickly you finish or which race you decide to compete in. The achievement of finishing an iron-distance triathlon changes your life forever. Are you up for the challenge?

Lately, triathlon has experienced such a boom and increase in media attention that it has led to a much broader understanding by the general public about what it is all about. Races are getting more and more competitive and participation numbers are increasing yearly. For many on the "outside" it may seem a bit crazy and over the top, but the uniqueness of combining the three most popular endurance sports together into one huge endurance fest is what makes triathlon so special and desirable to thousands of people.

Triathlon is booming worldwide and it is a highly addictive sport. There are over half a million licensed athletes in the US alone. Today, decades after the first triathlon, we are able to find a variety of race formats all over the globe. All levels of fitness take part in triathlon and pretty much all ages are able to race, from kids who take the step to complete their first triathlons to those 83+ year old Ironman® finishers in Hawaii. The legacy continues.

Fringe Benefits

Why do so many single discipline athletes choose to switch over to triathlon? The answer is simple; Triathletes are total-athletes. There is a big "wow factor" that comes along with being a triathlete. We constantly receive acknowledgment from others because of the challenge that we have taken on. If you finish an iron-distance triathlon, you will belong to a very small but elite group of individuals. Just imagine how it will feel when you are sitting around at the barbecue with all of your friends and family as you celebrate the completion of another big race. Imagine the recognition, respect, and approval you will receive, not just from them but also from all the people that you know and you will ever know. It is a crazy accomplishment that will give you wings forever, inside and outside of the sport But to earn this feeling you have to work hard to get to the finish line. It is work but it is more manageable when you know how to do it right. Don't be afraid of the unknown. This book will serve as a helpful guide to lead you along the way and I will be your own personal coach.

Once you reach your goal of finishing iron-distance event, or dropping your time down to your own personal best, you will have earned eternal bragging rights that will stay with you forever. You might simply be looking to finish one race or perhaps you've already been bitten by the triathlon bug and raced many events. Either way, you are forever bound to this amazing sport. There are always higher bars to set for yourself; better times, higher placements, and more profound experiences. Even after you finish just one race, you belong to an elite group of uber-athletes. The word triathlete speaks for itself. It shows your confidence and your courage, and your ability to execute a well-thought-out plan in order to succeed in achieving your goal. This reflects on all other aspects of your life as well. Your attitude and your drive will get a big boost to take on the challenge on the race course and also in everyday life.

Imagine how it will feel when you make it to the World Championships in Hawaii and you are hanging out at Lava Java, the typical hot spot in Kona, for everyone who wants to see and be seen. You sit down have a chat with the guys you've only seen in magazines, and everyone in the group accepts you because you belong. Triathlon is like one big family all over the globe no matter what skill level you are. Everyone recognizes and respects the commonalities we have with one another—the tough training, the sacrifices, and the hours and hours invested to get to the finish line.

One of the beautiful side effects of the sport is that it targets the entire body instead of just the upper or lower extremities as with other sports. As a result, this sport makes its athletes very body aware and pretty hot, I might add. It's that "wow factor". The nicest side effect of training for triathlons is that you will get a well-shaped body which you could have never imagined before. The sport and the exercise also keeps you young and dynamic. It's easy to get fit when you love what gets you there. Fitness levels increase as we train and confidence builds up step-by-step, pedal stroke by pedal stroke. Pounds are rolling off the scale and you will see a body transformation week over the week.

When you become increasingly aware of your physical shape it naturally leads to consuming a healthy diet. A race car doesn't run on normal gas, and a triathlete doesn't live on junk food. The aware and mindful triathletes make healthy choices because they want to, not because they have to. They treat their bodies like racing machines and push them to become superior in training by fueling with the healthiest foods.

Learning how to eat right, powers the body and allows it to shift up a gear during training and in everyday life. Simply being aware of what you eat is the first step to being healthy, and combining the input of healthy food and the output of smart training makes all the difference. Keep this in mind: Whatever you consume will later turn into one of your cells that will form your body—you literally become what you eat! The rule of thumb here is to focus on the 95%. We all have some weak moments and that is ok. Does triathlon training reveal the secret to the Fountain of Youth? Imagine yourself as one of those athletes, and then see your older-self being called up on the podium to receive your award at the prize-giving ceremony. Imagine all of the looks you will get when people just can't believe your age. This sport keeps you not only fit but makes you look younger. You will undoubtedly never tire of hearing the words "you look so young for your age!". This scenario is a standard one for triathletes, who have found the secret weapon to battle aging and tap into the hidden source of longevity. Feeling young reflects on your outlook on life, and you enjoy every day more when you have the energy and ability to do what you want. This means that you naturally feel more positive and confident when you approach life. You will soon officially belong to the "guess my age" crowd, and this will deliver a big dose of healthy pride in your accomplishments.

The health benefits of triathlon lead to an overall more powerful and more energetic life for your older and undoubtedly, wiser and fitter self. The joy of getting out in the elements makes you crave the pool, the bike lane and the running trail. Other people around you will notice it too, and they will realize that something has changed, but they might not be able to pinpoint exactly what it is. It might be your positive outlook on things, your level of happiness, and your fit body that draws others to you, but something about you is definitely different. Trust me on this, I have seen it so many times.

Thanks to triathlon, the fitness level that you achieve will help you live a longer, healthier and happier life. Exercise produces endorphins that act as mood-boosters. Plus, when you train for longer periods of time, your blood flow increases and widens any potentially clocked up veins and rapidly delivers more fresh oxygen into your brain. As a side effect, you will get plenty of new ideas and solve some of life's most challenging problems, pedaling along on those long rides. I had times when I took a dictation device with me on my long, easy rides, as my thoughts was going a hundred miles an hour. Top business professionals can vouch for this side benefit which contributes to personal growth and success in any field. It is not that surprising any more, that so many top managers and young professionals use this oxygen boost as their lunch break & cage-clearing activity to improve their performance. The benefits are numerous and the outcome, nearly immediate. You need to be on board!

> *"The goal of life is to make your heartbeat match the beat of the universe, to match your nature with Nature."*
>
> *~Joseph Campbell*

Life's an adventure and it becomes an even bigger one when you add triathlon to it. During training and competition we become more earth-aware because we spend valuable time outside connecting with nature. This makes you appreciate all of the awe inspiring gifts that Mother Nature provides us with. When we sink into that wonderful underwater silence, gliding through the pure water of a crystal clear lake, or when we hear the gravel beneath our feet playing along to the melody of our breath, the connection we have to the earth is pure and undeniable. We can use this connection in our everyday experiences, and it helps to ground us. This mentality informs our lives on many levels and helps us to be grateful for the beauty that the earth provides and challenges us to try to preserve it. “Thinking green” is just a natural result of being outside and “living green”.

Thankfully, being a triathlete allows me to connect with nature as part of my job, but it has also helped to create in me, a love for the outdoors that must be quenched. I personally have a real desire to get outside as much as I can. On my days off, you can often find me out on a boat spending time with fishing pole in hand. This calms me down and refuels my energy. I was a city boy but I mastered the patience and persistence of boating and fishing with the same drive and determination as my chosen sport of triathlon. As an answer to the high intensity of my bike training, you’ll find me bending the mountain curves with my motorcycle, the breeze conforming to my aerodynamic form. I am a badass with a soft heart. For me this is part of being in nature, connecting with the elements, a natural extension of the intensity of training and racing in the elements.

The human body is designed to adapt to the demands you impose on it. Triathlon accommodates with the ultimate demand. It teaches us how to handle stressful situations in races, mentally and physically, and as a result we are able to deal with life’s ups and down’s more easily. We know how to approach a situation that could be stress-inducing and how to remain in control. After you complete an Ironman®, everyday challenges will seem a lot easier to cope with, and with the help of a few tools like visualization and meditation, you will have all you need to deal with anything that life throws at you.

Despite the externalities that we cannot control, this sport teaches valuable lessons that can easily be applied to normal life. It schools us on patience and increases our threshold for the unknown. Sport science teaches us to have on and off days in our training blocks balanced with high and low intensity workouts. Learning and adapting this system of on and off time; switching back and forth between intense work and breaks; helps us to lead a life that has a higher quality. On some days you have to conserve your energy and on other you need to tap in your unknown resources. There is no wasted time, since taking relaxation serious is important too.

My coach once said, you only get better during the off days, as the body has to breathe and adapt after pushing through a crucial workout. More is not always better. It takes courage to do less at times. The key knowledge here is knowing when to push hard and when to rest and recover. One of the most valuable lessons that can be learned from a structured training schedule is that, as triathletes, we need to be efficient and effective at all times. This means no "empty miles" allowed and sticking to a proper plan is crucial.

Overcoming setbacks and obstacles is the primary directive in both racing and training. We don't expect smooth sailing all the time, and that's okay. Nothing worth anything in life comes easy, and we surely have to work hard to achieve our goals—but that is also part of what makes the sport so appealing. If it were easy, then everyone would be doing it, and the truth is that only a few can do it. Sometimes you just have to push through the rough patches and wait for calmer waters before you are able to set sail again. Everything about this sport is extreme, and the ups and downs are no exception. Learning to accept things as they are is part of what can give you an edge.

Revelations appear along the way, inspiring us and driving

us to persevere. We get out there each day and begin again because the stillness of the morning is too silent, because we crave that wind through the vents in our helmets and the sweat dripping down our face. We are fueled by disappointment and get back up when we have crashed. We accept the things that we cannot change and move mountains to change the things we can. Our alarm clocks are those that ring in the darkness at 4:30am; our muscles those that ache with soreness from the previous day's tempo run. Our hearts are the ones that beat out of our chests, pushed to the limits of their capacity, being forced to grow. We are first-timers, seasoned age-groupers, and professionals. We are all the same breed and follow our passion to become a better person through triathlon.

The Seasoned Traveler

I decided to write this book because I want to help people like you reach their goals quickly and effectively, with no nonsense. So many athletes are taught the wrong techniques or the wrong approach to training and racing. There are so many unsound methods I see and hear every day. Many athletes lack structure and just believe whatever they hear on the street, in the locker room, or from a part time semi-professional coach. I see athletes putting in endless amounts of miles and effort, wasting countless hours of training time, with no fruitful outcome. It hurts and saddens me to see people wasting their valuable time and money when they could be enjoying so much more success and fulfillment on their journey.

Having said that, you might wonder what makes me a successful triathlete? And how would I know the winning formula for completing your first triathlon, winning an Ironman®, or qualifying for Kona?

After a lot of questions and just as many wrong answers, I thought that there was a real need for an honest source of information, written from the desk of a successful, professional triathlete, about what actually works. In this book I will be providing you with the tools and the guidelines so you will be able to enjoy your triathlon journey, but remember, the effort to start is yours. I can only motivate you and show you exactly how to operate smarter and better than you can imagine. But when the rubber hits the road, you will have to lay down the work. That's what separates triathletes from the rest of the world's population.

If we have a plan and a clear goal in mind, we do the necessary work to get to the finish line, no matter what. You know this to be true. That is why you are here. So sit back and relax, and let me teach you all that I have learned over the past two decades in this sport. You'll achieve your goals in the most effective and efficient way. It is all in this book—and I am ready to share this with you so that your journey will become more meaningful and more fulfilled along the way.

Over the years, I've met the most successful and influential people in the industry, and I have picked their brains and put their theories to the test myself. There are many different approaches to training, but if you boil it down, there are always more efficient and effective ways to operate. If you cut out the unimportant parts you are left with precision training. I am giving you the necessary tools needed in order to build a champion.

You might be asking yourself, how do I get started? There are so many people out there who are giving advice on how to win races, how to train for your first race or how to reach that peak performance. Well, it's pretty simple really—you just start here, with me. The 27 plus years of experience and knowledge that

I've accumulated throughout my career are infused within this book. I have raced in all possible triathlon formats and have been successful at all of them. I have top results ranging from multiple half iron-distance and iron-distance wins to championships and racing at the Olympic Games in Beijing. I also have a well-respected reputation among athletes, professionals and amateurs alike, demonstrating that I am willing to share my world with others. I don't hold on to those secrets in fear that someone else might steal them. I answer questions honestly and I don't hold back information. My hope is that the wisdom that I have accumulated through treading my path will fuel your own journey.

When I started racing triathlon more seriously in 1992, I was just sixteen years old. From there on I climbed through the ranks of the German national team, collecting a world championship title as a junior and then making the German Olympic selection team in 2004. I was constantly improving. I decided to take up Luxembourgish nationality, after living and training there for many years and then represented my new country at the 2008 Olympics in Beijing. It was an amazing experience, where I led the race for over half an hour, in front of millions of spectators watching on TV, creating a worldwide name for myself in the process. This brought me the name "the bold guy from Luxembourg" when I started racing more in the US in the years to follow.

Once I was able to fulfill my lifetime goal and the Olympic dream became reality, I decided to change it up and graduate to the more prestigious iron-distance racing, which is where my talents seem to lie. Today I can reflect on over 27 years of triathlon training, racing and traveling—and trust me—I have seen and heard it all.

I have seen this sport morph from a relatively obscure,

extreme test of fitness, to a much sought after gauntlet of strength and endurance. I was racing when short distance racing switched from non-drafting to drafting legal in 1995 and when the first triathlon race debuted at the Olympic Games in 2000. I have trained and raced alongside the best in the world; from Germany's biggest names like Olympic silver medalist Stephan Vuckovic, Thomas Hellriegel, and Jurgen Zack; to the contemporary big names that everyone knows today. They all influenced me during my early years.

Growing up in the German National Team, I had a deep understanding of how Europeans train and approach their races. Then, once I moved over to the US to complete my education, I got a taste of how things were done stateside. Thanks to my cross country and swimming scholarship I was able to finish my studies while racing for the university team in Georgia and then later in Florida, where I finished my education.

The American approach to triathlon was different in a lot of ways, and I was very fortunate to be able to experience both schools of thought. I've even crossed over to just racing bikes on a number of occasions when I was picked up by the pro cycling team Leopard-Trek to train and race with the likes of Andy and Frank Schleck, Ivan Basso and Fabian Cancellara. I was always blessed to have the best and most qualified people around me in every area, from personal mechanics and physiotherapists to world class coaches and experts in state of the art technology. I've had the great fortune of utilizing cutting edge technology, from professional wind tunnel testing to running on "AlterG" anti-gravity treadmills, to help to increase my performance on race day.

Through the years, I have always had access to the latest developments and advancements in the sport. You name it, I have 'been there and done that'. Looking back at the humble bike I used back in 1989 versus the latest technologies in aerodynamics, there have been dramatic changes over the years and the shifts keep coming.

Through my experiences I could adapt and filter out what strategies were essential in creating a champion, and which were unnecessary and/or actually holding me back. After all those years of racing, I can proudly say that I have "outlived" a number of triathlon generations and managed to keep a steep learning curve, constantly evolving from the old school approach I took in 1989, to the modernized ITU short distance races, long distance classics and iron-distance races. Through the years, I molded myself into a top professional athlete with an impressive resumé over all distances—starting as an average junior, to participating in the Olympic Games, to several top ten finishes at the Ironman® World Championships in Hawaii, to winning several half and iron-distance events all over the world. I have been able to consistently improve as time goes on. Now, this is what I want to pass on to you.

But in this sport, it's not just the racing that's important, but everything it takes to get you to the start line. Whether you are a pro, aspiring pro, or a novice, it is important to be able to manage the logistics of training, racing, and life in general, while keeping everything in balance. This covers everything from daily training logistics to personal time management. I have learned a lot along the way, and am excited to share all of my secrets to maintaining balance while doing what you love.

I have learned a tremendous amount through the mistakes I've made and the challenges I've faced. I let my failures fuel my success to push me harder and further than I thought I could ever go. I have been able to get down to the root of problems, figure out clear-cut solutions, and accumulate an abundance of information along the way. This information will help you succeed, and I am going to share all of it with you here and now.

Throughout the years I have developed a reputation of being open to sharing my race secrets, even to other pro athletes that I compete with. For me, there are no secrets; there are just ways that work and ways that don't work. I may have wasted quite a few good years of my career trying to figure this stuff out, but it's my intention to save you from doing the same. So whether you are interested in giving triathlon a shot for the first time, or want to fine tune your current method of training and racing; these tools will offer concrete benefits to put you on the right path.

This book is not just a list of shortcuts or a kick-start for your triathlon racing. This is the pure essence of triathlon set in the backdrop of a life's journey, come full circle. This is the recipe for your success and the roadmap for the crusade of a champion. It doesn't matter if you are still sitting on the couch and trying to gather the motivation to start, or if you are already a seasoned racer but have decided that now is the time to step up your game and do it right. It's time to begin. It's time to change your method. It's time to join the team. No more empty miles. No more wasted time. No more money thrown out the window. Only the proven solutions that work best for of all of us; proven by science, confirmed by results, and guided by many years of experience.

Picture yourself being in control of every outcome in your life because you are prepared and you know exactly how to deal with anything that comes your way. This provides you with a great sense of fulfillment and a feeling of confidence and achievement. Every person strives for happiness in life and gaining personal satisfaction, and achieving set goals is one way to get there. It's time to take matters in your own hands and take control.

Let's get to it now.

Chapter 2:
Laying the Groundwork

"By failing to prepare, you are preparing to fail."

~Benjamin Franklin

The best advice I can give you at this stage in the game is that there is no such thing as over-preparing. It's in the planning stages that the rhythm of your race is revealed. It is my intention to give you the tools to create the strongest foundation for the test that is to come—race day.

There are no absolutes. Any advice that you get, needs to be filtered by your own life experience and personal priorities in order to be authentic and effective. However, good foundational planning creates the best possible solid ground for you to strike from, as you propel yourself as a triathlete. Consider the moral tale of Aesop's fable "The Ant and the Grasshopper". The steadfast ant plans for the cold of winter, gathering food for the season, while the undisciplined grasshopper whiles away the summer with no regard for the consequences. Much like the coming winter for the ant, you know the trials ahead. Best not to the keep company with the careless folly of the Grasshopper. Plan for the coming winter and your success will be evident.

Imagine you are building a new house. You don't begin the project by simply piling up bricks and hoping they will take shape. Once you decide that you want to build a house, you begin with a blueprint and plan for every phase of the process. The same applies to your preparation in training and competing. Let's begin constructing the blueprints for your successful journey to becoming a champion.

From the very first step, planning is king. Reducing the likelihood of easily avoidable mistakes will save you time and effort in the long run. Let's keep that in mind while we sit down together to plan your season. Do you have your pen ready? Taking some notes along the way will certainly help; now is the time to get serious. Let's use the power of action to get going and make use of the momentum that it gives you.

Where to Begin

Your current season should be your main focus right now. Whether you are in the middle of your race block, enjoying a winter break, or you are a complete newbie who is trying to learn the ropes before you jump in, you will find valuable information here that you can apply directly and integrate into your current approach. Ideally you should take notes, write in the margins, and make this book your own so you are able to wring out 100% of your potential. In case you are reading this mid-season, be sure to limit your changes to small, well thought through adjustments and try not to interfere with your current plan too drastically. Just implement a slight course correction if needed, and save the big moves for next season.

While motivation is fresh in your mind, you have to lay down the plan for the road ahead. Let's differentiate between two types of planning here; short term planning, which includes your weekly schedule (also called the microcycle), and long term planning, which includes a yearly overview (the macrocycle). To get an overview, it makes more sense to look at the long-term plan. Where do you want to race and what are your mid and long term goals? We'll start by filtering out which of all your desired races should be your "main event" for next season. Once you write it down, we can start to build around your main event.

Next there are a litany of questions to consider for all of your races. Is there enough time to sign up? Are there limitations such as qualifying standards? Will you be able to just sign up and go or will you face some time constraints? Do you have to race the equivalent distance in order to qualify for this race, or is there no qualification needed? For example: Could you qualify in a half distance event for a full distance championship event? Rules change each year so it is important to keep up with the regulations. Do your research. Check online and, if needed, call the race organizer and get a clear overview of the race requirements. Then, if you have to, make adjustments and corrections in your plan accordingly. Think it through and take into account all possible constraints.

Once you are aware of the constraints you have to work within, ask yourself how you can get to the final goal. When you know what is required then the game plan to get there is much easier to map out. It just takes a bit of time and reading to clarify things and make the most logical approach.

Locking in Your Goals

What do you want to achieve? Setting an attainable goal for yourself is key here. Your goal should be realistic but also challenging. Do you want to be in the top □ of the race finishers? Top 100 participants? Or would you like to break your personal record, or improve your swim time? Do you want to finish your first ever long distance triathlon or do you want to place high enough to qualify for a championship event? Goals are as diverse as the people that create them. Your goal might seem tiny compared to someone else's, or gigantic compared to another's, and that is completely normal and perfect. Don't worry about what everyone else thinks at this point—you are sowing the seeds of your future here and now is not the time to look left and right.

Now is the time to take some introspective moments to determine what is going to fuel your “tri-fire". Listen to the challenge that is pulling on your heartstrings. Meet that challenge using your own compass to guide you; pure and authentic. Maybe you always had this dream in the back of your mind but didn’t really bite into it up until now because you didn’t know where to start. Or perhaps you just didn’t think it was possible. Well, it’s time to dream big. Pick something that motivates you when you envision it. You might be climbing the epic “Solarer Berg” at Challenge Roth, surrounded by thousands of spectators. Or maybe it is making it to the finish line of the most mythical race, The Ironman® World Championships in Hawaii. Just about anything is possible with enough planning and hard work.

Pick a particular race on a specific date and location. It’s better to say, “I want to race at Challenge Roth next year” than “I want to do a triathlon one day”. When you set a specific goal it helps you to stay focused for a very specific amount of time, and it also helps you to be able to celebrate once you reach that goal (need an excuse to treat yourself, here it is). Remember, if you don’t have a specific goal in mind then you aren’t training, you are just exercising.

You will be able to measure your progress on your way to your goal when you set your milestone goals leading up to your event. I will go into detail about this in the next pages. Having a plan that takes into account measured tests will give you the confidence to approach your big event knowing that you are 100% ready.

Pick a goal that stokes your motivational fire. Realize that it might seem crazy, but so many things are possible if you give it enough time combined with blood, sweat and tears (yes, there is a good chance that all will be spilled on the way to your goal). If you are totally committed to achieving it, YES, you can. Make sure your goal is something that you are willing to go the extra distance to achieve, and therefore it needs to make your heart beat with intention when you think about it.

Be honest with yourself about how far you're willing and able to go to get to your goal. Only the sky is the limit here, and if you really want it, then you will work for it. There are so many accounts of the power of the human spirit when it comes to racing triathlons. Regular people with seemingly ordinary lives have done extraordinary things out there on the racecourse. The only difference between these people and others is that they wanted it so badly.

Take an inward look and see exactly where your motivation lies. Be real to yourself about how long it might take to get to your goal and know that sometimes it takes longer than you think. Don't be discouraged, if through this process you have to change some things around and reconcile your plan to the way your body is responding. You are still moving forward and that's what matters. Don't miss out on the scenery along the way. It's truly about the lessons you learn during this process more that it is about the end result.

It is also helpful to remember times in your life where you were able to overcome the odds and achieve something that seemed impossible. Maybe you learned a new language, moved to a new city, or quit a horrible job. Perhaps you walked up to that pretty girl at the dance and now she is your wife. Don't forget that you are already a hero, and that triathlon is just going to help you to remember it.

Now is the time to get your desired end goal down on paper.

You can also create a less specific mid-term plan that takes into account the next two to three years, along with a more distant and even more flexible five-year plan. Treat the planning phase for triathlon like you would a business plan. What's important is that you work your way backwards from the future goal to where you are now. From now until you reach your peak race (your main goal), you will set milestones for yourself that you will hit over time, and then even more frequently smaller milestones (i.e., test races) along the way. This will help you to realize whether or not you are on the right path to your main goal. I use a Milestone Chart in order to track my goals and develop short and midterm goals that get me to the end goal.

Don't get overwhelmed with a major five-year schedule; it should just be a rough plan that helps you to sort through your ideas, but nothing that is detailed. It is helpful just to see where you envision yourself down the road. The planning part helps you to get organized and get you moving. You've got to throw some paint up on the wall before you start rolling. Be aware that there will be changes and necessary adaptation that will happen on the road, so don't be a slave to your plan. It is a bit like being on a sailing trip and having a certain route mapped out in your mind. When the weather changes you need to correct your course. You may take a slightly different route, but your final destination should be the same.

Once you have a clear understanding about which race you want to target as your main goal, you then have to sit down and consider what kind of personal constraints and possible limitations you have to work within in order to achieve your goal. A professional triathlete who has the greatest support and lots of time on their hands to train will have much different constraints than those of a CEO working 60+ hours a week, or a mother juggling their kid's interests, cooking dinner, and training on the side whenever time allows.

No matter what else you have going on besides triathlon, it is important to realize that triathlon is not going to be 100% of your life—not even if you are a pro. You will need to have time for your friends and family outside of those 40+ hours you spend in your office, or in the pool, on the bike, or on the running trails. Keep your balance by revisiting and resetting your priorities as your life plays out. Blend your goals into your life with harmony not in opposition to the flow of your existence.

Considering your triathlon related goals over the next few years and think about how you will plan your life around them. You should ask yourself some important questions. Does your partner & family support and approve of your goals? Are they willing to make sacrifices so that you are able to reach your goal? If not, some complications could arise down the road, so address them now and expectations can be clearly managed on both sides of the relationship. Now is a good time to take a few notes about what your personal constraints and possible limitations are.

Consider the following:

- Exactly how much time are you willing and able to devote to your triathlon project?
- Is it possible for you to make a compromise by focusing on other parts of your life in the winter and then adding an additional 5 or more hours per week to your triathlon goal in the warmer months?
- What kind of physical constraints are you dealing with?
- Do you have any nagging injuries that keep you from doing specific workouts?

- Where is your fitness level at the moment and what is the status of your health? If you aren't sure, it might be worth consulting a doctor to make sure you get a green light to start training.

- Are ideal training facilities and conditions nearby? If not, are you willing and or able to commute for certain workouts?

- Where is the closest indoor and outdoor pool? Are you able to swim there year round? Do they allow lap swimming? When do the local swim groups meet for practice? Is there a 50-meter pool someplace within driving distance? Is it set up as long course or a short course pool? Does the pool schedule change based on the time of year? Are there times of day that are less busy than others?

- What are the best roads to ride on for an easy ride, and then for a long ride, and which will suit you best for tempo rides, with no traffic lights and stop signs involved for those longer, uninterrupted sections? What time of day do the roads have the least amount of traffic? This will give you an indication about when to ride.

- Can you start easy runs from your door? Where are the nearest trails for your long runs?

- When are group rides and group runs?

- Do you have enough funding for your project (think about start fees, travel expenses, training camps, and coaching)? How much can you devote to your project to procure material? Do you have a yearly/monthly budget that includes triathlon?

- If you already have a bike, does it need any upgrades? Are you at the stage where you are ready to invest in both a racing and a training bike?

- Are you able to borrow material from training buddies if you cannot afford them right now?
- Can you take time off from work to travel to your race, or do you have to limit your potential travel time?

Don't forget, it's all about location, location, location. Where you live will act as a constraint that will dictate your travel needs and when your most intense training will take place. Make sure that you take that into account before you pick out your main race goal. For example, if you live in New York, you may not want to plan to race in the heat of Mexico in January, since you won't have much of a chance to train in the winter up there. But, if you live in Australia, this might be the ideal time to race. Later on I will also address the concrete training material and race techniques that you will need. For now, let's just focus on this and consider your ideal schedule and those constraints that you need to work with, in order to create a realistic season plan.

When you create your weekly overview, mark the busy days and those days when you have more time to play with. It's best to place the longer sessions, such as long rides or the potentially more time-consuming swimming pool adventures, in those slots. I do this kind of planning with every athlete that I coach because even the best training plan does not work if it doesn't fit your everyday restrictions. I use the same strategy for myself. As I said, pro athletes have constraints just like everyone else, and most of the time, the more successful the athlete gets, the more constraints they have!

Create your new weekly schedule with the most important tasks blocked off first, such as work or picking up the kids from school. When you have them all listed, start with prioritizing them by adding numbers in front. One is the most important and should be filled into your new weekly schedule first. It helps to have the entire week listed, from Monday morning till Sunday evening.

Some might prefer the 5:30 am swims while others might like to start training after brekkie or even late at night on the trainer. Don't forget to take into account the weather and time of the year. During the summertime it's much easier to get up early and get out the door due to longer hours of daylight and warmer temperatures. In the wintertime it might be a bit sketchier and outdoor sessions might have to be replaced with indoor sessions. In case you have a holiday planned, you could also be free of working constraints and that could allow you to plan a bit more freely.

Out of experience, the pool schedule is usually the most difficult to work around due to the restrictions of opening times and lane availability. Sometimes it might be efficient to combine two sessions in order to have less time wasted driving back and forth. If the running trails are on the way to the pool or close by, it might be best to plan a combo session to free up some time instead of spending half your day driving to and from the pool and trails.

Your training schedule needs to work for you and not the other way around. If you already have a routine, review it and see where there could be space for improvement. There will always be room for a few little tweaks. If you work late on Thursdays, then don't plan big sessions that will make you exhausted and unable to focus. If the only time you can spend with family is on Saturday afternoon, then plan to wake up early to knock out your long rides before the kid's soccer games start. Make sure your priorities are in check and then you won't need to cancel or move sessions around. Be realistic about how long it takes to complete your session and how tired you will be afterwards.

You might not want a very detailed plan for every week, but it might help if you isolate the days where you have more time and those where you are crunched for time. This will give you a good indication of what sessions can work on any given day. If you are a semi-pro or a pro with a lot of obligations, you may be able to plan your administrative work around your training. If that's the case, you can build your schedule the other way around: First the training and then fill in the gaps. That's how I do things.

What an overwhelming amount of information to consider. I know, it's true. This is the crucial groundwork we lay to create a smooth path to your end goal. Careful consideration is required BEFORE the endless hours of training begin. This is exactly why I am addressing this topic right from the get-go. We will get through this process step by step. I have worked out a system to help you plan out your season goals in a realistic way, which works within your own personal constraints. Making everything fit is sort of like putting together a puzzle, so take your time here to think it all through and put the important pieces together first. Then the big picture will begin to reveal itself. Be patient but diligent.

Constraints are not bad things; they are what create a frame around your goal. They will make the challenge much more interesting and fun, and make crossing the finish line all the more rewarding. Constraints are what make racing worth it, and triathlons wouldn't be a true test without some limiting conditions and rules that we have to work within. The same goes for training and race preparation for any triathlon event. At the end of the day, juggling all of those constraints is what makes training, competing in, and finishing races so much of a joy. All of those sacrifices involved are the investments we make for that amazing feeling that we get when we train for that big race and the ultimate achievement: to cross that finish line in your goal time.

The Right Plan

I had just finished racing the World Championships in Hawaii in 2011, finishing 4th, just a few short seconds away from the podium. I had just missed one of my lifelong goals of finishing in the top three in Kona, but despite that, I was very pleased with my race. Just days after racing, my partner and I took off to drive to a deserted beach on the big island, in order to reflect on the season and to analyze the main goal of the year. After hours of chatting and discussing everything, we realized that I had to make a few changes in order to fine-tune my performance for the next year.

One of the key elements that we discussed was to cut out some of the stress we experienced during that season. I always seemed to have “energy draining“ circumstances that took place during my race preparation, which we decided it was about time to eliminate. We figured out that this was a key factor to increasing my performance. We also considered increasing my training mileage and including slightly different speed sessions (at the time I thought I was lacking in running mileage and long tempo runs). We also decided to reduce my travel time over the year. To start the next season off right and lay the groundwork, I came up with a few other ideas. Another key factor was not to gain too much weight in off-season so I would be able to get back into training much more quickly after the break and then wouldn’t have to deal with any injuries that seemed to come up because I tried to run with too much Christmas weight.

So, it was clear that there were some changes in store for the next season, which I needed to start taking into account right away. Since I wanted to keep my motivation high, I needed to be willing to get going on these changes right way. When you are motivated to do something, it is best to do it directly, using momentum to help keep you rolling.

The plan was to change a few things right away, and I wrote everything down in my Moleskine notebook, which I keep on hand for any ideas that strike me when I least expect it. I listed everything that I could improve upon, as I didn't want to forget a single detail of the fruitful brainstorming session that could only come from the emotion of just finishing an Ironman®. It's sort of like childbirth, or so I've heard, once time passes by you forget about the pain of the event and those little irks and negative points become a distant memory.

Among the changes, I decided to focus on a healthy diet in the off-season, instead of just when races were approaching. Of course I still allowed myself "reward food" and plenty of "reward drinks" after the race, but I tried not to drink too many calories and focused on eating healthy at dinnertime and late-night, when I often made poor food choices.

When I got back to the mainland, I only took two weeks off and then started back at it with mild training sessions. It's worth mentioning that previously I had been taking six weeks off and usually four of them completely off, where I would proceed to reward myself and sometimes overdo it and gain quite a bit of weight. This new adjustment allowed for some "off time" to recover from racing but also prepared me for the first block of training straight after the break. So, I stayed slim and fairly fit over the break and then got right back into my training routine.

My engine was pretty much running on idle during that time.

Just to avoid any injuries, we started with a three-week block of cross-country skiing (ski-skating in the Alps in Austria) to ease back into training and to extend the re-adaptation process. Cross country skiing is a great workout that enables you to work hard but still save your bones from ongoing impact that you feel during running sessions. It also limits the risk that you will get fed up with the swim/bike/run routine and reduces the chance of overloading your engine too quickly straight after the recovery period. Ski skating is a full body sport that requires you to use your arms as well as your legs, and it is tough! The skiing allowed me to be able to enjoy a change of scenery while also working hard on my fitness. The result was that I stayed injury-free while building up a solid base during the first block of training.

The next step in the planning process concerned my race schedule, where I set myself three main goals for the year ahead. Up until that point, I still hadn't won an Ironman®, so I decided to pick an ideal race that was someplace close to home and that suited my strengths well. I defined my three season goals of 2012 by choosing to race Ironman® Regensburg, ITU Long Distance World Championships (six weeks later) and the Ironman® World Championships in Hawaii at the end of the season. I wasn't shy about putting my goals out there, as I wanted to make sure that it was clear to the press that this was my only focus for this year, and that I would be ready for those races. I wanted to be measured by my results at these races, and not have any opportunities to look for excuses down the road. By announcing this early on, I also put quite a bit of pressure on myself. I filled in a few smaller races around those peak races to create a nice mix of sponsor obligations and "must do races" (Kona qualification races).

Exposure is good, but racing too much could turn into a disaster. The risk of injury is always present, and over-racing is draining, mentally and physically. On the flip side, if you race 10+ races per year, you are sure to have one or two good races. Many triathletes use this approach. The only problem with this outlook is that it is a gamble. For me there is no gambling, I need to be 100% certain that I'm in shape at that given day, not a week before and not two weeks after. Now, which scenario would suit your temperament? Which scenario appeals to the developing champion inside of you?

At this point in my journey I made the choice to outline my macro cycle in order make my race plan fit. I started with the big milestones and then filled in the gaps. It is vital that you work backwards from your main goal. Just like filling a jar full of stones and sand, you want to start with the big rocks first and then add the sand in afterwards, otherwise "filling in the gaps" doesn't work very well.

In my plan I also tried to integrate other date constraints such as very important family obligations, press and photo shoots, sponsor meetings, down time, etc. It's the same for everyone; you might have a business meeting where you have to fly out for the week and training is limited, or you might have your son's birthday party, or your wedding anniversary dinner. You want to make sure those obligations are clearly mapped out before you start the process of filling in races. Remember to prioritize.

For me, it all starts with the first big constraint, which is based on the previous season's Kona result. I can only create my season plan when I know that I have enough points to qualify for the next year's race. If not, then I decide whether or not I want to run around and race in order to gain points to qualify for Kona. If I do, I look at which point-scoring races I want to target as milestone races. If I have enough points to qualify, I schedule in more lucrative and interesting races as milestones instead of those races that I must do in order to qualify for Kona, which tend to be less fun, less lucrative, and less motivating.

> *"The best-laid plans of mice and men often go awry."*
>
> *~Robert Burns (adapted from)*

It is obvious that even the most sophisticated plan needs to be updated frequently. For instance, when my new team informed me that I had to attend certain training camps, I blocked that time off right away. The good thing about being a pro is that people understand that you need a lot of advanced notice before you can plan to attend any event. If you don't have the luxury of having a long-term schedule, you are going to have to be a bit more flexible.

Your race build up should make sense and your training should correspond to it. Plan around important dates as much as you can. Be aware that there will always be unexpected obligations that come up, and accept the fact that this is normal. It's called having a life! And it's the same for every person toeing the start line: Shit happens. I would even take it a step further and claim that no athlete is 100% fit for their peak races. We all have to carry our fair share of obligations and limiting constraints with us. The best athletes just make the best possible compromises and roll with the punches, getting as close to top shape as possible. It is not about perfection, rather it is about working around the uncontrollable and unpredictable constraints in order to come close. That's what we should all strive for, in competition and in our daily lives.

I personally have dealt with this on a number of occasions,

and have had to change my schedule tons of times because of things that come up. For instance, in 2015 I had an unexpected injury come up just a few days before the World Champs, and had to sit out of my two peak races. On top of that, I had to cancel my fly fishing holiday in the Scottish Highlands because I needed to wear a cast. It was hard at first, but I just sat down and sketched out my next steps, creating new goals and a new plan. Everything shifted from looking back in anger to looking forward in hope. It's an effort worth undertaking. The pages of this book are a living example.

Now that you have an idea about how to sketch out your season, when would be the best time to make your plan? The answer is, anytime is a good time. Ideally, though, it would be in the wintertime or after your last race of the year. Then your head is clear and you are open to evaluate and rethink a few points for the following year. I usually start the new planning phase for the next year after my last big peak race is done (usually that would be the World Championships in Hawaii). My next year's season is always influenced by how well I do in that race. If I do well, I don't have to worry too much about getting points and running around to do lots of races that I don't necessarily want to do. If I have a bad year in Hawaii, then I have to adjust my ideal plan for the following year accordingly, to make sure that I make it to the big dance in Kona, or whatever other race I set as my season goal.

Some constraints are unknown until specific points in time, so planning has to take place at a time when there are as many "known" constraints as possible. However, you must still be open to changes. My coach used to get annoyed with me as I always tried to have 100% clarity before I even started to get back into training. The funny thing is, the first few weeks of getting back into the flow of things doesn't come with too many surprises, whether you race in early March or the beginning of

May. Don't get too caught up into the details here. Trust me. It will all fall into place. After every rough draft, there is another draft, and then another and another…

Mind Games

After you have a fairly clear overview of all of the things that you would like to achieve this season, you might be a bit intimidated by all that lies ahead. You may ask yourself, can I really achieve these goals? Your new set of goals should be big ones and therefore they are not going to be easy. That's the point, isn't it? A feeling of doubt is pretty normal and it is something that everyone, even professionals, experience. This is why, within this planning stage, you should create a mission for the mind—one plan that focuses your intent in a more abstract way, bringing all of the specifics into one moment of clarity of purpose. A plan that creates a touchstone that reinvigorates your purpose when the sea of doubt creeps in. It is crucial for success; nourishment for the soul. This is how the plan becomes an achievement.

When I was on the verge of qualifying for the Olympics in 2008, I knew I needed a mental boost. For my "mission for the mind" I decided to contact my friend Simon Kessler, a former pro-cyclist from South Africa. After his pro career he went on a spiritual journey, which brought him to a place of great wisdom and understanding. Now he is a sort of a life coach for me, so I approached him about getting some insight into the mental side of my racing.

Simon and I met for the first time during my college years in Tampa, and I noticed right away that he had a certain calming vibe about him that I appreciated. I soon found out that he was an avid meditator, and after speaking with him about ways to improve my own mental game, I started meditating as well.

At first I just tried guided meditation sessions on YouTube and shortly after I got into a routine of meditating whenever I felt like I needed it. I still meditate twice daily and I really believe it calms me down and helps me to focus. I have learned to accept the world how it is, constraints and all, and resist the temptation to try and change it. We must recognize that our ideal situation is limited by those constraints, and accepting them can help us to not waste valuable time and energy that we need to invest in more productive tasks. Learning to accept things the way they are, can be a long process, and it requires a change in beliefs that slowly starts to permeate your life through the act of meditation.

Consider adding meditation to your bag of tricks. It only takes a few short moments of your day, but the effect on your life could be monumental. There are many different methods of meditation. The choice often comes down to personal preference and which method is most effective for your own sensibilities. When I started out, I had problems centering myself and got distracted easily by random noises, so I used noise-canceling headphones to achieve silence. The typical Yogananda position, with bent knees, didn't seem to work for me either. I guess my legs are too stiff for that. So I figured that a normal, upright sitting position would do the same job for me. The key is to focus in on finding your peace, regardless of where or how you do it; there is no right or wrong, just find your own path. Simply try it out and get started with it today.

Simon also taught me about the Ultimate Intention Statement (UIS). This is a written report that asks you to believe in what is yet to come by using positive feelings as a catalyst to allow yourself to experience your success before it even happens. It's like getting into a simulator for your life. Create it in your mind's eye: live it with conviction. Consider this approach for your own mental game plan. The basic steps are as follows:

- Write down exactly how you wish the race to unfold.
- Use a perspective of gratitude when writing it and involve the feeling you would experience when you imagine the race.
- Read it as often as possible; 2 times a day for 3 minutes, then once a week for 30 minutes. The key is to frequently read it and become familiar with it.
- Finally, you have to believe it. Only when you strongly believe it, will the UIS work for you.

Simon and I created a helpful YouTube video about The Ultimate Intention Statement. Use this video to further investigate whether this particular Mind Game will fit into your own mission for the mind.

Try writing your own Ultimate Intention Statement for an upcoming race. Don't focus on the concrete outcome or on the facts, like your position in the race. Instead, focus on the positive feelings and the emotions you will experience during the imagined future race. Start with those pre-race feelings that will come about on race morning and then go through the pre-race procedure, uniquely focusing on positive feeling. Then go through each discipline, remembering to put things in the present tense. Picture yourself as you are talking to a reporter after your huge success. Remember to only focus on the good vibes you will encounter, not a specific outcome or any hard facts. Immerse yourself in the process. It will give you a competitive edge and lead you to great success!

Before my first Ironman® race, Simon had me read my UIS

"report" twice a day over a period of two months. At some point I really started to believe what I wrote down weeks before, and was able to use the positive affirmations to my advantage. It took away my race anxiety and other negative thoughts that I may have had. These are powerful tools to use to bridge that mind / body gap.

Before I really got started with Ironman® racing in 2009, I had a hard time believing in these types of "new age" ideas. Now I use them all the time because I know they work and they really help me mentally prepare for races. When I considered signing with my new team in 2014 (Uplace-BMC Pro Triathlon Team) I had the chance to work with another mental coach and I believe there is still ground to be covered and enough space to improve mentally. Just think about how much we train our bodies compared to our minds. It seems like the mind is forgotten while we try to fit the brick workouts, tempo runs, and core sessions in. What we are doing here is simply creating a more even playing field between the mind and the body; a bridge to travel between the two. This consideration will be extremely important in your development as a champion.

Use whatever tool works for you, as long as it helps you to follow through with your goals. Focus on using them when you have doubts that creep in, or when you are lacking motivation. I highly recommend the work of Dr. Timothy Noakes from South Africa. He has written some amazing books about this component of sport, among other sport topics. He discusses the mental side of athletic performance, specifically how the mind controls the body. He calls the brain "the central governor" — in essence the maestro running the show.

For exploring options for meditation I recommend checking out the Headspace app, which comes with a set of free mediations that were developed by Andy Puddicombe, a

Buddhist monk turned entrepreneur. He also has a wonderful TED Talk which explains why mediation is so critical to our daily lives. Currently, I practice Transcendental Meditation. You can find out more about this type of meditation at www.TM.org.

I have found that the most important mental tool to use, specifically during training and before races, is visualization. It really is the strongest mental weapon in your artillery. Once your mind believes something, then your body will follow. Imagine your next race—maybe it is your peak race. By closing your eyes, you are fast forwarding the time and picturing yourself at the race. I find it even more productive to visualize while I am training, with eyes wide open, in a similar fatigued state as race day. I feel the pain, and prepare myself mentally for the suffering that's to come. I envision myself experiencing the sights and sounds of the race course, going through transition, and running through the finish chute.

These images help to deal with the upcoming reality. You can go through the preparations, the transition set up procedure, the starting procedure or simply see yourself out on the course, performing and achieving your goal. Imagine it and live it in your "dreams". This visualization process will help you to feel more at ease when it comes down to race day, as you already experienced it and have become mentally prepared.

The Mental Game in Action

In 2009, when I started racing Ironman®, I decided to shift my running stride from a short distance running style into a shorter much more frequent stride that was prevalent in long distance racing. The result was that I promptly got injured. I added way too many steps per minute to my stride cadence and I ended up with super tight calves, which later developed into plantar fasciitis (a nagging injury of the tendon underneath the foot, closely linked the calf muscles gastrocnemius and soleus). Basically, I couldn't run for the last 7-8 weeks before my first ever Ironman® race, in New Zealand. This is what I would consider very bad timing!

I adapted to my injury by replacing my run training with aqua jogging, cross training on the elliptical machine, and more mileage on my bike and swim. All looked okay until the last few weeks before the race, where I started to struggle mentally. So, we decided to step up the mental game. My partner had the crazy idea of ordering me a gold medal and engraving it with "Ironman® Champion". At first I felt terrible about having it on display because I thought I had to earn a win before I was able to hang it in my room. Then after giving it some thought I changed my mind and went ahead and hung it up next to my bed, where I looked at it several times a day. It was the first thing I saw in the morning and the last thing I saw before I fell asleep.

I used visualization techniques to imagine myself gliding through the clear water of Lake Taupo and exiting the water at the front of the pack, stripping my wetsuit off effortlessly, and mounting my bike to push through the crowd lined streets. I heard the sound of the spectators cheering me on during every run training session that I did through the roads of Taupo. Since I was able to train on the race course for 3 months leading up to the race, it was even easier for me to practice visualization and let the emotions and feeling of leading the race sink in on a daily basis.

Slowly, I started to accept the thought that I would actually be able to win the race, regardless of my running setbacks. Come race day, I was close, really close. I didn't quite make it to the very top that time around, but the quality of this experience fueled the momentum needed to make it to the podium, securing my Kona qualification slot. This was a win for me and it allowed me to win several races down the road. I still have that gold medal, and when I actually won my first Ironman® I couldn't stop thinking about it. The best bet is to always be on top of your mental game, even when your body seems to be in less than optimal shape. Use mental tools to your advantage and they will be ever valuable for you along the path to your personal goals.

I believe in the Law of Attraction, and I have proven its power to myself over and over again. It works—period. The Law of Attraction, which I initially learned about from the movie “The Secret” (introduced to me by my friend Simon), simply states that you will attract what you think about and believe in over time. If you’re hoping not to puncture on that bike ride when it starts to rain, you end up thinking about puncturing the entire time, and then what happens? You puncture. Emotions give beliefs weight, and fear is a strong emotion.

This is a negative example of The Law of Attraction, but it is obviously better to practice attracting positive things into your life. If you envision yourself finishing your race with a big smile on your face and overcome with joy, that will most likely be the outcome. The idea can also be viewed as your mind sending out positive thoughts and therefore attracting similar positive thoughts. Remember the saying: Once it rains, it pours? Or, when you think positive, good things will happen? This is also the basis of faith in many religions. When you have faith, you can move mountains and push watts you didn’t know you had in you.

Everything is possible if your mind is strong enough to handle the sudden changes and obstacles along the way. If you have these helpful mental tools in your toolbox; the UIS, visualization techniques, and the Law of Attraction; there is no need to fear failure. Try to incorporate these mental games into your daily routine and you will soon see the magic.

Building Your Support Team

The next logical step in your planning strategy is for you to decide how to structure and build your "support team". I like to place my support team in the category of "mental game" because it provides me with motivation and accountability. Triathlon is much more fun and so much easier when you have people surrounding you who motivate and inspire. Fellow athletes and friends, whom you can relate to, help you to enjoy a good time whilst on the way towards your goal. Your support crew is important on and off the course. If you are new to the sport don't worry. It's pretty easy to find a group to train and share your passion with. As a more advanced triathlete it becomes slightly more difficult to find the perfect fit in terms of training partners, but it is certainly achievable.

There are numerous ways to find your support team, even when traveling away from your homeport. You just have to keep your eyes open and meet people on the road, or alternatively you could take a more direct approach, like I do. Do some research. Get your computer and Google triathlon and the name of your city, and you will most likely find a group that is already organized and that meets regularly. Since the swimming part is the hardest to organize, start looking into this area first. I always use the website SwimmersGuide.com. This is a valuable tool because as a triathlete you will be married to locations that have lap pools.

Check out your local pool schedule online and since we live in the world of gadgets, take a snapshot with your smartphone. Then you will always have the various pool schedules with you wherever you go. This is great to have in case you're stuck somewhere without Internet and would like to check if you can sneak in a quick swim. Nothing is more annoying than driving to the pool to find that it's closed or kid's playtime is in session. There goes your workout for the day.

The lifeguards can always give you a few pointers about when masters swimming groups come in or even introduce you to some of the regular swimmers, which will help increase your support group of nice, like-minded folks. Since they spend all day watching the pool, they also might know the best time of the day to swim, in case you prefer to swim your own program during open lane hours. This pretty much covers about 99% of my swim sessions, since I like to do my own thing in the water. Consider what's best for you as you progress in your fitness over time.

If you prefer swimming on your own, I totally understand. For seasoned triathletes or people who were swimmers in their previous lives, all you will really need is a pool clock to show you your speed, and maybe a training partner or two to push you when needed during those extra long or fast sessions. You may even want to spice it up with a group swim every now and then to help with the motivation.

However, if you are a beginner you will need some help if you want to step up your game, for example, by taking some private lessons or talking to a swim coach. A very effective way of analyzing your swim is by simply asking someone to film you when you're swimming a solid workout. You'll see all the little mistakes in your swim stroke right away. Watch it a few times and then make a list of how to improve. Read this list before every swim so you are reminded of what to focus on during the next set.

If I am traveling and starting to swim at a new pool, the first thing I do is to check in with the lifeguards to get valuable basic information about the groups. If you are an advanced swimmer, then look for some faster guys to swim with. Don't be intimidated. You have to surround yourself with "better," or in this case "faster," people in order to step up and progress. This is the quickest and most effective way of improving. You might want to start out on your own, before joining the local swim team. This will allow you to get familiar and comfortable in the water. Don't go right to the fast lane. Start modest and then work your way up.

The coach of the Masters Team will usually advance you when they notice that you are too fast for the lane you are swimming in. Your willingness to let the coach do their job will be appreciated by all the regulars on the team. Remember, you are trying to build a support team around you, not create enemies. You need the members of the team so that you can progress. So treat them like you would a training partner. Treat them with respect so you can mutually benefit. And there you have it! You now have some members in your support team!

Much of the same applies to cycling. Depending on where you live, you'll most likely see plenty of people out riding, especially the weekend warriors. But if you're looking for more contact with cyclists, the local bike shop is the best place to go and ask about group rides. Bike shop crews usually ride themselves and have a good idea about when group rides take place and where the local groups meet up to train together. Maybe you aren't at a level where you feel comfortable riding with the fast guys yet. See if there are any slower groups that ride. Many times there is a mix of different skill levels on each ride. In fact most groups stay together till a certain point and then divide up into different distances and speed groups. It's a natural process that happens in cycling group training.

You may want to ride a few times by yourself to get comfortable and then take the step to join in on the group rides on the weekends. If you can make some contacts, it will be a good idea to start out riding with a few guys who are on the same level that you are on and who take their goals just as serious as you do yours. You will figure out pretty fast how to separate the coffee group rides from the serious guys.

For triathletes it's hard to find interval partners, as you should be working hard at a sustained pace, riding in the wind and not taking turns at the front like the roadies, where they are sheltered from the wind most of the time. Keep that in mind if you're planning sessions with more speed and let others know beforehand. This will save you discussions and your valuable training time (and of course some nerves). It is great to have company during those long sessions and it's fun to chat and learn about the people in the group. Along the way, I've made many friends, a testament to the balancing of strict training with the development of connections within the sport we all love. Don't underestimate the advantage gained from reaching out and sharing your training experience with others.

Running groups operate much the same. Let me tell you how I approached the problem of not having anyone to run with when I first moved to my winter base in St. Augustine, Florida. After running by myself for a few days, I got bored and wanted a change. So I Googled the local running club and emailed their contact person on their webpage, asking for some faster local runners. I promptly got a reply with the number of the best runner in town, Todd Neville, whom I cold called right away. Just a few days later, we met up and ran together for the first time. It turned out to be a great match. He was fast, focused, and he knew what he was doing. We ran together and chatted a bit, but after a while, we actually found out that we both just like to focus on getting the job done, and don't really like to chat too much during our runs.

After a few runs, Todd became one of my closest friends and we still run together today. After our friendship grew, he got the triathlon bug. One year, I had to fly to IM Florida by myself, and so I asked Todd if I could stay with him for a few days to acclimatize, as I was coming from Europe. I asked Todd if he would be keen on helping me out for the weekend, accompanying me to Ironman® Florida. He did and we had a blast. While I was recovering the next morning from the race, he secretly got in line and signed up for his first ever Ironman® race the following year.

From there on out, I helped coach him and get him ready to race his first ever Ironman®. In Florida, he qualified on his first attempt for the world champs in Kona! We trained quite a bit together during our Kona preparation and both benefited big time from "sharing the pain" during our sessions. After accomplishing his goal of getting a slot for Kona, he shifted his focus on growing his company and leaving his stamp in local politics, and has been hugely success at both. Isn't it amazing the ripples we create when we reach out and build our team. It permeates every part of our lives and those we invite in.

So, you can see how making random calls like this can end up developing into great experiences. Of course, you might not want to pick out the fastest guy in the group to train with for starters, but it is always nice to have someone at your level who you can train with. You will find that those long runs together will help you build up long lasting friendships, and separate the dedicated and hard working from the rest.

Remember to accept the challenge and surround yourself with better, faster training buddies. Remember to remain realistic in terms of your own abilities, not just in the swim, bike, run arena, but also in life. Only then you can grow as an athlete and as a person. This link is inseparable.

You might ask yourself, what else could I do if I don't find a tri club in my area? Well, I had the same problem back then. I talked to Todd about it and we figured out that there were several individual triathletes in the area but there was no club or platform to connect with one another. Shortly after that, we had a dinner with a few tri-guys at a friend's house. After a few drinks, we came up with the idea to create our own local triathlon club. We were in the tiny town of Elkton and we had a few International guys around the table. Here was the birth of EIT2: Elkton International Tri Team. It provided a platform for many local triathletes to connect and train together. Because we have our own jerseys and identity, it provides motivation and serves a higher purpose to many of us. And now, the baton has been passed to a new group who have expanded the team even further. The opportunities are endless to connect and share this love and commitment of triathlon.

The beauty of taking part in triathlons is that most triathletes have a lot in common. We are a certain breed of people. There are differences in our training approaches but the core value of hard work is always the same. We all love to work our butts off trying to achieve our goals but we also have fun while doing it. Triathletes are individualists in the sense that once the gun goes off at the start of the race, it is every man or woman for him or herself. There is no team in the race. But during training, despite the fact that everyone has their own plan, it is great to share the countless hours with good friends.

There is a time and a place for everything. Your key sessions should not be compromised when training with others. Other less important sessions can always be adapted to fit with what the others are doing. Of course, this is a two-way street. Sometimes you will need to adapt your training to fit in with someone else. Other times they can adapt their schedule to yours. Group dynamics are very beneficial as long as your efforts are measured. Pick out some training that you can do in groups and some you want to do on your own. A healthy balance is a healthy mix. You can select the most interesting comrades to share your “tri addiction” with and you can grow together. Training together helps many athletes strive for their personal best. It is part of the spirit of the sport, and it contributes to the fun and the value that triathlon can bring to your everyday life.

Photo courtesy of Kjell Schiöberg

Defining Your Goals

Now that you are done listing some of your goals, limitations and constraints, you will be able to create structure for yourself and provide a framework. Is your goal still the same? Are you able to work within your restrictions to reach your goal?

Write down your goals for this and next year. Read them over frequently. Once again, ask yourself WHY you are doing this. The 'WHY' is what will continue driving you. Whatever your motivation might be—it will fuel your passion. This is a very important part of the puzzle, as you will stumble across this question numerous times in your life, not only in sport but also in relation to your personal life. If you are able to define the why, you can get down to the how.

Once you know what you want and have your goal in sight, share it with someone whose opinion you value and who will hold you accountable for following up on your dream. This doesn't mean that you should use Facebook as a platform for smack talking or egotistically boasting your goals for the world to know. It just means that you should let people around you know what you are planning to accomplish and if that means sharing it in an honest (read: humble) way on Facebook, then that's fine too.

There is a happy medium between being true to your goals and being too vocal about your goals, so I will let you find your own way to that sweet spot. In any case, share your goals with someone, and don't just keep them for yourself. You are more likely to follow through if you share them with someone you care about. You can even start a blog if that feels right for you (we will talk more in detail about that later on). In addition, consider pinning your goal on your wall. Choose someplace where you will see it a few times a day (bathroom mirror, in the car, on the TV, etc.). This will help to remind you to put those running shoes on as soon as you get home, before you sit down on the couch.

When it comes to goal setting, I am brutally honest with myself and my support team. I even share my honest opinion publicly, by informing the press of my racing schedule at the beginning of my season. There is no turning back unless there is a significant reason for it and I have to change plans--which happens sometimes too. This was the case for my 2014 season, when I injured myself early on in the season while racing Ironman® Melbourne and somehow never recovered from it. Consequently, my peak race at Challenge Roth resulted in a sub-par performance and shortly after, I had to make the call to pull out of Kona for the year.

That was a well thought out, really tough decision, but it was unavoidable and necessary. Being honest and straightforward adds quite a bit pressure at times. I use that pressure as fuel to propel me toward accomplishing my objective. I simply accept it as part of the game. It is important to stay true to your word, so you and your friends know your word has value. If you don't know what you are capable of yet, then you can leave your publicly announced goal a bit more vague, but tell the people closest to you what you plan to accomplish.

Once you set realistic goals, and then get started, you will be able to see if your goals need to be adjusted slightly along the way. This is another reason why you don't want to be too specific with the "public" (i.e., social media) when it comes to your goal times. There is nothing more discouraging than when people set specific unrealistic goals for themselves that they are incapable of achieving. If your fastest Ironman® time is somewhere around 13 hours, then don't proclaim that you want to go under nine hours! If you do indeed go under nine hours, let that be a pleasant surprise to your friends. If not, then you won't have to worry about justifying your shortcomings to anyone.

It's great to be motivated, but big talk (the tri-geek's number one Achilles' heel) can really cause unnecessary negative vibes in the groups you have joined and the friends around you. The fastest and most professional triathletes don't talk about being fast—they let their legs do the talking. Try to be realistic about your own racing and your plans for the future. Be ambitious and excited but don't let your ego get ahead of itself.

Dream big—and live that dream—but make sure your dream stays realistic and challenging at the same time. Regardless of the way you put it out there, be ready to accept some criticism. There will be plenty of it. Knowing that upfront will help you to be aware of it and deal with it in a better way. Face it and let criticism be the fuel for your drive.

When I raced the German Bundesliga Triathlon Series in my years as a junior, my manager once told me that I am the world's best domestique (the guy that does all the work on the bike to help the big winners on his team win races) and that I should face the fact that I will never be a top runner and won't get very far trying to race triathlons. So, he said that I should just work for some of his favorite (aka faster) guys. Thinking back on that bit of harsh criticism, I can't help but see the through line to one of the biggest wins in my career, Ironman® Asia-Pacific Champs in Melbourne in 2014, where I ran down my competitors on foot.

Never let anyone determine what is possible or impossible for you, that's your right and only yours. Up until a few years ago, this negative feedback fueled my motivation in a big way.

Proving people wrong is a strong incentive. That's why we always have to remember WHY we chose to trek this path. It's personal. Everyone has different reasons, motivations and constraints. Define for yourself the WHY.

To help you with the HOW, it is also a good idea to improve your general knowledge of the latest news and developments in the world of triathlon. That means you should know when there are new rule changes, new technology, and anything else that could possibly influence your strategy and planning for the future. I highly suggest adding triathlon's most prominent website, slowtwitch.com, to your list of daily reads. It's not only the biggest, most thorough, and most up to date independent triathlon source in the world, but it also has an extensive forum where you can connect with other triathletes who love the "tri-life".

There is a lot of theory involved in sketching out the upcoming weeks, months, and even years of your triathlon journey. The motivation to persevere needs to come from within. To fulfill your dream you need to evaluate whether or not you are able to tackle it all yourself or if you need the benefit of guidance from a trusted and knowledgeable coach.

As for the early stages of becoming a decent triathlete, it might be good to start out on your own for a few sessions before meeting up with other fellow triathletes or a potential coach. You want to make sure you know the basics and get some easier training sessions done before you go out and hire the best coach that will work for you. By training with groups you will learn quite a bit already. You will meet new people and gain a fair amount of knowledge from the local "tri-crowd". For beginners, those guided plans in the tri magazines will get you off the couch and inspire you for a while, and it's a great place to start. A healthy mix between training on your own and in groups should be the next logical step.

Receiving an individualized plan by a tri-coach is the next natural step if you are to truly get the most out of your training. Once you are at a basic fitness level and you have proven to yourself that you are dedicated to your triathlon dream, then you could consider forking over the cash for a coach. In general, if you are serious about your goal, I don't recommend coaching yourself, simply because you are unable to see your own weaknesses the same way a great coach can see them. You need a different perspective, and a bit of pressure to make sure you don't cherry pick the fun sessions while training. You need to maintain your strengths, but also work the hardest on your weaknesses. This is the only way to get better. Even the best athletes in the world will run out of answers at some point and can benefit from having someone else there to gain some perspective.

Picking your coach is a very big decision, so make sure you weigh your options when you are on the market for that perfect mentor. Analyze the cost and decide if it's feasible for you to hire one. If so, then pick your top three choices and do your research. Talk to some of his/her athletes to get some references. Yes, it will cost you money, but it might be the right thing to invest in so you can keep your head clear and not go flipping around between the different training philosophies that are out there.

I cannot emphasize enough, how important it is to make sure that you and your coach match in terms of expectations. Not every coach fits every athlete. Make sure you are both on the same page about your coach's availability, how individualized your plan will be, and how often and how quickly you will have replies to your questions via email and phone. Will your coach travel to races? If so, will you pay for their travel expenses? The number one point is whether or not you have a good feeling about your coach. Have they coached any other successful athletes? Was their approach successful? How many athletes are they working with?

Don't forget to evaluate the runway for your coaching budget and whether your coach is fine with you just working with them part of the year, if needed. Your coach should be someone who will get you to work hard within your constraints. It doesn't help you out at all if you get the perfect training plan for 25+ hours, when you can only afford to train 12 hours per week. You should really analyze your picks from every angle.

So many triathletes call themselves a triathlon coach these days. Everybody seems to know the magic formula. It's a good idea to listen to people who are ahead of you in the tri-game. They probably went through a similar learning curve and have experienced things that could help you along your own journey. Remember, your coach doesn't have to be the greatest athlete himself in order to be a good coach. That is a myth. Some great coaches have never even raced, and some very poor coaches were world champions in their earlier careers.

Just make sure you exercise your due diligence. A good indicator of a top-notch coach seems to be an accumulation of years of experience and coaching due to passion for the sport and not for the dollars rolling in. If you choose a coach, stick with your decision for a while. Changes in training in endurance sport take time. Be very analytical. I like to compare this to physiotherapists and some doctors: Sometimes I prefer to go to the best physiotherapist in the area instead of going to a random doctor. A great sport PT often knows the body far better than an average doctor. Therefore knowledge, based on experience, should be good indicators.

There are plenty of good coaches out there, and it‘s a great stimulus for your training to change coaches from time to time, in order to experience a different approach. You would do the same with your job if you wouldn't like it. Pick what's best for your own development, but stay true to yourself.

Using knowledge, based on experience holds true for computerized training programs as well. I believe that if you really want to step up your game, and you have specifics that you need to work on, a standard plan probably won't work for you. I think the best plan is a well thought through, personalized one that takes into account your job, family, and all other important parts of your life. Have you ever thought about why computerized training programs sell for a fraction of real individualized plans? They are far off the mark from a personalized plan that works within your own, personal restriction.

As with building any strong structure, the foundation and planning stage is key. The tallest skyscrapers started out with many drafts to create a solid blueprint, and this takes patience. It is much wiser to make adjustments on paper before you go out and possibly build something that can't be undone later. Formulating your training plan, deciding on the possibility of a coach, and building your team takes time, but they are the cornerstones to a successful journey in triathlon. They allow the walls to stand tall and proud leading into the hard labor and construction phase. Attention to detail in your planning will allow for a more fluid transition to the heavy lifting of your training regime to come.

Chapter 3: Gear

"The expectations of life depend upon diligence; the mechanic that would perfect his work must first sharpen his tools."

~Confucius

Think of me as your human guinea pig. I've worked with the best of gears and the worst of gears. It seems I've tried it all. This is the part where you benefit from the ins and outs of my experience finding the right gear. Let's put this puzzle together step by step.

The Tools of the Trade

It is vital to consider all aspects of your gear when training and competing for a triathlon. These tools, in some ways, are an extension of ourselves; acting as contact points between our feet and the trail, and bearing all of our weight, pedal stroke by pedal stroke. We have to honor our gear for what it does in allowing us to do what we love.

Because gear is so important, there is a lot of information out there for people like us, who are looking for the next big thing that will shave a few seconds (or minutes) off our race time. But, it isn't that simple. One of the biggest myths in our sport is that speed can be purchased. Alas, you can't buy speed. Some believe that if you have the most advanced products on the market you will get the golden ticket to becoming a champion—but don't fall for that marketing trap, and don't let your ego get in the way here. Today's triathlon market is flooded with gadgets and gizmos and it can be difficult to decide which products are really necessary and which can be left on the shelf.

I am of the opinion that it is not about having the most optimal gear, but about doing what we can with what we have, and using gear upgrades as incentives to work towards. When I raced my first triathlon in 1989 (boy, that sure was a while ago) I used my dad's neglected Peugeot road bike with downtube shifters. The bike was way too big for me but it was the best that we could do at the time. In that first race, I tackled the bike portion fairly well up until a rather large hill was staring back at me. It was so incredibly steep that I had to stop and get off the bike to walk up. Because I was a runner, I was convinced that I could run up faster than I could ride, so I got out of the pedals and sprinted, Peugeot anchor beside me.

On the top of the hill I jumped back on my blue stallion and kept pushing. It was my first race ever and I managed a 4th place, so I took that as a good omen and continued training for the next one. My lack of perfect gear didn't stop me from moving forward. If I would have waited until I got a fancy bike before I started to train for and race my first triathlon, then I probably wouldn't be sitting here writing this book!

Triathlon is booming and has gained share of the sports industry. It's big business, but that doesn't mean that you need to purchase all new gear in order to make it even bigger. Let's get you up to speed on what exactly is worth spending your money on, what will benefit your overall strategy for success.

Upgrading

Shortly before my next triathlon adventure my first coach, Dieter Waller, gave me his old triathlon bike. His "old" bike was like a new one to me. It was a real triathlon bike with those good old Scott handlebars, and it rode like a dream. Once I proved my commitment to myself and earned my new ride, this upgraded gear boosted my motivation to not only succeed, but to excel.

Dieter was one of the first people to practice the sport of triathlon in Germany. Through the years he has won over 9 world titles. With his experience, advice and gifted bike, I was able to step up my game. Even though I didn't have the top-of-the-line gear back then, it was still a huge improvement to get his old, used tri bike to replace my Dad's roadie. I did well racing on Dieter's old bike and looking back, I think it was a great way to launch my efforts.

I find great value in the grass-roots, tried and true method of starting small and letting your material grow parallel to your commitment and success. I have always believed that I needed to prove to myself that I was able to work hard enough to "earn" myself the gear I needed for the next natural step. Once I started to get a bit more competitive and raced more seriously, my dad upgraded me to some nicer gear to fuel my passion. I still believe in that idea today; as you grow with the sport, you should earn an upgrade in your gear.

Now back to the myth that you can buy speed. If I had had a fancy new bike back then, I would not have been able to ride any faster—I was simply not capable yet. My preference is to use new gear as an incentive instead of a starting point. Assuming you have an old bike and have used it a ton, then of course you will experience a major change when you upgrade to a new one. You could, for instance, tell yourself that when you reach 5000 kilometers on your old ride, you will sell it on craigslist and use that money towards your new one.

This was my strategy and I think it's a great way to start out.

The key is to let the reward of new gear work as a catalyst for your success and not a barrier. That said, if you are a seasoned "tri-addict" that has earned his or her rank already through the years, and you have worn your current gear out, then there is potential to increase your performance by upgrading your gear.

Again, this is more relevant if you are fighting for seconds, which might be the case if you are trying to qualify for Kona or rank top in your age group. If you compare an entry-level bike to a top-of-the-line bike, you will indeed see a difference in the material, but across brands, there isn't that much of a difference between bikes of the same class or category. Just look at the Tour de France teams; different teams have different bikes and they all complete at the highest level. Do you really believe there is a major difference in the quality of the bikes between all of the brands? I can't imagine that this is the case. Trust me, I rode the seventh fastest time ever in Kona on a relatively unknown bike brand, which was my first ever TT bike.

It's really about where you are placing your focus and why. Chances are that you can achieve much larger advancements in your training, including your mental game, and are much better off investing more time out there sweating, or meditating, or investing in the right training support. Using this approach, you will see massive improvement, versus marginal ones for merely switching out your wheelset for race day. You can't buy speed—you have to earn it.

So what's the bottom line here? Start with the basics and upgrade as you invest more time and money into your hobby or budding career. Use upgraded gear as an incentive. Over the years, I discovered that the reward & punishment system works extremely well for many athletes. That not only counts for training but also for gear.

Rewarding yourself after a long period of training and a successful race is a great way to fuel your motivation. Once you do well at your milestone race, then you should get a treat. Whatever stimulus makes you tick, use it to your advantage and you will work even harder to get that reward. You may experience tough times in training, and during races it might even get tougher. If you set yourself a goal, then once you reach it, it's only right to celebrate and reward yourself for the work and time you put into your achievement.

At times, triathlon can get a bit complicated with gear requirements. It is my intention to make all of that a bit clearer for you here. Let me break it down into more detail for each discipline in terms of what is needed for training and racing. There are small but important differences between the two. At the end of this chapter you should be able to go through your gear and decide where you need a makeover, an upgrade, or a complete overhaul.

> *"Do not wait; the time will never be 'just right.' Start where you stand, and work with whatever tools you may have at your command, and better tools will be found as you go along."*
>
> *~ George Herbert*

Tools for the Pool

Swimming is the easiest part to suss out, because you don't need much gear at all. All you really need to be ready to jump in the pool are goggles, maybe a swim cap, your swim shorts and a bit of sunscreen. Those are the bare minimum basics. However, to allow yourself more advanced training you'll need to add a few more gadgets to make your swim assortment complete.

Goggles:

To get started, use a pair of goggles with a soft frame, especially for open water. It's okay to use the hard Swedish goggles like the pro pool swimmers if you are accustomed to them, but keep them in pool. For open water swimming and especially for triathlon races, they just don't work. Imagine swimming on someone's feet and then accidentally getting kicked in the face. Having to pull out of a race with a black eye is just too much of a risk to take, and your pretty eyes don't deserve that, so the softer ones are much safer for chlorine free zones.

There is a wide range of goggles out there, and the best way to find the one that works for you is to try them out. When you are in the store you might put them on and notice that they create an airtight fit, meaning that they stick to your face even without the strap holding them to your face. That's a good indication, but the best way to know for sure if a set of goggles is right for you is to give them a try in the pool. Everyone's face is different, and just because some pros wear one set of goggles, doesn't mean they are the best fit for you.

Once you decide on a pair that fits you well, get a few pairs to have as a reserve. This will save you time when you need a new pair, and you won't miss any training sessions. Taking backup goggles with you in your swim bag is always very useful. This tip has saved me from missing many a session over the years. They do break from time to time and then finding a random pair that fits you well is not that easy. Goggles have been an issue for me since day one, and I have always found it hard to find a good fit. Once you find the right fit, keep them in stock!

For daily use and for traveling, you should get your own

paddles, pull buoy, and an elastic band (to tie your feet together). Each of these important tools are key to helping you develop power in the pool.

Paddles:

Paddles help to develop strength. Unlike with biking or running, you can't train on varied terrain when you swim. Since there aren't big hills to summit in the pool, your paddles become the varied terrain. These important tools allow you to gain strength in specific swim muscles, which result in the muscles being able to handle fatigue better. Working with paddles will help you come out on top during the sprint in the beginning of the race or at key moments when you start getting tired towards the end. When picking out your paddles, remember to start small and work your way up. Just like when you are working out in the gym, your muscles and tendons need to adapt to the weight they are pushing. Be careful to pay close attention to your stroke form so it doesn't start to suffer as this can cause strain on your shoulders. Remember, remaining injury free is the key to keeping the triathlon party going.

Pull Buoy:

A pull buoy is essentially a piece of Styrofoam that is wedged between the thighs in order to keep the legs floating on top of the water. This allows you to isolate your arm stroke by not using the legs. Since swimming is intended to gain its forward motion from the arms (the legs meant to keep our body position horizontal), a pull buoy is key in keeping us honest and allowing us to do the work where it's needed: in the powerhouse swim muscles of the arms. There are also pull buoy / kickboard combinations that can be used for both arm and leg workouts. I use this option as I don't like to carry too many accouterments .

Elastic Band:

This band is to be tied around your feet when you swim a serious arm set, keeping you even more honest. For you resourceful types, you can make your own elastic band by making use of an old inner tube from your bike, as I do. You will puncture at some point on a ride, so just keep that useless tube in your back pocket till you get home, and then cut it up and tie it in a loop. You will hate swimming with it at first but the effectiveness of using this little tool is magic. It allows you to solely focus on upper body strength, which will help you to increase strength while doing your arm sets. It will undoubtedly make your swim session more intense, but this hard work will pay off on race day.

These additional tools will make all the difference in your training. In order to fit them all in one bag I use a swim net bag, which allows my gear to dry much more quickly after practice. These mesh bags can breathe, unlike normal cloth bags. Without the proper bag you may end up with a nice moldy surprise when you jump into the water and then realize that your gear has turned into a science experiment.

Of course, there is always something else that you can add to the list of items you haul back and forth to swim practice. These could include finger paddles, snorkels, kick boards, or swim cords. However, I would consider these non-essential. In my experience, I have found that the swimmers who carry the most random training accessories with them tend to be the ones who don't manage to swim as fast. I am not sure what causes this correlation, but personally I never used any of these tools and managed to be a front of the pack swimmer on the world cup circuit. So, less is definitely more in this case.

Despite the typical misconception, there is no need to swim with your watch on. Every pool has a deck clock, so get used to working with it, as it will help you to keep time during your interval sets. It's very convenient and easy, once you get used to the clock. Try timing yourself based on break times, for instance leaving 15 seconds breaks between a set of 100s, instead of using more complicated methods of timing yourself. When you are tired you won't want to have to think about math. Also, remember that swimming with a watch is additional drag and doesn't feel right during your stroke in training. Swimmers shave their arms and legs to reduce drag and triathletes add a thick GPS or stopwatch on their arm. It really doesn't make much sense.

Most pools actually have some gear available for public use, such as kick boards or pull buoys, but if you get used to bringing along your own, you will never run into any problems. These are pretty small and inexpensive items and they are easy to travel with. Usually I leave mine in the car, so I always have them with me everywhere I go. I'm always prepared to sneak in a swim when the opportunity arises.

Pool Protocol

Apart from the tools for the pool, it's helpful to beef up on some good swimming etiquette. When going for a swim, you might want to bring your sandals, a towel and maybe shower gel as well. Personally, I usually don't use the shower gel unless it is the last session of the day, because I train several times throughout a day and don't want to OD on soap. If you train a few times a day, you will also shower a few times and the skin, paired with the amount of time spent in the sun, will need some support as well. So make sure to apply some lotion after sessions to help your skin recover. For bald headed guys like me, it is a must.

You can tell when you meet your buddy who just swam, not only due to the fact of the frog eyes thanks to the tight swim goggles but also due to the dryness in his face. The skin tends to turn white when it is dry and this is a sign that it needs to build back up the natural oily layer that the chlorine strips off. So, apply some lotion or natural oil to your legs and arms. You need to take care of your body and maintain it, since it is the only vehicle we have in this life. Anyway, muscles always look better when they are well moisturized and then reflect some light. This makes your muscle tone stick out even more. You worked bloody hard to get your body so lean and defined, right? So why not show off what you have?

An additional item that I always keep with me, are cotton swabs. I always have water in my ears after swimming and these help to dry my ears out very effectively (be careful not to wedge it too deeply into your ear though). It might also be useful to purchase “swimmers ear” drops if you start to notice that you have trouble with water in your ears after swimming. It will help to avoid infection and discomfort. You can also make your own version from rubbing alcohol and vinegar.

To recap. Make sure your swim bag contains the following:

- Goggles
- Swimwear
- Paddles
- Pull buoy and band
- Swim cap
- Sunscreen

- Towel
- Shower gel
- Sandals
- Q-tips
- Lotion

It's good to have a place to store all of your backup items so you know where to find them when the time comes. I call this my "tri-box," which is more or less a treasure trove of duplicates of gear I value most. I always keep an elastic band (you can easily make 2-3 out of each punctured tire) and some spare goggles. These seem to be the items that get misplaced most frequently. Online ordering can takes 2-3 days, but sometimes you can't wait for the postman to come or the shops to open to start your session.

A Word on Wetsuits

Swimming in a wetsuit in general might feel foreign to most of us. It is sort of equivalent to being stuffed like a sausage. However, this is part of the job and we have to get used to it! Picking the right wetsuit requires testing several suits, but my suggestion is always to look at the fastest swimmers in triathlon and see what they are using (short-cut method). After doing the research, I would narrow it down to your favorite three suits, and then try them on, and preferably swim with them on. You might be able to borrow one from a buddy who is around your size, or you could try them out at a race expo where many wetsuit companies have test suits available. This is worth the time it takes, as wetsuits are a minor investment when compared to other items on the triathlete's shopping list, but the right fit can potentially result in much faster times.

It is very clear that the long arm wetsuit is better than the sleeveless suit, although the sleeveless suit might feel more comfortable at first. It comes down to the fact that the long arm suit provides more resistance during the stroke, when your arm is under your body, so you push more water on your arm stroke. It does feel like the suit is heavier on the shoulders, but this is purely subjective and you have to look at it this way. The fact is that tests have shown that the long arm suit is faster than the sleeveless suit.

Consider the following:

If you have a specific swimming weakness that results from buoyancy (i.e., your legs sink too far down), then you should make sure your suit has a thick panel on the upper leg area (5 mm for instance, instead of the thinner 3 mm ones), which will improve your water position. Also, try to find suits with thin neoprene in the arms in order to insure free movement during the stroke.

If you find that you have folds of extra neoprene around the stomach area and water enters the suit when you are swimming in open water, your wetsuit is likely too big. Be advised, testing for wetsuit sizing in the pool is not accurate as the force of pushing off of the wall will mimic the same effect even with proper wetsuit sizing.

It's a good practice to keep an older wetsuit and a used swimskin handy for normal training sessions, so you don't have to worry about ruining any material and you can keep your race material new and fresh for when it counts. Swimskins are also nice to use when the pool is a notch too cold. On cold days it doesn't hurt to have one in your swim bag.

Maximizing the effectiveness of your wetsuit:

- Cut your wetsuit 2-3 inches at the bottom of the leg, which will facilitate easier transition in T1. This is something I learned during my Olympic distance days, and it can prevent the common occurrence of getting your feet stuck in the leg of the suit. Many times just being smarter can earn you valuable time that would take a lot of effort to gain from training.
- When training with a wetsuit make sure you use Vaseline on your neck in order to avoid chafing, especially in saltwater. This is a mandatory step and prevents you from looking like you tried to hang yourself and failed.
- If a wetsuit is dry when you go to put it on, it is useful to have either a plastic bag around your feet or your socks on to help slide into the leg of the suit.
- When the wetsuit is wet, the only way to comfortably put it on is to do so in the water.
- Make sure you are conscious of your fingernails when putting on the suit. Good wetsuits are very sensitive to surface tears. Unlike diving suits, triathlon wetsuits are not as rigid and can easily rip and leave moon shaped gauges in the material if handled the wrong way.

A final caveat: you should be very comfortable wearing the suit once race-time comes around, but there are some negatives to wearing it too much. As mentioned earlier, a wetsuit helps to keep your body in a more buoyant position, and therefore cheats your training slightly. If you train with a wetsuit all the time, you may lose the “feeling of the water” and your natural body position, which is something that you should be sensitive to. So, do all of the real work in the water without the suit.

Then in the last 2 weeks before the race put on your wetsuit, particularly during hard sessions that simulate race situations and during longer sessions.

Swim: Training Gear vs. Racing Gear

For race day, you will need to have different swim gear available than what you need for your standard training sessions. What you use will depend on the type of race you are competing in. Some races are wetsuit legal (depending on the water temperature), while other races on your calendar might be non-wetsuit swims and allow for swimskins. It's important to be prepared with the proper attire. Wetsuits will keep you warm and buoyant, and they usually benefit the slower swimmers by narrowing the gap between the front and back of the field (which is something to consider when planning your race calendar). Think of your wetsuit as your second skin during the first leg of the race. As you put it on you can envision yourself putting on your armor for battle. Your gear is an extension of you, and the wetsuit and swimskin set the stage for the grand opus that is to come.

Unlike a wetsuit, swimskins offer no buoyancy, but instead offer a slight advantage in terms of their make-up. They are made out of a textile material, covering your body with a faster-than-skin armor. Be sure that your choice of swimskin does not contain neoprene as this may disqualify you for the race. The swimskin is always sleeveless and can be either short or long legged. For long distance racing, it is worn over your normal tri-suit for the swim, and then shed after the swim portion is over (similar to a wetsuit). Since it is faster than your own skin, it is much better to use the swimskin than to go without one.

Because most races have rules that don't allow for the shoulders to be covered for non-wetsuit swims, remember that your tri-suit needs to be short sleeved as well. If you opt for a t-shirt style tri-suit (one piece suits that cover the shoulders in order to increase aerodynamics on the bike), then you have to roll the top portion of the tri-suit down before you put on the swimskin. Then, once you run into transition 1, you have to peel off your swimskin and pull back on the top part of your tri suit (which will be a bit difficult, since it will be wet). Evaluate the benefits of having a suit with aero sleeves that will benefit your bike segment versus having to deal with a rolled down suit under your swimsuit (less hydro-dynamic) and the added time in transition to put it on over a wet body during the hectic moments of the race. These considerations, in choosing the right swim race gear, will make your race day run much smoother.

Swim gear that is ill-fitted will feel like you are dragging a parachute behind you when you swim. Before you go out to buy a wetsuit or swimskin, go online and look up the sizing chart for the brands you are interested in. Then you can narrow down your search to just one or two sizes that will most likely fit you. The easiest way to know whether or not the suit fits is to swim with it. The same goes with goggles and tri-suits. They have to fit otherwise you'll get too much water inside and it will cost you valuable time. Many sport hotels, wetsuit booths at race expos, and training centers have wetsuits available to test. This is really the best way to ensure a perfect fit.

Your racing goggles should be the same type as your training goggles, but they should be designated as race goggles so they stay in good working order. Your racing pair should be a bit tighter than your training goggles, as you will be swimming in open water and possibly saltwater. Swimming in open water is different from swimming in the pool in the sense that you have a lot of force (people and current) that could potentially knock your goggles off. So, make sure your race goggles fit tightly, particularly for a beach start where you will be running into the water or when jumping from a start pontoon.

Some athletes like to use swim caps during training, and some don't. I always hated swim caps, and since I shaved my head I have the luxury of never having to wear one in training since bald guys get exempt from the mandatory swim cap rule. I love that! In most races, however, the use of swim caps are mandatory for all competitors in order to aid in identifying athletes.

There are two types of swim caps to choose from: thinner latex caps or thicker silicon caps. Typically, the silicon caps are used for colder weather. They are also more comfortable and easier to put on. They work like magic when it's freezing cold outside because your head is wet and is constantly in and out of the water. With the additional component of wind and colder air temperatures, a warm swim cap can be quite useful.

The Dos and Don'ts of Swim Gear

Dos

- Use sunscreen before your swim and lotion after your swim. The water reflects and could easily burn you; it also causes wrinkles and skin cancer. "Rule No 1" is to look good, so don't get totally sunburned out there.
- Have spare goggles in your mesh swim bag.
- Keep your racing gear separate from your training gear. Train only in gear that is designated for training

purposes. The only exception to this rule comes in the final week(s) before your race, where you will be testing your race gear.

Don'ts

- Don't wear a GPS watch or a wristwatch in a pool. Try to learn to swim with the pool clock (like the real swimmers do).
- Don't go oversize with your paddles. Start slightly bigger than your hand, not with the size of a frying pan—you'll risk shoulder injuries if you do that. Paddles are for building strength and you can increase the size of your paddles step-by-step, over time.
- Don't wear board shorts when you swim. You will add a significant amount of drag to your swim workout, and also run the risk of painful chafing.
- Don't buy a wetsuit or swimskin without trying it out and testing it beforehand. Wetsuits really need to fit properly to avoid drag.
- Don't tighten your swim goggles too much; you will have frog eyes for hours after your swim
- Don't forget to lotion up afterwards

Bike Gear

The basics required for this leg of your journey include your bike, pedals, shoes, and a helmet. This would be enough to get out and go for a ride--all of the additional things that we think we need are just extras that can help us along the way. Let's explore your options.

In case you decide that your bike needs to be upgraded or replaced, then be aware this will be the most expensive purchase you will make towards your triathlon goals. Make sure you do your research. You can scout an unbiased third party source like slowtwitch.com for the latest trusted reviews, and ask questions on the forum if you are having a hard time deciding on which bike to purchase in your price range. People can be a bit die hard about their bike brands, so try to look at things objectively when deciding on which bike to purchase. Remember to keep in mind your ideals as well as your constraints when making a big purchase decision.

If you already have a bike you can always make it work. So go for a ride and train. You can get the job done, if you are up to the task, even if it is not the top of the line bike. Remember that training is about developing your fitness and not about how fast you go. If it's not yet time to upgrade, this shouldn't be an excuse for skipping a session.

Read through the advice below to get the best bike fit for your personal needs. Don't let the guy in the shop twist your arm by telling you what you should buy—remember that he needs to make his commission too. Do the work upfront and use him as a supplement to your own research online on sites like slowtwitch.com or other sites with unbiased 3rd party reviews. Keep in mind that pros are paid to endorse their bike brands, so you really can't believe what they say (I know, the irony is not lost on me here). Also, be careful when looking into forums for advice because views are so subjective. Be an educated consumer and consider your sources.

Road vs. Tri Bike

One of the most important decisions you will make is deciding which type of bike to purchase. Once you are ready and have really proven your dedication to triathlon, you might consider acquiring multiple bikes. Again, this is definitely not mandatory and should really be earned over a longer period of time. Many pros and some more dedicated age groupers that have been around a while, might have the magic number: three bikes on hand. These three bikes are: 1) a training road bike, best used for easy sessions and in the off season; 2) a race TT bike (Time-Trial, also known as a tri bike) that stays in the garage until shortly before the race and is always in 100% top condition and ready to race; and 3) a training TT bike with the exact same configuration as the TT race bike, but with parts that are timeworn, so you can put all the training mileage on this bike.

The key here is to have the same geometry (measurements and position) from frame to frame. If you want to save some money here you can always use cheaper components and wheels for your training bike versus your racing bike. This arrangement would be the best situation for someone who has pledged and proven their allegiance to their triathlon goal by many, many hours in the saddle. We will look at the pros and cons of different bike setups in the next pages.

A road bike offers the advantage of easier maneuverability during group rides. It is easier to pack for travel and it allows for a more upright position that is easier to get used to for beginners. Road bikes can be adapted for use in triathlons by clipping on aero bars. This set up is ideal for short distance, drafting races (since you don't need to have such an aggressive position and you will be able to ride in the group more easily) and easy rides for more advanced riders who like variety. In contrast to that, the triathlon or TT bike is made for long distance and non-drafting races. The position in this bike is much more aerodynamic and the handling is very different from an agile road bike.

So, if you plan to race half distance triathlons or longer, you would be much better off with a TT bike from the get go. You will find various bikes in a range of price points for both types of bikes, but TT bikes do tend to have more bells and whistles and therefore can start to get more expensive once you start adding on the accessories, or the "schnickschnack", as we call it in German.

I would say there are 4-6 top bike brands, and then another few that are very close in terms of aerodynamics and quality. Some are "no brand" bikes that are made in China or Taiwan but still offer a good product for the money spent. All in all, if you aren't racing in order to put food on the table, you just need a solid bike that does the job without bringing financial ruin to your household. Remember, you have to prove your dedication to yourself before you consider bringing home that beauty in the bike shop window. In any case, it will depend on whether or not being a few seconds faster really makes that big of a difference to you. As with most triathlon gear, general performance isn't what determines which bike you should purchase. It also comes down to how a bike looks and feels when you are riding.

Consider the weight of your prospective bike when making your final choice. Bike weight has long been a topic of discussion among the tri crowd. How much is someone willing to spend to save a few grams of weight? In triathlon, weight it not really as big of an issue as it is in road cycling because we don't usually climb massive mountains during our races. Most triathlons are either flat or feature rolling hills, where weight isn't a big concern. Of course, it does make a difference for those hilly courses, so this may be something to consider when you look at your race calendar. Be aware that a TT bike will always weigh more than a road bike and your bike will be considerably heavier if you add tons of nutrition to the frame.

Another point to consider, when making your bike choice, is your bike position. You might need the long version of a specific size frame, depending on your body size and position on the bike. Remember that sitting very aerodynamically is usually a trade-off for sitting comfortably on the bike. For triathletes, comfort is important, because we sit in the time trial position for a very long time and we have to run after we get off the bike.

Never try to mimic your road bike position on your TT bike because the more you sit in the "classic position" (on the back of your saddle, pushing forward when pedaling) as you do with the road bike, the more you will use your hamstrings. By using these muscles so much on bike portion, your run will consequently suffer. The more "aero" you are (also known as the "American position"), the more you use your quads which is more beneficial in triathlon as you have to run after you get off the bike. Considering these points will help you choose a bike to support your most effective body position and will transitions your body more efficiently into the run.

When choosing your bike saddle, make sure you get a chance to figure out what works for you. I don't mean to get cheeky here (pun intended) but everyone's bum is different. Keeping said bum happy requires a discriminating choice of a saddle for your steed. Do you prefer a short TT saddle or a long triathlon saddle? Do you prefer a split nose version that is designed to release pressure on the soft tissue in order to deter numbness? Make sure you use different saddles for your road and TT bikes, since they fill very different needs due to the changing positions. Ideally, you would want to test a saddle before you buy it, so check with your local bike shop or even a tri-friend of yours to see if you can try one out before you commit to buy one.

So, let's move on to the nuts and bolts of the bike: the components. These are the parts that make the bike move and it is important that everything works smoothly with as little friction as possible. It was love at first shift for me when I tried out the Shimano Di2 electronic shifters back when they first came on the market, and I haven't looked back. The sound of the shift is addictive and the fluidity of being able to shift uphill when my hands are out of the aero position saves my energy. The Dura-Ace Di2 and other wireless shifters are the crème de la crème, of course, but Shimano also makes a lower priced Ultegra version that could be a good stepping stone from traditional shifters to electronic.

If you are ready to upgrade your pulleys and bottom brackets for racing only, you could consider changing them out for ceramic ones like those offered by CeramicSpeed. This will cut down on friction and shave time off as well. They even offer specially coated chains to reduce friction. These little upgrades can act as incentives for you when you are ready to reward yourself for a really hard training block or a race well done. You deserve it!

Of course, there is more to a bike that just its functionality. Your bike is your race day chariot and needs to look the part as well. If you are looking to customize your ride for race day, there are limitless options available. I always like to color coordinate when possible, as it give me an added boost of confidence and just makes me feel faster. I think it also adds a bit of intimidation to the mix as well, which is always nice. Look the part and your actions will follow suit.

This photo shows me with a prototype frame that was about to be introduced to the market. Like the Tour De France riders who get to present prototypes of new material, we triathletes also get these fun privileges out on the course in Kona, Hawaii. I received a lot of coverage that year, and of course this meant great PR for my sponsor at that time, as well as for myself. To be honest, I think this was my favorite paint scheme of all time.

Another point for you to consider, before you sign on the dotted line, is how you are planning to transport your two-wheeled-wonder when you have to travel or fly out to a race. Depending on the type of car you have, it could make sense to get a bike rack. A friend of mine has a mini-cooper and still manages to transport two bikes on top. I usually drive a hatchback so I can easily fit all of my gear inside the car. This reduces the need to clean the bike of the nice variety of bugs that hitch a ride on the frame and it is much better at deterring thieves.

In addition, if you are going to travel by plane, you will also need to consider how you'll pack your bike. You can either purchase or borrow a hard or soft case, or you can simply use a cardboard box from a bike shop (most bike shops will give them to you for free). When you take your bike apart, you will need to make sure that you tape off or mark the seat post and handlebar position to ensure accurate reassembly. Make sure you have all of the proper tools, as well, so you can put your bike back together with ease without any help.

Particulars for a perfect ride:

When purchasing bike training shoes, make sure they fit well and are ventilated but solid. They should have a least 2 straps on the front side of your foot so you get a solid footing on the upstroke. With proper bike shoes come proper pedal systems. For those of you who are just starting out, click pedals can take some getting used to, but everyone had to do it at some point down the line. As a beginner it's ok to start slow. We all started out in a parking lot someplace, or way outside of town, so don't be embarrassed. The key is to get started and use your momentum. Make sure you have enough play in them so your knees are free to move. If your foot is 100% fixed on a pedal, the chances of knee issues down the road are very high.

You will also need to get a road helmet, some glasses, a few sets of cycling pants, jerseys, and socks. Depending where you live, you will most likely need to get arm warmers and knee and leg warmers, perhaps some long sleep gear, as well as wind vest and rain jacket. There are plenty of additional items that you can purchase along the way, but these are the main items that you will need.

TIP:

If you are looking for nice triathlon gear, but don't have the money to invest in expensive new items, try reaching out to some of the pro athletes out there. If you see a pro riding a bike that is drool worthy, then write them a private message on Facebook or send them an email and ask if they are looking to get rid of it at the end of the season. Many pros have deals with their sponsors that let them keep any material they use.

You can also check the slowtwitch.com list called "what are they riding now" and see which athletes have recently changed sponsors. Chances are, they are going to want to clear out their garage to make way for all of their newly acquired bikes and wheels. They will probably be pretty eager to get rid of the old stuff at oftentimes very discounted rates. Make sure you ask if the bike was a training bike or was just used for racing, since racing bike are tweaked with the best gear on (and off) the market, and are generally barely used.

Bike: Training Gear vs. Racing Gear

Once you are ready to go for the optimal gear at the highest level for racing long distance, you can consider a top-tuned TT bike. As we touched on earlier, there are two options to consider. You can either have one bike that you use for both training and racing or you can have separate bikes for training and racing. Both options work and I have been down both of these roads. You will need to consider a few things before you decide which way to go.

The One Bike Method:

If you choose to have the same bike for training and racing, you will need to change a few things out before every race in order to make sure it is ready to go. Your wheels are the biggest component that needs to be subbed out. This means that you will need newly adjusted brake pads as well. Carbon rims require cork brake pads, and since they wear down pretty quickly, they should definitely only be used for racing. Adjusting the brake pads can sometimes prove to be an involved process, as the width of disc wheels is different from road wheels. I have run into situations where I went to put on my disc before a race and realized that I needed a mechanic to do the adjustments to my derailleur, and all of the bike shops were closed. I would hate to see anyone else painted into a corner like that so be prepared for each adjustment necessary to transition your bike to racing status.

You might need to change the number of bottle cages on your race bike to get it race ready, since oftentimes you need less bottles or more aero bottles for race day than you need for training. You may opt for a bottle cage behind your saddle, for instance, in order to create less wind resistance. Storing bottles on the frame is the least aerodynamic position. Putting them behind the saddle is smarter and one bottle would be more aero than two in this case.

You will also have to exchange your road/training helmet with your aero TT helmet. A road helmet could also be used for racing in extreme heat, as was the case when Chrissie Wellington and Craig Alexander raced Kona in 2008 and 2009. They both went on to win, having chosen to use the better-ventilated road helmet. However, from the research I have seen, the TT helmet still offers a much larger advantage than a road helmet, even in heat. Craig Alexander came to the same conclusion when he switched his trusted road helmet for an aero version to break the world record in 2011.

The problem is that road helmets offer ventilation at the cost of aerodynamics—which once again demonstrates that aerodynamics is usually an advantage that is traded off for comfort. The more you get into it, the more important aerodynamic issues become. The balance between comfort and speed starts to shift as you are making your way up the ranks in the field of competition.

The one-bike option can work well for you, but make sure to have a professional tune-up before the race. Your one bike carries a heavy load between training and racing so make sure she gets that extra special attention from a qualified craftsman. Make sure they clean and grease all of the "joints" of your bike. They will need to check the use of the chain and go over the gears with your race wheels set up properly for your upcoming race. She'll get you through it if you pay close attention to transitioning her from your training status into racing posture.

The Dual Bike Method:

When utilizing two bikes in your program you'll be spending more money but gaining comfort and ease. If you have separate bikes for racing and training, you won't need to make any last minute changes and your racehorse will be sitting in the stable, prepared to get to the racetrack at any given moment. The setup features the same geometry, same type of bike, and same position which makes the swap really easy.

This bike could be equipped with all kinds of fancy race components to add to the badass factor. To have a killer race bike, you could tune it up a bit more by adding components like ceramic bottom brackets, special ceramic pulleys and wheel bearings, as well as race chain lube and pre-coated ultra-fast chains. Some of the over-the-top items can be very pricey and unnecessary, but if you have the budget and the inclination, there is no limit to the upgrades on market to make your bike candy dreams come true.

Don't use your race set up too many times in training. To save the tires and have everything perfectly dialed in, you should ride it just a few times before the race to confirm she is race ready. You should take special care to be sure your gear is 100% ready BEFORE you fly out to a race. This will save you the headache of trying to find a bike mechanic with skill and time on sight. Don't forget all of the time and effort you invested over the past few months in order to get to where you are. A technical issue could derail all of you efforts even before the race has begun.

Since I race a lot, I often travel with a mechanic who sets up my bike for the race. This is of course a convenient way of handling the packing and rebuilding of your race bike. But even most pros don't always enjoy these kinds of perks. If you are smart and plan accordingly, you won't have to finance your own private mechanic to make your race setup 100% perfect.

Regarding cycling shoes for racing, I use a lighter triathlon-racing shoe with one or two straps in front. This makes it easy to get into the shoe and tighten it up. Some shoe brands offer the same sole with a training and racing option for the upper, which is an ideal scenario, as your foot loves to have consistency and doesn't like changes before your race. You could use any shoe with one or two straps, as long as you are able to get into it quickly. We will talk about this technique in detail in the upcoming chapters.

Along with considering the one bike method vs the dual bike method, you'll also have to decide between a one wheelset and a two wheelset option. You can either have separate training and racing wheels, or just use your training wheels for racing by simply changing the tires to racing tires before race day.

I ride aero wheels in training, which are made of carbon with a max of 5 mm deep clinchers on aluminum rims (just the last part of the rim is aluminum, where the rubber meets the rim). I feel that this type of wheel is the easiest to change in case of a flat, which is ideal for training. Using deeper rimmed wheels in training will help with your adaptation to the slightly different handling (particularly in corners and at high speed). I don't suggest using tubulars (fully carbon where the rubber meets the rim) for training as this will get a little pricey when you puncture and also requires some skills to be able to replace the tire (which I still somehow never manage to do myself). Another major concern with the carbon rims is braking ability when the wheel is wet. Carbon rims lose this test compared to the aluminum rims here as well.

If you opt for the two wheelset method (training on clinchers and racing on tubulars), save your racing tubulars for the last few days before the race. This way you train on wheels that are easy to fix if needed and you also save mileage on your racing equipment.

Remember, when using a full carbon rim, the brake pads might have tiny aluminum pieces from your training wheels stuck in them which could ruin your race wheels. Before you change the wheels out, make sure to file down the pads in order to get rid of the small particles or exchange them with special carbon specific pads.

If you opt for the single wheelset method, you can use the same clincher wheels for training as for racing. Remember to have a close look at the tires. It's best to use a separate racing tire for the race, so you have a light, smooth, new profile. For training you need just the opposite, such as Gatorskin tires, which will keep you rolling through nearly any hazard out there on the road. The size of the tires for racing should be 23 mm or 25 mm and should fit the width of the wheels. The thicker the width of the wheel, the bigger the tire size. For training, anything goes.

How do you know which wheels to use at which races? For races where it is allowed, opt for a disc in the back and a deep rim in the front (either clincher or tubular, based on whether or not you are using the one wheelset or two wheelset method). The heavier you are, the deeper you could choose to have the rim in front, due to wind and steering ability. For me, at 170 lb. (76 kg), a 6-8 mm rim is perfect for the front. If it's crazy windy, I would go 4-5 mm deep in front, while keeping the disc in the back.

I would also suggest this for the smaller and lighter athletes—but remember that the best aerodynamics won't help you if you can't keep you're your bike moving in a straight line due to the wind. So choosing a lower size rim, such as 30-50 mm, could be a better choice in certain circumstances. Test ride and then decide. Clincher tires are much cheaper and easier to change. One of the only benefits that tubulars have is that you can ride longer on a puncture. Don't get too caught up with such details. Just weigh the benefits vs the weaknesses and make a choice.

Both types of tires have their pros and cons and I have used both successfully. Being in a team structure for the past few years, I've always gone with the advice of the top mechanic.

That advice has led me to choose tubulars for racing and clinchers for training. Apart from the occasional puncture during training, I've hardly ever had a mechanical issue during a race that has cost me any time.

There is plenty of debate on the issue online, so feel free to dig deep here. The bottom line is same. It comes down to personal preference. I've never had an issue so far, either way. Please bear in mind all those little decision will not influence your race or your performance, it might just make your life slightly easier. So don't waste too much energy on it. Be decisive and get it done. Then you'll have more time to train and make an actual difference in your performance. Remember, you can't buy speed; you have to work for it.

Here's the bottom line: If you can afford it and are racing at the top level, get a low rim clincher for training and a medium deep tubular in the front and a tubular disc in the back for racing. For super windy days during racing, choose a 40-50mm tubular in the front and a slightly bigger 60-80mm tubular in the back. That is three wheelsets total, one for training, and two for racing. For 99% of my races, with various distances, this has been sufficient for me. Remember, all of this is not cheap. If you are on a budget, then try borrowing or renting gear.

If you want to be self-sufficient during races and maintain the ability to change your tire, you should stick with clinchers for all of your wheels. The difference in rolling resistance between clinchers and tubulars is minimal, and risking sitting on the side of the road for large gaps of time (or having to DNF) is certainly not worth it. You will have to decide what is more important to you.

STORAGE TIPS:

- Nutrition can be stored anywhere during training. It just needs to be easily accessible and not require you to take your eyes off the road for too long a period of time. A little extra drag in training is actually a good thing. Racing, however, is a different story. You buy the most expensive bike and then you tape bars and gels all over the frame, losing out on all of the aerodynamic benefits that you paid good money for. It makes sense to store your nutrition in a bento box to maximize aerodynamics and utility. A Bento Box is a small zipper pouch that sits on the top tube behind the stem.

- In terms of fluids, there are quite a few options out there. You can store a bike bottle between your arms on the aero bars, where they create less drag than the traditional positioning on the frame. There are quite a few companies that produce material that will aid in this aerodynamic setup, or you can create your own as I have done in the past, with a bottle cage and zip ties. You also have the option of storing one or two bottles behind the seat. I personally think the best option is to have a special aero-bottle for the handlebars, which can often make you more aerodynamic than you would be without it. Of course, there is always a tradeoff between aerodynamics, and comfort and convenience. Traditional bottle cages allow you to switch out your bike bottles with those that are offered at the aid stations on the course. If you are racing half Ironman® distance races, then this won't be such a tradeoff. If you are racing full Ironman®, you might need to consider how you will store the extra fluid needed for the longer race.

- Choose the size and number of bike bottles based on

your pre-calculated personal nutritional needs. Mix the solution for your drinks between 6-8% (details to follow). If it's cold you will drink less fluid but need a bit more energy in your bottle mix than during a hot day.

Technical Tip:

- If you ever get a crack in your bike frame, it is important that you see a specialist who can tell you if the crack is in the carbon or just in the paint. Obviously paint scratches are merely aesthetic (which, if they bother you, can be touched up with either fingernail polish or paint that can be color matched by an auto-body shop). Of course safety is always priority so don't take any risk by riding a bike that is less than 100%

TIRE TIPS:

- I usually check my tires before I fly out to a race, since it doesn't really make sense to fly halfway around the world and then notice that a tire is about to go. Tubulars need to be glued and therefore have some lag time to prepare, so make time in advance of your race if you are using tubulars.

- During training, you will usually know when it is time to change a tire because you will keep getting punctures. Since you know that this is really annoying for you and your training partners, you won't need too much reminding to replace your tire. It makes sense to double check your tires after a long wet spring, and before group rides.

The Dos and Don'ts of Bike Gear

Dos

- Get a bike that fits your needs and your skill level. Get a bike that you like. Choose the One Bike Method or the Two Bike Method. In case you are a total "tri-geek" and are as addicted to the sport as I am, then you can start your own collection.
- Get a helmet and please wear it. It's a must these days—it's better to be safe. Helmets are light and well ventilated today so there no excuses.
- Get used to the click pedals—practice if you are a beginner. Practice someplace where you won't be too embarrassed if you fall. Don't practice downtown where there are lots of stop signs.
- Know the basics of how to repair/fix your own bike.
- In training, always carry a puncture kit with you, including Co2 cartridges, otherwise you will learn the hard way as you stand on the side of the road waiting to get a lift back home.
- Learn how to ride appropriately and safely in traffic. Use hand signals to turn and indicate to the rider behind you. YouTube videos about group riding are helpful, if needed.
- Get lights for the front and back of your bike. I even use lights during the day when training in areas with a lot of traffic and in countries where bike riding isn't so common.
- Buy some chamois cream for your sensitive saddle

area. After a few rides without it, you will understand why this is essential to your gear list.

Don'ts

- Don't attempt to be aerodynamic by lowering your handlebars so much that your chin nearly touches the front wheel. We are racing triathlons and not high-speed prologs in the Tour de France. Find a good balance between comfort & aero in order to ride fast but also produce a solid run off the bike.

- Don't try a bike in the shop, get all the info and then go home and order online. It's not fair to the shopkeeper. You can always get your info online. If you want to talk to someone personally, at least give the local shop a chance to match the price (plus a margin for his time and helpfulness). The good karma always comes back to you. If you are not sure which bike to buy, then go to a few shops and try the ones you are interested in. You might get it cheaper online but it can be very beneficial to have a good relationship with your nearest bike shop keeper. You will need it sooner or later.

- Don't train in your race gear more than necessary. You obviously need to test your gear at some point, but there is no need to run a 5k in your tri one-piece race suit. No Sunday group rides with full on race gear, aero helmet and speedos please.

- Don't pump up your training and racing wheels too much. Even if they hold 11 bars, you don't need to fill to capacity. More is not always better. I use this guideline: 7 bars for training and 8 for dry racing. Adjust to 7 bars for wet racing surfaces to have the best possible grip (7 bars equals 102 psi, 8 bar equals 116 psi).

Run Gear

Your swim gear is pretty easy to organize, and the bike gear is definitely the most expensive and complicated part of your program. We'll finish here, with your running gear, which is relatively straightforward. You don't need very much to be able to get out there and run. The beauty of running is that you just put one foot in front of the other, simply falling forward, and you're off.

For training, you need shoes that fit properly, socks, maybe a watch and some running specific clothing. To get the perfect pair of running shoes, it's best to go to a certified running store and have them evaluate your needs. With only a short test run on their treadmill, they will be able to tell you exactly what type of runner you are and what kind of shoes will be best for your running style and foot type.

Experts can tell the difference between a neutral runner, and one with supination (emphasizing the outside of your foot) or pronation (emphasizing the inside of your foot). This is important to know, as it tells you where you put your foot down and where your shoes would eventually wear off according to your stride. They have special shoes with stronger outside or inside support. High or low arches can benefit from insoles for support. The path to excellence is often paved through delving deeper, seeking information from trusted sources and adapting your equipment on the road to an upgraded outcome.

Your running shoe should be slightly larger than your normal shoe, as it should have a bit more space for your toes to spread out when your weight is on your forefoot. Normally it is one half to one full size larger than your normal shoe size. No worries, you won't slide around in the bigger shoe, as the top of your foot is tightly fixed. Choose a well-cushioned shoe for longer runs and a lighter shoe for shorter more speedy runs. By varying your choice of shoe, your foot is always adapting, which creates hardy, fit feet.

Apart from the shoe, you need some specific running socks. In thin Lycra socks you will find that you sweat less than in thicker cotton socks. Sweating means chafing and with wet feet that means blisters. I actually get my socks a size smaller than my shoes, as I feel like they stretch out after a few uses.

As for additional running gear, it generally comes down to personal preference. I do recommend avoiding cotton T-shirts. I would choose T-shirts made of a synthetic material, which will help with the cooling and the transportation of sweat away from your body. Depending on the temperature, of course, you will need a variety of clothes. Generally you will need a running top and a pair of running shorts. On cold days you can use running pants or tights and a long sleeve running shirt.

I realized, during my time in college, that in Europe people prefer tights when it's cold (despite the apparent exhibition factor) whereby in the US people tend to wear shorts even throughout the winter. Over the years I have rarely seen men in the US running with tights, although they seems to be catching on as of late. Have you seen the picture of some crazy guy from NYC running with a hat, gloves and a long-sleeve shirt, along with shorts? That's nonsense. Staying warm is key for your muscles to work properly and even more importantly to avoid injury. So try to keep the muscles warm by covering up. There is a saying: Keep the engine warm and well-oiled and it will run for many thousands of miles.

Apart from training clothes I highly recommend using a GPS watch for pacing your workouts. It will teach you so much about your speed and you will get a feeling for pacing yourself, which will help you a great deal for racing as well. There are a few out there that work well, but I always used the Garmin and now I am really hooked on it. I am known for running a very constant pace in my races and people always comment on it—so that's my secret—it is so simple. Just keep your race pace steady (taking into account form and fitness, of course). My coach always told me that the fastest way to get from A to B is by holding the highest average pace. Those are words to win by.

Running: Training Gear vs. Racing Gear

For triathlon racing we use the same light running shoe, or race flat, as road racers use but with the addition of an elastic lace system which helps us get into the shoe quicker. I create my own laces by using the same elastic that seamstresses use. I've done it that way for over 25 years and it hasn't failed me yet. You can also use laces with a fast lock system which are fancier elastic bands that have a lock mechanism. These specialized laces save valuable time in T2.

Some of the more up to date tri shoes even have a drainage system built into their soles. Carefully placed holes allow water to easily flow out of your shoes while you are running. Imagine you are running in the heat and you pour several cups of water over your head to cool yourself down. What happens to the water running down your body? It ends up in your shoes, and if there are no holes in your shoes, it remains there, throughout the race. Consequently, your shoe gets much heavier, your feet get waterlogged over time and it doesn't take long until you get your first blisters. I have even drilled holes in the soles of my favorite shoes, which worked fine as well.

In case you plan to do this with your inserts or your choice of shoes, then choose your drilling point wisely. Use areas where there is not too much pressure on your foot, such as between the toes. Then you won't run into any issues. A shoe that's made of water repellent material will also help you to avoid getting water in your shoes through the fabric, but it won't do much for the water that runs down your leg into your shoe. Remember that a marathon requires a lot of steps and a few grams of water-weight per step piles up massively over the distance.

The Dos and Don'ts of Running Gear

Dos

- Consider using a GPS watch. It lets you track your runs, comes with an extensive software and you know exactly how long and how fast you are going. It will teach you a lot during your session but also later for analysis.

- Vary your running shoes. I use a well-cushioned shoe for long easy runs, and a less cushioned shoe for middle distance runs as well as tempo runs.

- Make sure you know what foot type you have in order to have the right fitting shoe (neutral, supination, or pronation). A good foot evaluation will avoid injuries in the long run.

- Always walk in your new shoes a day or two before running with them. To avoid blisters and prevent injury, never break in your new shoe with a long run.

Don'ts

- Don't get new shoes just before a race.
- Don't forget Vaseline on long runs—you don't want to fall victim to "bloody nipples" because your running singlet rubbed you the wrong way. This is also helpful in shoes and shorts if you are prone to chafing.
- Don't train without socks. My buddy used to run without socks and it ended up costing him an injury. The Achilles tendon is the backbone of your run. Always keep it warm by wearing thin, light, Lycra socks!
- Don't buy shoes for their looks. Always get the shoe that fits your running style. If you are a neutral runner, don't get a pair of shoes that are made for pronators. It might give way to injuries.

Chapter 4:
Training

"We are what we repeatedly do. Excellence, therefore, is not an act but a habit."

~Aristotle

It's time to do the work. I'm here to motivate and inform you along the path. Prepare to shake up your routine and inject your game with all of the knowledge that I have gained throughout my career.

Success Is In the Details

This is one of my mantras. In a life that involves work and dedication, there is no overlooking the small parts of the big machine. In the part of Germany where I was born, we like to say "schaffe schaffe Häusle baue". In English this translates to "work, work, and build your house". It takes effort to yield the desired result, and in Germany we hold this to be true, and there is no hack to substitute for hard work. This is where the seeds of my work ethic were planted and the soil was toiled until it yielded fruit. It is perhaps the context from which the advice in this chapter originates. This is the secret of the success of my growth, passed on to you.

You've fashioned a plan and you've gathered your gear. You've made the decision to take the leap into triathlon. Now let's get you started on the meat of triathlon; the training. The knowledge I am about to pass on to you will help you to understand the details and science that will transform your future performance. For many of you, this information will fine-tune your training and deepen your understanding of the complexity underlying your buildup to becoming race ready.

Like any goal worth attaining, your triathlon aspirations will require frequent time in the pain cave where you will face your demons and possibly experience some dark nights of the soul. That's all a part of the path that you are now on. Use this section as a map of sorts, to help you find your bearings and eventually watch the sun set on your old self, revealing the champion within. It is your tool to train effectively, without wasting any more time. As they say, if you give a man to fish, you feed him for a day, and if you teach him how to fish, you feed him for a lifetime.

As we touched on in Chapter 2, many athletes, including myself, use the "3 to 1" — "2½ to ½" approach in our regular training schedule. Stretched throughout a 7 day workout schedule those numbers make out to three days of training followed by one day off. Then beginning again with 2½ days of training and a ½ day off. A recovery swim is perfect for that ½ day workout to finish off the week with a "leg free" session. I've worked this training path extensively with my coach Michael Krueger. We have found that it has served me very well over the years. This training system will give you solid training time but also time enough to recover, as you search for balance not burnout.

I will not be giving you one meal here, rather an endless supply of nourishment for your triathlon mind. This section is not about getting a pre-programed training plan that promises instant success, it's about laying the groundwork for your goal by getting you to think about your training as a champion does. You will be able to face your challenge head on with advice that will guide you through your everyday training. Meld these techniques and tactics into your day to day living to create a fuller, more integrated existence. You will emerge a more efficient and effective triathlete.

Swim Training, a Primer

Bring yourself into the arena as if you were beginning an actual race. We are fresh, rested and full of energy but reaching for our mental game to put everything into perspective. You recognize the mountain of a race in front of you and yet you begin. Here is the backdrop to begin a successful training regimen.

It seems like swimming is the least-liked part of triathlon. I know it's not always easy and enjoyable, but if you are able to swim well, you will come off with a clear advantage. The swim is an opportunity to give yourself a head start in your next big race. No matter how difficult it might seem to organize the swim session, always ask yourself the question: How bad do you want it? Then you will figure out if it's worth the trouble of working on your swim. The degree of dedication towards your goal is in your hands. My goal is to get you going on the path to discovering new avenues to turn you into an excellent swimmer in the shortest time possible, so you can enjoy your time in the water and see results of your hard work. Swimming is complex and technical, but it doesn't need to be approached in complicated way. After all, it's just about going with the flow, isn't it?

The best way to gain valuable time in the swim is to do the obvious: SWIM! A lot of triathletes don't put in enough time in the pool because it is the most inconvenient discipline. Swimming is the only discipline that we have to schedule according to facility availability, so it is not always the easiest to plan around those slots when lap swimming is allowed. Adding in an additional one or two swim sessions per week will make all the difference and improve your speed much more than any material or even the best training plans. It is all about the time you spend in the water.

When I started with triathlon back in 1989, I was a hopeless swimmer. At the age of 14, during my first tri race, my main goal was to beat my girlfriend at that time and to survive the swim. My times were stuck at around 23 minutes for the 1500 m swim, and no matter what I did, they didn't seem to get any faster. Eventually, I joined the local swim team, started to train hard with them, and started to see gradual improvements.

A bit further down the road I decided to join the team for a two week training camp. It was great fun. The camp itself was great, but I had a hard time adapting to three training sessions in the pool per day, and the overall volume. It was overload for me, but good fun. That was the first time I broke 45,000 yards in one week (that is slightly over 40k a week). Shortly after that camp I dropped 3.5 minutes during another race and started to make significant progress in the swim. I even started to race for the swim team and I began to swim more competitively. Somehow that camp helped me to get a lot of things right, and I stepped up my game substantially.

We are what we repeatedly do, so the best way to improve in the pool is to put in the hours. I know it's not the easy answer, but the point is well-founded. Once you put in enough time, you start to move in the water in a different way. You feel the gliding and the current and the subtle differences between the angles of your body. With a bit of technical guidance from a knowledgeable coach and lots of time staring down at that black tiled line, you begin gaining physical endurance as well as speed. Something just clicks. I can't tell you when that moment will be for you but I can tell you to hold space for those expansive moments. Be patient. You will recognize it when it happens. Things just start to come around, and when you look back you see a grand canyon sized gap between who you were when you started and what you let the water carve out of you.

After narrowly missing the German Olympic team in 2000, I started playing with the idea of going to the US to combine college and semi-professional training in the NCAA. In my opinion it was a perfect opportunity for me to combine my studies with improving my swimming and running by joining the competitive college teams. Since my biking was already top notch, I knew I needed to work on my two weaknesses if I was ever to live my Olympic dream. I decided to transfer to the University of Tampa, where I found what I was looking for. I was admitted with a full scholarship by splitting my athletic ability into two parts: the nationally ranked swim team and the cross-country team.

The coaches there were awesome and understood my passion for triathlon. I was the oldest athlete on the team and by working very hard I gained respect from all the others. This enabled me to manage a two-sport team schedule while getting my education on the side. Once I arrived in Tampa and got settled in, my times improved drastically. The Uni race schedule didn't really mesh with my international tri season, but I swam and ran well and received my Bachelor's degree to boot. I mostly took 3-hour night classes, so I had all day available for training. On one of my study-free nights, I met my partner…and the rest, as they say, is history. My life expanded both professionally and personally; perhaps my first venture into recognizing the merits of balancing and integrating all of the treasures in my life.

During my three years at UT, I morphed from an average swimmer into a front pack swimmer. Thanks to the volume of training I accomplished in Tampa, I was able to race internationally in triathlon and my swimming and running got much better by the day. I was able to use the accountability, camaraderie, and competitive support of my team to propel me towards my goal. Since training with the swim team benefited me so much, I always advise people to join a team or a Masters Squad. In the beginning, swimming by yourself is mentally challenging and it makes it all the harder to improve. Once you get to where you are excelling in the swim section, then you can always go back to more individual sessions if you want. Again, the group dynamics I was talking about in your planning phase are very useful in this training scenario as well. No way will you miss a session when you have all of your buddies waiting for you on deck!

Now that I have overcome my swimming obstacle, I tend to swim by myself a lot more. This works well for me, now that I've learned technique and understand how to execute a training session. If I feel I need support before a big race, when training is at its peak, then I tend to join in groups or organize training partners to help me get the job done. I've learned all the little tricks over the past 25+ years and this is what I've filtered out that works best.

Most of your work is done in the pool, and if you can choose 50 m over 25 yards, please do so as it is more "race-like" than the short course pools. If there are no nearby options to swim long course, try to find a longer pool within a reasonable driving distance so you can get in at least a few sessions before your race. This will better prepare you for non-stop open water swims.

Timing and focus are key. This means that you should aim to arrive at the pool when the least amount of people are there to distract you. Once you are at the pool, focus clearly on your swim routine. I see so many athletes hanging out and chatting instead of getting started with their session or with their warm-up. Of course when training in groups, everyone needs to be clear about what's on the menu for the day, but don't waste your time chatting up a storm—you are there to swim.

We all have our own schedules to follow but the less time you waste the more time you have left to play. It's hard when your buddy wants to stop you to chat because he is leaving early. Keep it quick and this will save you lots of swim time over the season. Other people understand that this is your "training time". Respect that within yourself as well. I am a big believer in not lallygagging (aka faffing around). Time is scarce and if you only have your lunch break or 1 hour after work, then you better make it count. Be careful not to shut out all socializing though. A balance must be achieved. The ability to find that sweet spot of hard work and play is a worthy goal to work for. Your intent should be to maximize your time and effort while also enjoying the ride.

Try multitasking by warming up on deck or dry land, as they say, while you chat with your comrades. It will make the transition to the real work much smoother. If you are swimming in a group, you will probably have to wait on other people and start all together. Even waiting time is your valuable training time, so use it wisely. If you are early, why not jump in and start warming up with a few laps before everyone is ready? If you are on deck, then stretch and do some basic core exercises since you are there anyway. Try tapping into some visualization exercises. Sprinkle in your mental game. It's always better to use your time wisely instead of just hanging out.

Always remember what your desired result is and prepare yourself for each step along the way. What is your big goal and are you able to reach your milestones on the way? You know where you are at this moment and where you need to be. Is your next race in a wetsuit? Have you tried it out lately? Picture yourself swimming in a 25 yard pool over a long period of time and then going to your first race where you suddenly have to swim in a lake or even in the ocean. Just the thought would scare many triathletes. Building in the proper engagement with actual race conditions is vital for effective training.

Open Water

Before you head out in the open water to train, you should first get really comfortable in the pool and learn the basics. When you do make the transition to swim open water, I advise you strongly not to go by yourself. Going alone is not only unsafe because of potential accidents, but it keeps you from the advantage of having people around you to push you during your sessions, or just to help you zip up your wetsuit.

I admit that I am a bit of a sissy when it comes to ocean swims. The thought of a shark coming up from the dark of the ocean floor to meet me for lunch just freaks me out. Even though I'm often scared shitless, I still bite the bullet and get the job done when necessary. Luckily I have put in enough time in shark infested open water that nowadays I am fast enough to maintain my position in almost any front pack.

Photo courtesy of Rick Dole Photography

If you are afraid of open water swimming or have ever experienced panic while out there alone in the water, (don't worry, virtually everyone started out like this) then you have to overcome your fear. Open water swimming is not to be taken lightly but any potential panic has to be normalized by exposing yourself to the source of your fear over and over and over again. When you become an authority on something you gain confidence, and your fear dissolves. Most fear is birthed from unfamiliarity, and the easiest way to rid yourself of this fear is to let the source of your fear become your new best friend.

When NASA planned to send their first astronauts to the moon, they recreated that day hundreds of times, from waking up and having breakfast, to boarding the aircraft, they exposed the astronauts to the experience of landing on the moon, so many times in fact, that it became second nature for them. Any fear dissolved over time and effort in the simulation.They couldn't afford to screw up that mission and neither can you. Be patient but diligent and over time your fears too will dissolve.

Training in open water is useful because it gets you accustomed to swimming longer distance without the breaks that each lap turn gives you in your pool training. It's also necessary in developing proper orientation. Practicing orientation in open water requires breathing on both sides, utilizing sighting exercises to help hone your navigation skills and finding buoys despite large waves. Be sure to practice your sighting by using landmarks in the distance that line up with the direction of your desired path. This way you can save time and energy and keep yourself on track more easily.

You will want to breathe when you are on the crest of the wave instead of in the trough, so you are able to see where you are headed. If you don't live near open water and cannot practice far in advance, then you can use the days leading up to the race to practice. Because you will be tapering, once the race gets closer, you will have a bit more time and energy to sharpen your open water skills.

Becoming accustomed to swimming effortlessly through an ocean full of competitors is vital to your success. Try and reproduce this scenario in training so there are no surprises come race day. Simply get in the middle of a few guys when swimming in open water to recreate the feeling and hone your method of operation. Discover whether you like to swim directly behind the swimmer ahead of you or halfway on the side, having your head at the height of their hip. Both of those positions will provide you with the best possible water draft while swimming. This is the most efficient way but be aware that it might not work well in rougher water.

Wetsuit Considerations

Preparing yourself for race conditions applies to your gear as well. If you will be racing in a wetsuit soon, it's a good idea to use your wetsuit every other time during your open water training to get used to it. Fine tune your routine of putting on your wetsuit which may include having somebody close by help you zip it up. Get in the water and swim with your wetsuit. I suggest you use a wetsuit when you do speed workouts, as this will mimic the feeling of being in a race and therefore it will better prepare you for what's to come. Little things, such as putting your wetsuit on when you are nervous and sweaty, will mimic pre-race condition. So try it out a few times and there will be no surprises before your race.

Remember to always work your way back from the main goal, and then you will know what you have to do in order to be prepared for a wetsuit or a swimskin race. I usually start getting used to the wetsuit during race week. I prefer to do the workload in the pool and when I am down to my last few hard sessions, I put on my wetsuit. To simulate racing conditions, I put it on a bit quicker than a training session and swim a short warm-up of 200 m. Then I get all the water flushed out before I imagine the gun going off to start the race. No need to overdo it in every swim, but doing this few times will help to refresh your memory for race day.

There are certain temperatures where a wetsuit is allowed. Sometimes it is optional and on some occasions it is not allowed at all. If the race isn't "wetsuit-legal," depending on the temperature, you will be wearing a swimskin. In general, unless the water is freezing cold, the swimskin is much more comfortable. Most age group races are wetsuit-legal, so if you are an amateur there is no doubt that you will have to get used to your "second skin". Make sure you are able to swim a solid distance in your wetsuit and don't restrict yourself to just a few hundred yards. Your training schedule should provide the time you need to feel at one with your suit.

In most cases, if the water temperature is below 76.1 degrees Fahrenheit (24.5 degrees Celsius) wetsuits are allowed. Generally, if the thickness of the wetsuit material exceeds 5 mm, you will be disqualified. In terms of temperature regulations, there are minor differences for pro and amateur athletes and for WTC, Challenge and ITU races. The rules should be checked before each race in order to avoid any stress, causing confusion on race day.

The Nuts and Bolts of Swim Training

Where do you begin when constructing your own personalized training routine? How do you build on your current routine and adapt it as you improve? I think the answer to these questions usually begins with a good sample training routine from a trusted source. Let's take a look at my routine and discuss how to adapt to your own stage of the journey.

I believe in the beauty of transitioning and I try to avoid jolting my body and adding unnecessary stress between various activities. Fading into and out of intense work is crucial if you are in this for the long haul, as every machine needs to warm up before it goes into action. I usually spend a few short minutes to build up heat in my body at beginning of every session, doing some dry land exercises to get ready. A dry land warm-up is also crucial as some races don't allow for a swim warm-up. This is a useful tool to get comfortable with as it could be a warm-up swim replacement before the actual race. The basic and really necessary movements that you should do before every swim, as a warm-up, are as follows:

- To get started before your swim, just jump up and down a few times and then shake out your arms and your legs (you can check out some videos on YouTube as to avoid looking like you are starting a new-age dance trend). A solid 1-2 minutes will begin warming up your body temperature.

- Now start rotating your right arm forward slowly and let it circle a few times. Keep increasing the speed of your rotation over a few seconds. This mimics the arm stroke and you will prepare your muscles for the swim. Do the same with your left arm. Start easy and then increase the speed of your arm rotation. Now do the same rotation exercise with each arm but now start doing them backwards.

- Move down to the floor and start warming up your knees and ACLs by bending your legs slightly, placing your hands on your knees and then making a circle with your knees in one direction and later in the other direction. This warms up all your knee tendons. It looks a bit funny, but if you don't take this step, and then you try to swim breaststroke, you run the risk of hurting your knees.

- To loosen up between exercises and warm-ups, do a few stationary light jumps to activate the calf muscles, your Achilles, and your ankles. Imagine yourself pushing off from the walls during your swim and imagine how you extended your feet into a streamline position.

- Do the streamline stretch for your feet before you start swimming. Simply bend your toes inwards and carefully put weight on the inwards bent toes, so you feel a stretch in your shin area.

- A quick stretch of the latissimus prepares your torso for the work to come. Do this by holding both arms straight over your head, folding your hands and slowly bending to each side. Hold there for a few seconds, then switch to the other side.

- One last important pre swim stretch would be for your triceps, which is your main swimming muscle beside the chest muscles. Put your left arm over your right shoulder and hold your elbow up straight in front of you. Then use your right hand and slowly push with your right hand your elbow towards your right shoulder. You will feel a nice little stretch on your left triceps. Stretch both arms for a few seconds.

Now you should be prepared for your swim. You can always add a few arms stretches or shaking your arms around to open up the shoulders. Some prefer to do a few pseudo water strokes by bending your upper body forward and simply simulate the swim strokes by rotation your body to left and right while pretending to swim. During those few short minutes you prepare your body for the swim and you have time to chat with your buddies or simply check out the pool scenery and decide which lane you will take over.

This is pretty much the same warm-up I use prior to the swim start of a triathlon race. You may have seen the guys out there that spend hours stretching and doing interesting yoga poses before the swim. That's not really necessary but you could decide to do a bit of dry land exercises such as a core stabilization warm-up, before your swim. I generally try to avoid jumping around in the middle of the pool deck and prefer to do my work off to the side (just be careful where you swing your arms. I have seen a few triathletes whack their wrists into the wall more than once). The more interesting the "pool scenery" is the longer these sessions usually last, I know, and that's okay. Boys, if there is a Baywatch alert, simply keep stretching and wear sunglasses, so it is not too obvious. Nobody likes a gawker.

In terms of style and show, most triathletes are worried that they will never look like pool swimmers when they swim, but it really isn't a big deal. We have to train differently than swimmers so don't compare your stroke and your swimming style to the likes of Michael Phelps. There are plenty of swimming exercises that we don't really need to know how to do, while others are important. One that belongs to the latter group is the flip-turn.

Many triathletes believe that there are no flip turns in the ocean, therefore they are not necessary. It does seem odd to learn a skill that has its use only in training, but alas, I am firmly planted to the importance of the lowly flip turn. I do understand that they don't need to be perfect, but there are many people that don't even bother to use them. Every swimmer who really wants to improve, tries to incorporate flip turns into training as it helps with the flow of other swimmers in the lane and makes for a more fluid training session. It takes just a few swims to get comfortable with it; you just have to force yourself to do them all the time, even when you think you don't have enough time to breathe when you swim hard.

Flip turns also help you to staying focused on your swimming as they don't allow you to stop and greet everyone who passes by. The pool lane is not the place to socialize. Plan to go for a coffee and refuel together afterwards. When you are in the water, it's time to work. There is nothing more annoying for other swimmers than people standing in the lane, discussing their life, while another one tries to do his interval and can't even turn due to loitering athletes. Take it as a given and you will get used to training with flip turns in a short amount of time. Remember, success is in the details and this little details is just as important as any other.

The Finer Points of Your Swim Training

Depending on your skill level, and which part of the season you are in at the moment, there are certain programs that make the most sense to swim. For instance, you might need longer endurance, building sessions in the beginning of the season or when you are doing a base block, or you might need a session with more sprints and resistance when you are working on building strength and speed later on in the season. You will find various swim suggestions and swim plans online and in all the tri magazines, and they can help you spice it up a bit. I like to fly over some of them to get new ideas from time to time, but make sure they match to what type of block you are in at the time, whether it be a base block, speed block, taper block, or pre-race block. The key is to make sure that you have some kind of structure to your training buildup and the ebb and flow of it all.

Swimming is the discipline where you have quite a bit of variety of types of training sessions compared to riding and running. During winter and spring, the swimming focus should be on stroke technique and a good variation of the four different swim strokes (butterfly, backstroke, breaststroke and freestyle). Moving into summer, freestyle will become your main swim stroke focus. That is why it is important to create this strong core training with all of the strokes so you avoid injury. Some athletes avoid all other strokes but freestyle, but this could lead to injury if you aren't careful. Overloading your freestyle specific muscles, versus your back muscles, very often causes your supraspinatus to act up. If that happens, a great counter movement, while training in the gym, is doing reverse butterfly which builds up the opposing muscle group.

Practicing all four strokes allows you to build up your overall fitness. What I like to imagine is that I am creating an overall balanced swim body that is prepared for an intense freestyle race. All of the supporting muscles have been paid attention to during my training so they are present almost as a counterbalance to the hyper-focused work of a freestyle race.

Have your training set up in blocks. There is a warm-up, a drill set, main set, some kicking and a mixed cool down. Focus on each block, understanding the mission of each block may shift as you move through them. Get a feeling for what works for you and don't focus on other people. Keep the predetermined flow and the speed for each block.

At the beginning of your warm-up, start swimming easy and slow to get into your session. If you jump in and start hammering away, you might run the risk of getting injured by pulling a muscle. The best stroke to ease into your warm-up is freestyle. In general, you should minimize the amount of time you train with breast stroke as it can aggravate your knees. Just be sure to take special care to warm-up properly beforehand, incorporating the breaststroke kick on dry land into your warm-up. Once you start your session, ease into each of the strokes carefully and let each muscle adapt.

The base period should be spiced up with some sprints and even some threshold sessions as well, but the main focus should be on creating your swim framework while maintaining fast twitch muscle memory with short intervals and drills. During the summer, right before the races start, you will need to increase the load for freestyle and adapt to the race pace while maintaining a high volume of base.

Keeping your interval breaks short during a base session is crucial. These workouts make up the majority of your swim training and as a rule of thumb, you should try to keep breaks between intervals short when you swim at base speed. For example if you do 12x 100 m freestyle at base pace, then there is no need to spend 1 minute between each of the 12 intervals. Keep working them off with short breaks until you are done and then after a block of 6-12x you can take time to catch your breath. Try to work in blocks and work yourself through up until a certain point where you know you deserve a rest. I use this rule all the time. Remember that you will be swimming nonstop in a race, so short breaks will mimic your race swim more accurately and this will help improve your speed over time.

Your interval breaks should increase the harder you swim. I've made a habit of not calculating my starting times, such as 5x400m leaving every 5:15 min as a lot of people do, which involves figuring out how long you will swim, plus the break, and remembering it for each rep. I feel it is easier to keep a certain amount of seconds (for example 10 seconds) between each set. Or if I have to hammer these 400s then I would probably take 30 seconds rest between and then take a longer break after I made it through the set, say 60-90 seconds in this case.

It can be confusing keeping track using the starting time method if you swim at various pools with 25 y, 25 m and 50 m. Therefore I try to simplify things and use the interval rest time as a guide. Of course there is a formula to perfectly match swim times between pool lengths, but be easy on yourself as you can get confused, and remember to keep track of your break time instead of your start times.

Remember to keep in mind how you will swim in a race. You

will start with many others at the same time and you won't have all that open space to yourself. From time to time you can practice this scenario, as your swim stroke might be influenced by others swimming close to you and you will mostly likely need to use a more compact stroke. The best technical drill to practice this is the high elbow swim stroke, where you touch your shoulders in the middle of every stroke. Push off in the back, high elbow, then touch your shoulders quickly and then proceed with your arm stroke and reach to the front. This exercise is very helpful for developing a compact stroke. It's also helpful to simulate the swim start from time to time when there are 2-3 swimmers in your lane. In a race, you will start faster than your average swim pace, so adapt to this in your training, and get used to being a small fish in a huge school.

There are countless numbers of training techniques and swim programs out there. Here are some examples of a typical threshold session to practice the high swim start pace and then settling in your race pace for the remaining session. Picture yourself surrounded by several other competitors waiting for the swim start. The key is to get away to have clear water so you can actually swim instead of swimming over other athletes.

<table>
<tr><th colspan="2">Sample Swim</th></tr>
<tr><th>Basic</th><th>Advanced</th></tr>
<tr><td>Warm-up:</td><td>Warm-up:</td></tr>
<tr><td>400 m Nonstop mixed stroke (10 sec break)

300 m Nonstop mixed stroke (10 sec break)

200 m Nonstop mixed stroke (10 second break)

100 m Nonstop mixed stroke (1 minute break)

4x50 m freestyle kick w/10 sec rest (1 min break)

6x50 m Heart Rate Build Up w/ 15 sec break between each 50 m. Use 4 different speeds in each 50 m, start easy and finish with a sprint

100 m easy (1 minute break)</td><td>Same warm-up, including kicking and Heart Rate build up.</td></tr>
<tr><td>Main Set:</td><td>Main Set:</td></tr>
<tr><td>8x100 m - 25 m all out sprint / 75 m base pace

w/15 sec interval breaks (1 min break)

200 m mixed stroke easy your choice (1 min break)

5x200 m (with 30 sec interval breaks)</td><td>4x200 m

• 50 hard/150 easy
• 100 hard/100 easy
• 150 hard /50 easy
• 200 hard w/ 15 sec break between each 200 m

100 m easy
4x200 m</td></tr>
</table>

• 50 m all out sprint	• 50 hard/150 easy
• 50 m medium pace	• 100 hard/100 easy
• 100 m base pace (1 min break)	• 150 hard /50 easy
-200 m mixed stroke easy (your choice)	• 200 hard w/ 15 sec break between each 200 m
-3x 600 m nonstop base pace freestyle with 30 sec interval break	**400 m** recovery/easy **2x800 m base pace** • freestyle - 45 second break • Paddles and Pull buoy
Cool Down:	Cool Down:
200 m mixed stroke at your own pace.	200 m your choice

Mind Your Manners

Know the Rules! When in Rome, do as the Romans do, literally. In Europe and the USA, the protocol is to circle swim up on the right side of the lane and down on the left. If the other lanes are full, it is standard to let another person share your lane by splitting the swim lane. Each swimmer keeps to one side of the lane and swims up and down exclusively on that side. If there are three or more swimmers, then circle swimming is standard. It is common courtesy to let people join in your lane, but don't forget that courtesy goes both ways. If you join a lane, show the other swimmers some respect and signal before you start swimming, so the other person is aware that another swimmer is joining in. Hitting your head on someone else's really hurts, so make sure to give a signal and pay attention to whether it's a circle swim or if you are splitting the lane. From then on, head down till it's done. Careful, our mates from down under are known to swim the opposite way! So if you happen to be in any Commonwealth countries be ready to switch up the courtesies.

At most pools there are lanes labeled with signs for fast, medium and slow swimmers. Don't let your ego get in the way. Choose the lane that's equal to your level of swimming. This helps everyone to get his or her training done in the best possible way. You can leave room for a motivational challenge from time to time by seeing if you can keep up with some slightly faster guys. But keep your eyes open and realize when you are in the way and your speed doesn't match the speed of the other swimmers. I always encourage others to leave five to ten-seconds between swimmers so that faster swimmers are able to pass.

Be careful not to let lane rage get the best of you, or let somebody else's bad mood impact you. Sometimes it might take a lot of self-control, but use that as part of your mental training. Swimming is a sport where you come in close contact with others, and you don't get much of a physical buffer between you and the next person. During a recent training session in Chamonix in the French Alps, I actually had someone punch me in the face under water and claw at my back, scratching my skin. I know it sounds crazy, but he just didn't like it that I was swimming faster than he was. I literally still have the scars to prove it. It took all I had to contain my anger and continue my session, but I managed to hold it all together. It's not worth the risk of getting kicked out of a pool because someone else is having a bad day.

If it's getting too crowded in the swim lane, reduce the medley sessions and focus more on your freestyle. It is extremely frustrating when slow guys jump in the fast lane and do super wide breaststroke kicks, covering the entire lane. When this happens, there is a good chance that this person is also swimming in the middle of the lane. We have all been there and we know exactly how annoying it is. Pool awareness is important. Do your best and hope that the crew you are swimming with falls in line.

When using short interval rests for a base training session, keep your socializing to a minimum. Use the time after a block or an entire set for any communication. When there is a solid break, you can catch your breath and have a quick chat. It's not uncommon for people go to the pool to focus strictly on their session and choose not to socialize. If this is your style, don't be self-conscious about appearing aloof, as long as you are respectful. There's a time and a place for connecting with your fellow athletes. You will find your own comfort level and may find yourself getting seriously addicted to focusing strictly on your job. Either way, the results will be evident.

Making the Most of Your Pool Tools

When swimming with pull buoy you have to swim a bit faster to make it effective. It's not a floating device to help you swim more easily. Heaps of athletes misunderstand the importance of pull buoy swimming. Their function is to eliminate your leg kicking and significantly increase your arm work. In addition to that, you can use a band around your feet to prevent your legs from supporting your stroke. I highly recommend swimming with the band around your feet when utilizing the pull buoy. This will demonstrate the strength of your arm stroke. Start with very short distances and work your way up. While doing this exercise you might feel like you are moving very slow and you may feel it ineffective. Trust me, you will gain speed in no time.

The pace clock is an often underutilized tool in training. Try to get used to the pace clock that most pools have on display. They are so much easier to read than your little wristwatch. Real swimmers never swim with a watch unless they are in the open water. Using the pace clock will allow you to get a better feeling for the times you produce.

If you are new to the game, train with your wetsuit or swim skin periodically to get used to them, especially when open water swimming. Don't forget to practice getting in and out of your wetsuit. If you can, avoid putting your wetsuit on when soaking wet; it is a nightmare, especially in the hectic pre-race situation. If it is wet, putting it on in the water is much easier. Watch your fingernails as they could easily leave cuts in the suit. Use your fingertips. Some athletes like to use plastic bags over their feet when they step into their suit, and this surely helps too. You can do so for your arms too, if you have issues getting your suit on. Trial and error will allow you to discover what works best for you. That's why it's important to use your training time to sort out any pitfalls before race day.

Keep sipping from your bottle every now and then, even if you don't realize it, you are also sweating in the water and therefore keep your electrolyte levels and your water storage up. Plan ahead for what your body will need after your workout, whether you're swimming with the early birds or with the night owls. A protein rich snack is always good to have on hand, as swimming makes you hungry. We will get into that later on in more depth, but planning ahead is the key is to maintaining a healthy blood sugar level. A banana and homemade protein bars in the car is the perfect snack on the way home. Don't run into the situation where you are stuck somewhere hungry and are forced to reach for something unhealthy on the road.

Body awareness means paying attention to environmental

conditions before, during and after training sessions. You may not feel cold after exiting the water but you must still be aware of the temperatures outside or indoors. You just finished a training session and your body will have an elevated temperature. Fluctuating temperatures can wreak havoc on your system as you move through your training routine. You might enjoy the air-conditioning but it could also affect your health and get you sick. Outside you might underestimate the temperature as your body is still in work mode, so be aware. Falling ill is always a bummer and so let's try to avoid those risks when we can. Daddy Dirk says put on your hat to stay warm, and make sure you dry your ears before heading outdoors. You'll thank me later.

If you're measuring the 3 disciplines of triathlon racing, the swim section is the smallest proportion of the race. Have that in mind when managing your training week, but don't underestimate it, as a lot of people do. Age group racing is very often influenced by the big packs that come out of the water and to have a chance to be up there in front, you need to be in that first group. That's an edge worth preserving by paying the right amount of attention to your swim training.

Swimming is a crucial part of triathlon and many people struggle with it due to the complexities we've discussed thus far. Knowing the pitfalls and creating a solid plan will help you to manage it better and more effectively. If it works smoothly then the fun will increase and you will enjoy it more and more. When you pay attention to your state of mind while navigating your swim train regimen, the flow in and out of your day to day life will feel natural and supportive. Happy training; happy body; happy life.

The Dos and Don'ts of Swim Training

Dos

- Do your pre swim warm-up each time you start a session, but just a short one including only the necessary exercises. Build a routine.
- Start swimming easy for the first few laps and let your body and swim specific muscles warm-up before hitting it hard.
- Adapt and accept circle swimming if necessary, pay attention to what might be marked on the signs posted for your lane. Remember to adapt when you travel, to clockwise or counterclockwise circle swimming.
- Pick the proper paced lane for your swim workout.
- Have your swim gear with you, and use your paddles, band, and pull buoy.
- Bring a drink bottle to the pool with a light energy and electrolyte mix in it, to refuel during your swim
- Go easy on the paddle size at the beginning. Start hand size or slightly bigger and work yourself up gradually to avoid shoulder issues.
- Use short breaks (such as 10-15 seconds) during base sessions, as well as technique and kicking sets. Use longer breaks when during speed workouts and at the end of longer blocks.
- Avoid injuries by swimming a variety of strokes, especially during the winter. The more you swim freestyle, the more you should swim backstroke as

well. Always work the opposite muscle set to avoid body imbalance issues and potential injury.

- Cool down properly after a set. Reduce your body temperature down by swimming a few easy 100 meters.
- Keep it loose. When back on deck, stretch out your triceps and loosen up your shoulders for a few seconds.
- Pause before skin hydrating. You will be sweating the first few minutes after a session, so wait with the lotion for a little bit before applying, otherwise you will be sweating even more.
- Plan to take some post swim fuel with you, best is always something homemade from whole foods, not processed and packaged.
- Always bring a spare pair of goggles and swimwear along. It will save your session a few times over the year.

Don'ts

- Don't hang out at the end of the lane and chat, blocking space where swimmers need to do their flip-turns. The pool is not for chatting--it is for swimming. Clear your lane when you are done.
- Don't push off right when someone is about to turn right in front of you, he might be faster and has to pass you right away. Allow a few seconds distance between you and the swimmer in front of you to allow for gaps where other swimmers can pass.
- Don't just use your pull buoy as floating support. Use it to work your arms!

- Don't overuse paddles and pull buoy. You swim faster with equipment, but just try the ring around your feet alone, without any pull buoy, if you want something more challenging.
- Don't be too serious out there, but be focused on improving your swim. Remember to keep things balanced.
- Don't get lane-rage. If you are having a bad day, don't take it out on fellow swimmers — use your workout to get out your frustrations and stress. Public pools are made for everyone, so try to be courteous and respectful of others.
- Don't make huge lane-width arm strokes that get in the way of other swimmers. Triathlon swimming in a race requires you to have a compact stroke, since you will be in a pack in the open water with plenty of others around you. You can practice this in the pool.

Cycling Training

The bike section of any triathlon race requires a mental toughness and stamina through the longest part of the race. You are required to reign in and redirect all of the fear and doubt that your mind throws at you for 4, 5 or as many as 8 hours. You sit with the burn of your efforts for such an extended amount of time that you begin to play with the voices in your head always chiming in with opinions. These are the conditions we remind ourselves of during our training.

Spending time in the saddle will be the most time consuming part of your triathlon journey. In the US, it is common for cyclists to drive out of town to a much quieter place to ride their bike. For a Euro, this is a pretty strange thing to do, since we just get on our bikes and go. This may be due to the fact that Europe tends to be more walkable and bikeable, and drivers are used to cyclists on the road, so there is less need to go to a remote area to ride. Of course no matter how you get it done, find the best possible way that works for you. If your city is a bit too crowded and the roads outside of town work better, then make the trip. This might involve a bit more planning and will add more time to your sessions.

Weigh the advantage of better road conditions against the time wasted traveling to a more desirable location to train. After doing this commute a few times, you will figure out how effective each option is for you and how much time is required. If you are venturing out of town, you should plan to have post-workout clothes with you and also some additional food and fluids. This will help you to recover faster while you drive back home. I prefer to start from home if there is a reasonable way to do so. I don't mind a bit of traffic as long and I am not stuck at too many red lights. For me everything is about effectiveness and efficiency, so I prefer to use the 45 minutes for recovery instead of driving.

The Finer Points of Bike Training

What is the measurement for improvement when charting 1000s of miles of bike training? To shave the minutes off your bike section, begin with an evaluation of a basic 20 minute time trial test. This will give you a baseline of what your abilities are in terms of wattage output. You have to make this 20 minute time trial test an "all out" endeavor. Hold back a bit when getting into the test but once you reach your maximum, stay strong and steady. Constant is the key word here. You are looking for your highest possible output for 20 minutes. This will give you an average watt output as a baseline. Set that as your base to measure your improvement and goal setting.

Most of your bike rides will be base rides. That means typically they range between 2-5 hrs, all in a steady pace with a lower average heart rate. There is nothing to it other than riding at base pace and getting the job done. We call it time in the saddle. Up until two weeks before race day I have really long tempo rides at race pace and also some shorter sessions that are much faster than my average race pace. The final two weeks are more for recovery, so not too much speed involved.

You'll start with your winter base mile training, then around spring time you should have accumulated quite some base miles in your legs and are ready to bolster. Typically 3 months of solid base training provides a proper platform to build on. From there on you will start adding a few tempo sessions to your normal training, which we call intervals. There is plenty of variety to make this interesting. You could do intervals in the form of hill repeats, which are usually done with a low cadence (around 60-65 rpms / rounds per minute). Focus on staying in the saddle and pushing a heavy gear uphill in order to increase your power output over time. I like those sessions a lot, as you don't have a super high heart rate, your watts are high and the training effect is great. When going uphill, it is much easier to hold the watts high compared to a flat, tempo ride.

Let's talk about a sample Interval. warm-up 45-60 minutes in base training mode. Then slowly increase your heart rate adding 3x2 min in heavy gear in the flat to prepare your legs for the heavy gear pushing.

Then you would do 5x3 miles uphill section, where you push a low cadence around 60 rpm and keeping your heart rate under control. The focus is on the heavy gear, keeping the rpm in check and just letting the legs do the work by keeping your upper body still. Between the 5 intervals, turn around and roll down to the bottom of the hill, possibly adding another few minutes spinning on the flats before heading up the hill for the second time. That provides enough rest between (typically 5-8 minutes).

To finish up you would then spin out the legs and add anywhere from 30-90 minutes cool down to make this a solid session. Remember never go below 60 rpm as we need our knees for running unlike pure cyclists who can go as low as 45 rpm. No need to risk injury for such marginal gains. The pace on the uphill sections should equal your Half Ironman® watts. This means the same watts you would push on average during a Half Ironman® triathlon. The downhill sections is used for recovery, where you would spin your legs out for active recovery vs just rolling downhill. Once you are at the bottom, roll another 1-2 minutes in the flat to get the feeling back before doing the second interval.

Another example of an interval session could be doing a time trial (TT) in flat terrain. Let's say you have to do 3x30 min efforts in Ironman® race pace. Your watts will result from your most recent test, so you have your baseline for various distances. To keep your watts up in the flat you have to push quite hard, and so of course it makes sense to do those sessions on your TT bike, in race position, laying on your aero bars. Therefore it's good to have a TT training bike with the same set up as your race bike.

The warm-up would be similar to the hill repeats, warming up for an hour at base pace, then getting your legs ready and your heart rate up by doing 3x2 min medium paced time trials to slowly increase the pace to prepare the body for the intervals.

Now you would do your 3x30 min efforts at your own designed pace, let's just say 300 watts. In between you would spin easy for 5-10 minutes and then repeat. Once you are done with the final interval, spin easy for recovery and then back into base pace for the remaining cool down time.

Once you get close to your peak race, the session are tougher and longer as you are fitter and you need to get close to race speed and distance. As a rule of thumb, the closer you get to race week the harder the sessions get. You want to be able to know exactly how hard you can go during the race, and you will learn this by adapting to various paces in training over time.

One of the hardest session I recall was before my win at Challenge Roth in 2013. It started with a 6 hr ride consisting of a 3x45 min interval at Ironman® pace (=300 watts for me), followed by a brick run of 30 min. So the 6 hrs. were always split into 1:15 h base then 45 minute interval, three times through, nonstop. The intervals needed to be progressive. Coach's order was to increase the wattage each interval. (1st at 290, 2nd at 300 and the last one at 310 watts) That is fast. Once I arrived back home I had to transition to a run off the bike. Coach's orders were: 20 min at Half Ironman® pace, then 10 min medium. That was brutal. Even though it was only 30 minutes, I was at my limit. That was an example of total exhaustion 12 days before my peak race.

When adding intervals training to your base training, you will realize that you will have to pay way more attention to the traffic around you. The increased speed adds more fun but also a bit more risk. So please be aware of your surrounding when doing speed and choose a quiet road with less traffic. At times I even had my coach driving behind me to protect me from the cars when traveling to the races where we were uncertain of the conditions. That can help a lot, but obviously not all of us have that opportunity.

Safety in Numbers

We have already talked about the benefit of joining formally organized group rides to experience the group dynamic. Those weekly group rides are very often known for being faster sessions. In Europe there are also base group rides but from my experience, most weekend rides are for the “weekend warriors” to test themselves. So if you show up, know what to expect. Some of the rides could be pretty dangerous due to crashes that happen in the middle and back of the pack, so you have to calculate the benefits versus the risk involved.

If you are sick of riding by yourself, group riding offers a nice change. You can use them as a speed session or you can stay a bit further back and just ride along. It is usually possible to fit your needs to the group ride. Just make sure there is good communication about that before the ride so you are not expected to take a pull and then you disturb the pace line.

If you’re not too familiar with the pace line, think of it as a grown up version of taking turns and playing nice. Everyone lines up in a pack, and then each athlete takes a pull at the front of the pack for a bit, working hard without the draft of other cyclists. Since you can save a solid amount of your energy if you are in the pack versus in the front, the best way to work as a group is to let each person have a turn at the front, before falling back into the pack. Birds flying south for the winter practice this same technique, spelling each other by taking turns at the front of the flock. So, cyclists take a hint from nature and implement this on two wheels.

Sometimes it might be easier to pull through and go to the

front when you are tired, but just do a short turn. Then you'll maintain the rhythm and fairness within the group, and others won't be disturbed. Not every triathlete knows how to behave in a group (after all, this isn't a team sport). Please inform yourself to avoid looking like a fool.

For instance, a key rule in group riding is not to lie on the aero bars in the middle of the peloton. It's not safe and will scare a lot of people around you. If you are pulling in front and you are a strong guy, it's not a problem to lie down on the aero bars and put your head down for a while, but in the middle of a group it is a no go. Lots of cyclists dislike triathletes because of that fact. So, learn to do it right and adapt to the group riding style.

Each group ride usually has some fast sections, some easier sections and then some intermediate sprints. The big final sprint is usually where everyone goes all out. Be a bit careful in this part of the ride, as I have heard plenty of crashes happen behind me during this final sprint. Stay out of the mix if you can't really keep up, as this is frowned upon. Most weekend warriors aren't super strong and they try to hang in there till the very end, sometimes going way beyond their limit. It can get a bit unpredictable. You might not want to sit on the wheel of one of these guys. You will only know who "these guys" are with time and observation.

Be careful when training in groups. Training with different people in bigger groups could also cause some issues from time to time. There are always one or two guys that need to show their egos because they simply feel great on any given session, even on a two hour easy ride. If you train yourself or if you look at your Sunday ride as your highlight, you may find yourself letting the group dynamic influence your planned training session. If you fall victim to this temptation of the ego, you may experience peaks in performance in haphazard and unexpected patterns. So, you might peak a few weeks before your race and show up exhausted on race day.

Remember that you have a bigger goal here and you need to keep focused on the big picture. Make sure you know what to do, and when to do it. That's why having a coach can be very helpful. Sticking to your plan is key to move forward and to develop your personal skills. Otherwise your form will be a gamble when it comes down to racing your peak race.

I often see age groupers being used as training partners for pros in training camps (mostly men, age-groupers being used as work horses for female pros). My advice? Don't be the "training bitch". Be careful here. The coach will want to get all his athletes together for a camp to add to his coaching value and you end up doing the wrong sessions just to make it fit for everyone else. I see that all the time.

Don't get this idea confused with simply training together and helping each other out. Camaraderie in training is a good thing and is desirable. Many top female pro athletes are doing heaps of training with other male amateurs, and this is usually a great fit for plenty of the training sessions. Just be aware that you are not being used to pull someone around and by the time you have to do your second or third training session of the day, you can hardly move because you used up all of your energy for someone else's benefit. Training together does work to some degree, but there's a fine line between mutual benefit and exploiting the situation. Make sure your plan is tailored for you and your needs and not just a copy of someone else's.

During my ITU short distance days I took part in group rides regularly and had good fun. Nowadays things have definitely changed. To be honest I've hardly gone to any formally organized group rides since I started my long distance career in 2009 because I consider it very dangerous and I just can't afford to crash due to someone's else's mistake. The risk is too high for me and there is too much at stake.

Back in the days of ITU racing I used group rides to prepare myself for the criterium-like racing style (aka crit) that short distance races have. For Ironman® training it's not really necessary though. Our goal is to ride a high pace, very steadily and for a long time. So when training for short distance (high intensive) races, formally organized group rides are very beneficial.

In contrast, when training for Half Ironman® or Ironman® distance races, these types of group rides are not ideal due to the constant shifting of the pace. When going long, a consistent steady pace is desired and it is tough to apply in a typical group ride. Group rides work in the very opposite way, so aren't the most beneficial. The sprints and unrhythmic acceleration are too fast and after these sections the pace gets very slow. This is where we triathletes need to continue to keep the pace high in order to use it as a long effort. So, if you are training for longer events, it might be better to organize your own smaller group of long distance tri focused athletes, or just meet up with a couple of your buddies in order to share the pain for the long haul.

At group rides, you often see guys with race ready bikes. A lot of athletes want to show off their fancy new stuff, but you have to decide for yourself if this is necessary. It might be true that the dog that barks doesn't bite. Training is a place to work, and not a place to race. Your race gear could also easily get damaged if you train with it a lot. So don't show up in your tri top, with compression socks, aero helmet and race wheels.

This is a big etiquette no-no. Most cyclists don't like it, and to be honest, neither do other triathletes.

It will, however, be necessary to test your race gear before your next race. I normally do this on my own or in a small group. Imagine if the former World Champion Faris al Sultan, famous for racing in his speedo, would show up for training rides in a banana hammock? That wouldn't be pretty, wouldn't it? Well, it would be pretty strange. So save your race specific stuff for the race, and definitely not for group rides. Always bear in mind that you could get a tiny leak in your race tires, so save your good stuff for race day, just make sure it is 100% functional and well broken into.

Tips for Healthy, Happy Bike Training

Have you heard of the 20 degree Celsius (68 degree Fahrenheit) rule? It's a typical Euro idea, but it is the rule of thumb on when to use short sleeve jerseys and shorts vs. long sleeve clothing. It's always smart to stay at bit warmer instead of getting too cold. If you are always riding in cold and wet conditions, there is a much higher risk for injuries and sickness. In the cold you also need more energy to stay warm. As a rule of thumb, try to remember that your joints and tendons don't like to be cold, so keep them toasty.

Your bike jersey has big pockets in the back, so use them. Roll up your wind vest and take your puncture kit with you. They might come in handy, and if not, then it's also no big deal. Better to be safe than sorry, as they say, right?

You should pay particular attention when riding in the mountains, as the weather changes so unbelievably quick, and you never know what you will end up with. Check the weather forecast before your long rides. I tend to bring too much on most of my rides, but I don't like to be cold, so I have my wind vest, arm warmers, a hat and my puncture kit with me pretty much all the time. If the weather turns dark then you can still ride and get the job done. It's all a matter of having the right clothes for any occasion. My coach always says: There is no such thing as bad weather; there are only bad clothing choices. Weather is never an excuse. If you have the right gear, you can make the session happen, no matter what.

If you're going to meet up with some other athletes, try not to rely on them to bring a pump along for the ride, and just check your bike before you throw it in your car. A few key items will do the job: Check the functionality of both brakes and the tire pressure before you hop on your bike. Pull both brake levers and rock the bike back and forth. By doing this you will find out if your handlebars or anything else is loose. If your bike passes the test, then you are good to go.

To inflate or not to inflate, that is the question. The public debate about tire pressure is an ongoing one and nobody really knows what's best. I remember, back in the days when we pumped up our tubular tires to the very max.

I finally figured out that that wasn't the best way to approach it when I joined the professional cycling team Leopard-Trek. During my very first race in 2012 (Abu Dhabi International Triathlon) I had a team mechanic with me. Three days out of the race I had to do a short TT and we tried out the entire race set up to make sure all was functioning perfectly. He pumped up race my tires to just 8 bars. I looked at him and wondered why he all of the sudden stopped pumping. He revealed the secret: For training rides the guys from the Tour de France team use a tire pressure of around 7-7.5 bars (which is 100-115 psi) and for racing they use 8-8.5 bars (115-125 psi). If the road is wet and they have to race in the rain then they use even less pressure than that, roughly 7.5 bar. That gives the tire more surface for gripping, making it less slippery and allowing it to connect to the ground. If it's good enough for Cancellara, it's good enough for me.

One of the myths is that you have to pump up your tubulars to 11+ bars (160 psi) like I used to. I was wrong, but you don't have to be. It's all about rolling resistance versus puncture safety. I will address topic again in the upcoming chapters and also show you how to tune up your bike and tires right on race day.

We talked a bit about click pedals in the gear section but it bears repeating here. The benefits of using click pedals are huge and no cyclist ever rides with normal shoes. In case you are a novice with the particulars of bike training, and you want to get used to the new click pedals, it might be best to get out of town for your first rides out on the road. It is also a smart decision to try it out by yourself first, instead of meeting others for a ride.

The clicking in and clicking out is very simple. You just need to get over your fears. Hold on to a pole or something near you while you sit on your bike and start clicking in your shoes, then click them out again. Make sure the mechanism works fairly easily, so you can do that back and forth a few times without too much effort. The easiest way to avoid falling down when you are at a standstill is to remember to keep the foot up (i.e., on the upper part of the stroke) that isn't getting clicked out. This will prevent you from falling over because it will allow your weight to stay on the foot that is on the ground.

Once you feel comfortable with clicking out in a stationary position, start riding and look for a place you plan to stop. From the point of leaving the stationary position, you need to stay focused on clicking out. Start clicking out a few feet earlier so you feel comfortable doing that at your designated stop. It is just a mind game to be ready to click when you have to. Simply push your heel towards the outside and you will click out. The reason that many people fall is because they forget to prepare to stop when they should. So don't be afraid. The worst case scenario is that you will just drop to the side and get back up again. Try it out a few times and you will get over your fears.

Ever try to describe your location to your significant other only to be met with a head full of question marks? Next to the area with all of the trees! Where the potholes end and the hill starts! Well, my partner never understands what I am talking about here and now she doesn't have to. I started using a handy tool: the "find my iPhone" application (or Apple's new "Friend Finder" app). These little apps are highly appreciated by your partner and/or family. They track you (assuming you have your phone with you) at all times.

From time to time it happens that my partner is waiting at home wondering why in the world I am not back from my ride yet. With the app she can easily see that I just added a loop or am still hanging with the boys after my ride. Imagine an emergency situation where you break down in the middle of nowhere. If this happens then your partner will know exactly where you are and can come and get you. God forbid you get in an accident and can't respond to your phone, then this would be the only tool that would help to locate you.

But it's not just for emergencies. The app can help your partner have supper ready for you when you get home, or to know exactly where to meet you for impromptu brick workouts where he or she is to deliver your running gear to you after X number of kilometers. It is very useful. It has helped me a few times over the years, on and even off the bike. Here is the catch though. Just remember, if you want to get off the leash or get off grid, then you need to turn the app off. You are trackable at all times by people who have access to the app. Remember that, before you text back some interesting locations of where you supposedly are—as they will know!

Since cycling is the most time consuming part of your training, try to keep it interesting by avoiding repeating the same loops over and over again. Of course if you ride 2-3 times a week for just around two hours, then it's not a big deal and might be nice to just get away and let your mind drift off. But for those of us who ride more than 25+ hours a week at times, it's all about making the ride interesting.

In most training camps the standard roads start to get boring after a point. Be a little creative and ride the loops the opposite way or listen to an audiobook or a podcast on your easy rides. I love it and have even listened to some Spanish classes on the bike. If you do decide to take this approach, you should only put your headphone in one ear (the one that is furthest away from cars), so you still hear what's going on around you, and only use them when you are in low traffic areas; safety first.

If you listen to your book or music while riding with others it could add a little tension since you can't really chat. What's the point of riding together if you ignore one another the whole time? I suggest using it for your hammer sessions or your long workouts when you want to be alone anyway. Sometimes I change up my routine and ride at different times of the day, just to have different stimulus on the way.

Biking adds the technical and mechanical component to training. Get used to doing some minor repairs on your bike, as it will save you a lot of time instead of running to the nearest bike shop every time something is wrong. Most repairs are pretty simple and there is always the "How to..." section of YouTube that can explain most repairs pretty clearly. My training toolbox includes an allen key set, levers, a spare tube, Co2 & adapter, my phone and some cash. I take this kit with me on every ride. I keep everything in a plastic bag, ready to go. Weather permitting; I will add a wind vest and/or rain jacket and arms or knees to the mix.

In a non-drafting event, if you ride your highest possible average speed from the beginning until the end which will get you to the finish line as quickly as possible. You can take it a step further by using your average power, which takes the terrain into account, allowing you to create the steadiest output. I suggested you utilize a power meter to measure your output. The power you produce is measured in watts, and the most reliable place to measure power is in the bottom bracket. To determine your best-fit average power for race day, you will need to do a few all-out tests. A coach will generally advise, that after a 20 minute warm-up, you put the hammer down for 20 minutes straight, holding your best average. This test is generally repeated before every new training block of roughly six weeks, and this shows your progress and also impacts your training for the next block, and eventually your race day power goal.

For the purpose of measuring power, I love my SRM power meter and I cannot imagine training without it—this is definitely the gold standard when it comes to measuring power, and you should accept no imitations. Your heart rate can always fluctuate due to form, temperature, fatigue and other outside factors, and your speed can also fluctuate depending on the terrain. However, you can always maneuver your watts. If you know you can ride 300 watts for 1 hour, then you know exactly how to pace yourself. During the downhills your numbers will drop significantly, so despite what people think, this is where you have to step on the gas. Downhills are not made for recovery in our sport! On the other hand, during an uphill climb, your watts will skyrocket. Learn to evaluate your watts to your advantage. You can always go above your estimated average, but only for a short time, otherwise you will end up losing too much energy for the effort and it will negatively influence your race later on. So, pacing is your number one goal.

If you can afford it, get one. It will be the best investment in maximizing your pacing strategies. This is the one of the very few gadgets that I really think helps you to learn how to push your body in the most effective way.

Variety is the spice of life, as they say. I found out that when I get bored of just riding on my TT bike, it's fun to ride on a road bike once in awhile. I change up frequently and enjoy riding on the road bike for my easier or some of the base rides. It seems to help me to pass the time better and it adds to the fun. On the road bike you will experience a totally different riding style and therefore your sensation will be very different as well. Don't miss an opportunity to sharpen your body awareness. Try it out and see if that helps you to trick your mind into getting motivated to face your session head on.

So much of training is about playing mind games with yourself. Bring in your mental game with your training practice. Take my advice. Being mindful in your everyday training has a significant effect on your ability to follow through in both your training and racing. Be aware that it all starts with your mind. We train our bodies but the mind leads you through every aspect of your triathlon experience. The more you understand the psychology of what motivates you, the more benefit you will have come race day. This is self-awareness; body, mind and spirit.

The Dos and Don'ts of Cycling Training

Dos

- Always bring some cash or your CC and an ID with you.
- Bring your own puncture kit when going out; don't rely on others to cover for you.
- Bring your own training snacks (bars, gels, bottles). You can even make your own ride fuel, which is what I do a lot of the time. Fuel properly, especially on long rides.
- Check weather and pick adequate clothing before your ride (especially the longer ones).
- Perform a quick standard check before every ride (tire pressure ok? Brakes working? Skewers tight?).
- Always wear your helmet when you ride. Just get used to it from the beginning if you are just starting out. Times have changed since the days when the wind in your hair was worth cracking your skull.
- Use proper precautions. If you ride early or late: use some blinking red lights in the back and a white light on the front to be seen my others. You can also use these during the day if you are riding in an area with a lot of traffic, which is what I do a lot.
- Familiarize yourself with the cycling jargon (pace line, take a pull, and elbow and hand signs).

- Learn rules for riding in the group, such as pointing out hazards on the road for those riding behind you.

- Try to get your position right and have somebody who is well experience help you dial it in. Then ride a few times by yourself before you join a group. Bike skills are crucial in groups.

- Get out in front and use the wind as you become a more advanced triathlete. The wind is your friend and it will only make you stronger.

- Monitor your heart rate. If it's too low in the group, pick it up, or simply go to the front.

- Be alert and awake at all times, especially when you get tired towards the end of your long rides. This is where most stupid little accidents happen.

- Always bring a Ziploc bag for your phone, as sudden rain might surprise you and if there is no rain, the sweat also affects your phone's functionality.

- Have your chain oiled frequently, there is nothing more annoying riding with someone who has ongoing squeaking music coming out of the their bike; and of course your gear will last longer if you take care of it.

Don'ts

- Don't take risks on the bike. Learn where your own limits are without crossing the line (speed, quick turns, pacing).

- Don't take an aero position in the middle of a group, unless you are very skilled with your bike, and even then, you really shouldn't.

- Don't lose your focus. Whatever you do, remember there are guys riding right behind you and their reaction is delayed after your own. Try to think ahead in traffic.

- Don't free spin too much, letting your legs sit still. You waste your training time and this will annoy the guy riding behind you.

- Don't show up with countless gadgets and compression wear from head to toe. You might be the joke of the next few rides if you attempt it.

- Don't use your cycling gear as street wear. Cycling gear is meant for cycling and it is not supposed to be the outfit you wear around in the hotel for breakfast. This is typical Mallorca hobby cyclist behavior, which should be avoided.

- Don't be the new guy in the group and tell everyone how they should ride. In sport there is a sort of hierarchy. Meaning the big boys usually lead the way and make sure everyone is okay. Take your time to see where you fit in.

- Don't show up in a stinky jersey when you ride with others, it's a nightmare for the guy behind you. A rule of thumb for number of times to wear your kit is a very max of 2x per jersey, and your nether regions will be happy if you change pants every time you ride. Use antibacterial chaffing cream to avoid problems.

- Don't run every stop light. We want the drivers to accept us on the road, so then we have to act appropriately and show that we accept the rules. Of course, this can vary from country to country, so adapt to the status quo.

Run Training

Running is a bit more individual than biking. There is no hiding and drafting behind someone. Running is very honest and pure. It's the easiest part to organize of all three disciplines, though it can be the toughest part on your body, especially when it comes to racing. Almost anyone can run, at least at some level. Regardless of weather and temperature you can always sneak in a run. It might not be perfect and exciting but you can always get the job done. The beauty of this discipline is that you will get the most accomplished in a short amount time. I believe it is the toughest part in triathlon--mostly because it's at the end of a race and you are already tired, but also because you must carry your own body weight, unlike for swimming and biking.

The Finer Points of Run Training

So in training, we set the stage for racing conditions both mentally and physically. At this point, during a race, everybody is suffering physically. But what does your mind do with that pain. When you realize the number of miles in front of you how does your mind convince you that you have what it takes to push through? We get comfortable moving through a simulation of your state of mind on race day, exhausted from a long bike ride. Now we train.

Most run sessions at base pace are clearly defined by a certain pace, such as 4 min per kilometer, or in US terms 6:15 min per mile pace. In addition to that, the pace is principally based on a heart rate range that was determined by a test (such as keeping your heart rate between 130-140 bpm). This is similar to a FTP bike test. During this Functional threshold power test (FTP) you determine your highest average power output (measured in watts) as well as you heart rate. From this 20 min test, you can determine all other training zones, such as your base endurance place being 55-75% of that test and so forth. You would do a test run to determine the parameters for the training such as a 5k (3.1 mile) run test to see your potential. Average heart rate and pace could be a base line where you can draw conclusions and training recommendations for the following training blocks. The running test is very similar to this 5k test. In order to track your fitness progress, those test would be repeated during the season to adjust the date.

Similar to biking, you would also determine various speeds such as base training pace, interval pace and race pace. For example, a 1 hr base run, is usually at a 4 - 4:15 min/km pace for me. I personally prefer working with clear times that are carefully controlled by a GPS watch, using the heart rate as a secondary training feedback device. Heart rate can be touchy, easily fluctuating due to a crappy night of sleep or simply elevated by talking during your run. So I advise you all to use it more as an informational tool than a strict training control tool. Most athletes are so data focused nowadays that the joy of simply doing the sport is taking a back seat.

Your run training will include intervals on the road and on the track and hill repetitions. When running uphill intervals you are emphasizing the glutes, our biggest muscle in the body. This builds your strength and stamina. Be careful when running downhill as this potentially causes injury over time. Many athletes opt for the treadmill to avoid nagging injuries. Here you can run uphill at a steady given pace and when it time to ease up and recover, you simply run flat, adjusting the slope of the treadmill. Many athletes prefer this as you have the opportunity to perfectly adjust your pace in an air conditioned environment, plus you can have your drinks with you and analyze your running form in the mirror in front of you. The downside is that sometimes the mental toughness needed to push through is absent when simply staring at the wall in front of you.

Before your hill repeats, you would also start with a 20 min warm-up jog followed by a few easy stretches, just a few strides to loosen up the legs and adapt to a faster running pace, preparing your body for the workout to come. Strides are short 100 m runs, where you are starting from a normal jog and steadily increasing the pace to a sub maximal sprint towards the end. Think from zero to 100 km/h. Then walk / jog back and repeat 4-6x. That will bring your heart rate up and kick starts the system in preparation for the high heart rate hill reps.

Now choose a steady uphill section where you could run uphill 1-3 minutes. It could be 2x 8 repetitions, meaning you will run up and down 8x and after the first block of 8 repeats, you will take a 10 min easy jog, in a flat section, in order to recover and then jump in the second set of 8 repeats. The rest between the 8 repeats could be an easy downhill job, and even an additional 1-2 minute jog in the flats before hitting it again.

To make it even more fun, the first 8 reps could be medium pace and the second block of 8 reps could be all out. I am starting sweating typing this. It's vital to add a proper cool down after the repeats as this also helps to prepare the body to loosen up afterwards and to prepare the next session.

Apart from hill repeats you could also go to the track. A typical track session would include the same 20 min warm-up as a hill repeat, a few stretches and also 4-6 strides. The main dish would be 6x 1 mile repeats made up of 2x at 5:10 min/mile pace, 2x at 5:00 min/mile pace and the final 2 at 4:50 pace as an example. As interval break you would use a 3 min active recovery jog. Once you are done, you need to catch a breath and then add a proper 15-20 min cool down.

There is so much variety in track sessions and I believe the key is to keep a good mix in order to keep it interesting because, at the end of the day, you are simply running around in circles for hours. Another good example for track sessions are the pyramids. A sample main set could consist of a 400m/800m /1200m/1600m/1200m/800m/400m. When running pyramids the pace can vary a bit. The shorter the distance, the faster the pace becomes. And the faster the pace the longer the breaks are in order to recover between. For advanced athletes it is beneficial to have active recovery during the sessions, and not just walk and stand around until the next interval starts. This helps to keep the system going, but it's tough. A super easy jog pace for 2-3 minutes is best between those long intervals.

Whatever sessions you prefer, It is nice to use the same key session over a period of time in order to track your progress. Since 2008 I rarely train using track sessions. Stepping up from Olympic distance to long distance racing, I found it more beneficial to run on trails utilizing my GPS watch for distance or time alerts. So it is basically the same thing. I guess after so many years of training I got a bit fed up with running around in circles. I believe one of the reasons I was able to enjoy such a long career is that I changed the scenery a lot and focused on keeping the training interesting. Outside stimulus was always important during my career.

My favorite interval sessions were the brick runs. Sure they are tough but there is nothing more triathlon-like than hammering out a bike session and then flying in hot, quickly changing into running gear, grabbing the gel and a sip of water and storming out on the run. Those sessions have to be prepared beforehand. Your running gear needs to be laid out as well as the nutrition. This is a perfect simulation of a hectic race like situation. Out on the run, this is where I always pictured the spectators cheering for me as I was leading the imaginary race. The cheering was then converted into positive energy which helped me on my run.

I hardly ever run more than a 45 min brick, simply to keep the pace high and in order not to get too tired after one single session. This would negatively influence training the next day. So giving your muscles a kick is ok, but not too much. Usually a 30 min run is divided into 20 minutes of hard running and 10 min medium/easy. If they are increased to 45 min then the pace would adjust to 30 min hard running, finishing up the session with 15 min medium/easy. The pace would vary according to which training period I am in or which race I am about to prepare for. It usually ranging between Half and Full Ironman® pace. It might not sound fast, but remember the 6 hr bike ride before Challenge Roth? Yep, you are slightly cooked before even starting.

As many triathletes know, during a triathlon race, once the first few steps of the run are behind you, it starts to feel like you forgot your running legs at home. Don't worry. You can indeed run, but it will always take a little time to get into the zone. The longer and harder the bike is, the more difficult it will be to find your running rhythm. For me, sometimes it takes me 20-30 minutes to feel like I am running normal. Training using brick workouts definitely helps us to get used to the changeover. This is critical for your training. Every champion knows that the more you do brick workouts, the faster you will adapt to running off the bike and the easier it becomes.

It's very difficult for a great runner to maintain his running ability in a triathlon. Running after a long bike ride is a totally different feeling than just running a road race. In triathlons we need to train our bodies to perform under heavy fatigue and running is a key factor in having a successful race. Every athlete is tired from a long ride and now it's up to the strength that's left in the body and mind. You can avoid being too tired on the run by pacing yourself properly on the bike and choosing the right pace once you get off the bike. In training we can simulate those sessions by doing brick workouts.

Brick workouts are combinations of swim-bike or bike-run workouts that simulate race conditions by introducing a transition. You will learn more about the benefits of these types of workouts in the next chapter, but just remember that in training you need to slowly adapt your body to performing when it is tired. It's not the athlete that goes the fastest that wins, it's the athlete that slows down the least. By dealing with fatigue and making it your best friend, you will more easily be able to deal with the fatigue that will come on race day.

Given the fact that you have put in the necessary training on the pure running part as well, bricks make sense, as the next step to linking all of the disciplines. You can't simply train like a runner to perform well in a triathlon. Even average runners can shine in triathlon if they are very skilled at absorbing the bike section and transitioning the body through each discipline. Those athletes aren't too worn down by the time the run comes along and can show off more of their potential.

As you can see, it all sounds pretty simple, and that's because in principle, it is. Through repeated brick training sessions your real running potential for a triathlon will be revealed. It's following the narrative of a race through your body's physiology, pushing your legs to the very limit. On the mental side of it, bricks train the brain to push through the pain threshold, adapting to the extreme discomfort. Getting familiar with this burning sensation in your legs teaches you that your body will transition and be able to carry you through to the finish line.

A sample brick training scenario might start with a swim-bike brick session. During your swim, all the blood rushes to your upper body where the intensity of the workout is focused. Coming out of the water, your body recognizes the shift and begins diverting blood flow back to the legs as you jump on the stationary bike and start pushing your legs to their limit.

During a bike-run brick scenario, you would jump off of the bike to begin using your running muscles. Your mind and body recognize that fatigue is setting in. Here is where you trust that your legs will not fail you in this final leg of the journey. You are teaching the body the transformation from one discipline to the other. You are proving to your mind that the body can learn, adapt and succeed. To keep it all together is the definition of a champion.

Triathletes are usually stronger built than typical runners due to the strength component needed in all disciplines. Always bear in mind that you need to customize your training and modify your race strategy for triathlon, not road racing. You will be evaluating your current strengths and weaknesses against the cadence needed to navigate the gauntlet of triathlon

I recall being one of the slower guys when I ran the 10k on the road; most of my friends on the German team back then were flying on those 10k tests. I seemed to function very well under enormous fatigue but not that well in a tapered 10k pure running test. The same was true during college. I ran good enough but there was no comparison to how my body fought under fatigue. My goal was always to run well when my body was tired, and I guess that's why I had a more successful career in Ironman® racing than in short distance, where you don't really have time to get very tired.

In contrast to cycling, you don‘t have to have much material or gear to get your running training done. Apart from the training content and the mileage involved, your overall health and avoiding injury are key elements. Therefore I can't stress enough how important it is to have the right kind of shoes. As I hinted earlier, get your running stride checked out and find a shoe that fits your specific needs. By knowing what works for you, you can avoid a chain of unpleasant events that could lead from one injury to another.

Listen to your body. Maybe barefoot style running shoes work well for you while they are horrible for other people. Just be sure to slowly adapt to any new gear you take into your program. From there you should be set and you just have to focus on putting in the miles. The right amount for you should be evaluated by your coach based on years of experience, and it should integrate a feedback loop that comes from you and your time on the trails. If you don't have a coach you'll begin building a foundation of training to work from. And of course most committed triathletes naturally develop a support system of like-minded folks that act as a sounding board to your developing training. Lean on that and through experience you'll move your training forward.

The beauty of running is that it is very natural and we all have the basic capability to run. You can also run pretty much everywhere and in all possible conditions. I always tell people, there is no excuse not to run. Time cannot be a limiting factor, because with just a 30-45 min run, let's say three days per week, you could gain great strides in your race performance. This might not increase your running performance by a lot, but it should maintain it. You could even spare those few minutes during your lunch break if you needed to.

How much mileage is too much mileage? That is a very

individual and could vary quite a bit. Upping the mileage in your running program could lead to significant improvement in your running form but could also could increase the risk of injury. Try to follow the guidelines mentioned here and avoid pitfalls. Wear good shoes, run up 80% on trails if you can, stretch after each session, get massages, use a foam roller, do core stabilization exercises, and take recovery seriously.

For example, I use my Normatec compression boots, which pump air into space chambers of a leg boot, that you wear while sitting on the couch (in my case, while watching Netflix), at least two times a week on a regular basis. In addition to that I also get at least two massages per week. The best time to get massaged is at the end of the last day before your rest day, so you benefit from the effects overnight but also the entire next day when you are resting. All of those little things make the difference in the long run.

As with swim training, run training is highly individual and requires a core body of knowledge that should be combined with listening to your own body. You are the only one who lives in your body and you are the only one who will know when things are too much or not enough for you.

Another important point is to keep your joints, muscles and tendons warm during your run. Like a well-oiled, warmed up car engine, it's better to be warm than to be cold. This is to avoid risking getting injured down the road. Your knees and ankles, and especially your Achilles tendon, needs to stay well-oiled and therefore warm. Just be extra conscious when you head out in the cold to keep the lower extremities warm as much as possible. Keep that head covered. You lose a lot of heat from your head, so make sure to wear some headwear, especially my fellow bald guys.

On average, a high percentage of runners enjoy running by themselves, as it's tough to find the right training partners when you get to a certain point in your run development, and some people just have crazy schedules that require getting out the door alone. I find training with a partner highly beneficial and I always encourage others to find running buddies. It just makes the journey so much more memorable and takes our focus outside of ourselves which fits in with this journey we are on together very well.

It's pretty clear that you need to find a bird of a feather—someone that thinks like you do. It won't help you if you prefer to run with your music on and your partner in crime loves to chat about his latest weekend adventure. I believe it's easy to find a good fit if you take the time to look. Earlier, I talked about my friend Todd from St. Augustine. We both love to train alongside one another and just run. We chat sometimes but we need quite a bit of oxygen at the pace we run, so normally there isn't too much chatting going on.

I see plenty of running groups everywhere I go and I am sure that everyone can find a nice training group that will help them out. Not every run session is ideal for sharing with the group, similarly to the bike groups we talked about before. Some workouts you might have to do by yourself and depending on your time investment, you might only have some support here and there. Running is easy to organize and you can run anywhere.

Consider your turf. Ideally you should try to run around 70-80 % of all your runs on soft surfaces, such as soft trails, forests or gravel roads. The physical pounding of your weight has three to four times more impact on your body that your actual weight. Several studies hint that there is a slight variation on this figure depending on if you are a forefoot, a midfoot, or a heel striker. So be nice to your joints and have solid cushioning in your shoes.

Finding those trails might be a tough task, depending on where you live. If you live for instance in Boulder, Colorado, you have more than enough trails to choose from, but it's not like that everywhere. In many places you have to drive to find the trails and then it becomes something that you have to account for in your daily time management. It sure makes sense for the long runs, though, which should be a minimal requirement. If you have to drive to all of your workouts, you'll spend way too much time in the car, so it might be good to combine some of the sessions in order to save some time.

Back in the planning phase we talked about finding the nearest pool. So if you find a perfect town with tons of trails, low traffic and various terrains for riding, and on top of that have access to a great 50 meter pool within walking distance—please let me know so I can move there! No but really, I have indeed found a few pretty awesome places throughout my career. Of course, lifestyle is also huge on my list of priorities too, so a few nice coffee shops are also a must!

Time effectiveness is key in the life of a triathlete. You have to figure out what is easier for you--a combo session and then a longer break or if it is easier to just get out the door and get it done. Everyone's priorities are different. You'll know what works for you as you sample different methods. I think the key lies within your own intuition. Listen to that inner voice and trust.

Even the best training plans don't work well for you if it they don't take into account your typical weekly schedule. In our busy days there are always unexpected demands that come up and sometimes we have to adjust our training. As a basic rule I teach my athletes to try to get the session done, but if it's too difficult for whatever reason, then their second step should be to keep the volume of the session but reduce the speed of that session (downgrade from a speed session down to base training, or from base down to a recovery session). If even that is too tough, then the third step is to reduce and cut the volume down, let's say your 1:10 hr run is too long and you suffer badly in the heat, then you could either run the second half on the treadmill or you could cut it down to 45 min.

Don't make a habit of this sort of compromise in your training. Use your instincts when choosing to pare down a training session. The adaptive capability of the body is amazing and it will get used to the pressure you put on it. You just have to give it some time. The very final solution, and this is if you really can't go on, is to cancel the session and take a nap. It happens to me too sometimes, and as long as you are being honest to yourself then you should be careful not to beat yourself up about it. Remember that triathlon is a way of pushing yourself and loving yourself in the process, so don't get into a negative self-talk spiral.

Running is tough. Don't try to run hard every time you get out there. Use all your "gears". Easy runs will help you to recover and will also do their part to bring you to the next level in terms of your endurance. Just like you shift your bike gears up and down to test the functionality of your bike, let your body move through its running gears throughout your various workouts and you will be ready come race day.

The Dos and Don'ts of Run Training

Dos

- Change your running socks frequently as to prevent blisters, odor and possibly athlete's foot.
- Choose the perfect running shoe that provides comfort but also cushioning. Have various shoes for long runs and tempo runs.
- Alternate your running surface and try to run on soft trails when possible. The closer you get to the race, you might want to get more used to the concrete (= hard pounding). Be aware that your muscles could get a bit tighter. Use enhanced recovery measures if that's the case.
- Keep your joints, muscle, tendons and head warm during cold days. You can always take off layers of needed.
- Pay attention to your fuel intake. Find out for yourself what you can eat before your run and what causes heartburn. It could make your workout a not so nice experience if you eat heavy food right before your run. Eat easily digestible food up to 90 minutes before your run.

Don'ts

- Don't run with headphones in your ears at all times. Enjoy the silence when out there and let your mind drift without stimulating your brain with loud music. Music sure helps sometimes, but not on every run. The reason to get out there is to embrace nature and not just push through to get the run done. Mix it up and see what works best for you.

- Don't overuse your running shoes. Have several pairs of shoes to choose from. Check the sole frequently and if there is significant wear, change them out for new ones. Good shoes are crucial for staying pain and injury free!

- Don't forget basic safety procedures out there on your runs. Be careful when running in the dark. Use reflection gear and be extra cautious. I once had a shoes sponsor that produced glow in the dark shoes, which were pretty helpful!

Be your own trainer. Assess your efforts. Try rating each of your training sessions (swim, bike and run) from one to ten. Ten being the best grade and one being you should have stayed in bed. Needless to say, you can always strive for a minimum of eight out of ten. If you work and only have limited time to spare, each second is really worth a lot and you should try to get the most out of each session. Efficiency is key and this rating could help keep you honest. Once you train you should work and not just move your legs; get something out of your session otherwise it might have been smarter to simply stay home and hang out with the people you love. It can happen sometimes, but it should be really rare. You can use your coach as a soundboard to help decide what is best in situations where you feel like you are putting in empty miles.

Train hard and recover with intention. Listen to what your body is telling you after each training session and give it what it needs. It could be as simple as an Epsom salt bath or as luxurious as a full body massage. It could be a decision to take a recovery day early or tone down a workout after a stressful day. Training is as much about evaluating feedback as it is about swimming, biking and running. Communicate and listen. Creating harmony in conversation between your body and mind allows us to move toward becoming the champion we envision ourselves to be.

Training is the core of the triathlon experience. We weave this effort into our daily lives to integrate it as part of the tapestry of our existence. The daily pressure we put on our bodies forces us to expand our reality, convincing us that we are capable of so much more that we once were. The daily grind is what gradually sharpens our tools for battle come race day.

Daily training can be painful at times but is necessary in order for us to shed the person we once were and become who we really are. This is what the epic voyage is really about. It is as much mental as it is physical, and through the process of shaping our bodies, we also become aware of our own mental strength. Our minds make choices that make the machine run, and through this daily reminder of another session in the books, the mind and body prepare for battle.

"All things are ready, if our mind be so."

~William Shakespeare, Henry V

Chapter 5:
Getting ready to race

Dorothy Parker:

"Exactly what do you mean by 'guts'?"

Ernest Hemingway:

"By 'guts' I mean, grace under pressure."

~New Yorker Magazine Article

"The Artist's Reward"

Repeat after me.

SUCCESS IS INDEED IN THE DETAILS:

Imagine yourself both mentally and physically prepared for the expedition ahead. You've done the work now let's make a subtle but important shift to transition to race day. There's no looking back. Let's push on ahead.

The final weeks leading up to a race require a special touch. This shift in your training is meant for your targeted peak race as well as every race you have slated for your schedule. These guidelines give wings to your efforts. Treat each and every race as an elevated stage, honoring the blood, sweat and tears that you have relinquished on your path to this day. It's time to get into pre-race mode. It's time to practice a little grace under pressure.

Imagine you are closing in on your first big race. You did the work in each discipline and now, a few weeks out, it's time to weave these three separate disciplines together. You have the choice between utilizing the classical approach or the reverse periodization approach. If you chart your path using the classical approach, you will be putting in the base mileage first and then adding the speed progressively, the closer you get to the race. The reverse periodization approach flips it by focusing on speed first and base mileage second.

I have used both, depending on where I've trained. For instance, in altitude (starting roughly at 5000 ft or 1600 m, if not more), I may focus less on speed, even if I am getting close to my peak race, and instead work on power and base miles. Regardless of which approach you use, it's crucial to get adapted to race speed with block training when you get very close to the race. Organize your sessions more specifically the closer you get to your race. Coming off of a base block of several weeks you may lead into more specific speed block sessions and in the final few weeks before your race you will likely add in some brick sessions. This wakes up the muscles and helps them remember that "this is what it feels like when you are flying on race day".

Shifts In Training

Tapering, or gradually dropping volume of training as the race approaches, is the fun part that most athletes really look forward to. The intense fatiguing phase is finally over and now you just have to put your feet up and eat boatloads of pasta, right? Well, not really. Tapering is a very important and very individualized phase of the process leading up to the race. For most athletes it is a rule of thumb to maintain your typical training structure in a weekly rhythm, while just decreasing the volume of your training. This gives your body more recovery time, moving toward becoming race ready. Your body begins feeling powerful and equipped for the approaching contest.

Tapering doesn't mean it's off time. This is very often misunderstood. Imagine your body has become accustomed to constant work and suddenly you have all this rest. Your body goes crazy. This might be the reason why plenty of hard working guys get sick during their holiday time. The body finally gets the rest and then takes all that it can get. On the other hand, an athlete who only trains 8-12 hours a week, won't need a recovery drop that significantly, as he won't be too fatigued from the overall weekly volume.

In the final tapering stage, about 10 days out from the race, this system has a few variations that add in more rest days. For the lead up to the race I usually apply tapering using a 2 to 1 system (2 days of training, 1 day off). This tapers the volume of training off from the standard 3 to 1 — 2½ to ½ regimen. Once race day approaches (about five days out) I sometimes even switch to one day on and one off to get the maximum possible rest, while maintaining the workload during full-on training days.

Again, this is what works for me, but this is very unique to each individual and may take some time to perfect. Try out different models and make sure to take notes so the adaptations to your methods are properly noted. You might have to fine tune a bit during your next taper if you realized that you were either too rested or too tired once your test race day came along. This is pure communication with your body. You will begin to work out methods that suit your own personal relationship with your body dynamic.

By maintaining your training rhythm you can reduce the overall volume while increasing the speed (to race pace). Then phase into shorter distances and increased speed (faster than race pace). If you only push to the level of race pace you will get used to it and it will be hard to break through that plateau. We have to make sparks above that pace in order to adapt to higher potential speeds. Intervals will get shorter and faster and recovery breaks might increase a bit so you don't get too fatigued. You have more time to recover between sessions.

For example: for an athlete training 30+ hours a week, stepping down to 18-20 hours gives the body the additional rest it needs. Once race week rolls around, you can subtract your race time from the weekly quota. For instance, if you are stepping down to 18 hours a week of training, and you plan to race a 10 hour Ironman®, your race week will consist of 8 hours of training plus, 10 hours of racing, which equals your 18 total hours for the week.

In general, every change is a shock to the system, and by shock I mean a different impulse or stimulus for your muscles. This definitely applies to changes in training. Just as you are taking tapering and rest seriously, you are also taking time to adapt your system to avoid potential shocks on race day.

Brick workouts are a good way to get race ready during your tapering phase. Bricks link the different disciplines together, which is key for us triathletes in order for us to get used to having to deal with continuing the burn from the swim, onto the bike, and into the run, without stopping for air. You could swim a hard session and then head out on the bike, or do a bike-run brick which takes you from two wheels to two feet.

Be careful though. A common mistake is making these brick workouts too long, which causes fatigue and doesn't guarantee much benefit. If brick sessions are too long, it increases the stress hormone cortisol, which slows down the recovery process. So you might have knocked out one monster session but you will pay the price later when your body can't recover, causing a black hole of fatigue. It is always more beneficial to favor consistency in training over single massive workouts. Imagine how much you could have trained during those additional three days where you were overly fatigued and had to skip or reduce sessions? It's always about the big picture here.

During bricks and tempo sessions get used to the GPS watch settings that you will use in the race. Some watches have the option to vibrate or beep to remind you to look at your pace time or to take in nutrition. As mentioned earlier, when it comes to racing, GPS pace watches are really beneficial to most athletes. The key is to know your watch, so you can easily flip through the massive amounts of information that these devices hold. Streamline your settings so that you only see the information that you need at any given moment. These convenient gadgets can only help when you utilize them in an efficient manner. When you are tired and on the last leg of your epic battle, you don't want to have to think about complicated watch settings.

The final weeks before your race is the time to do the last small experiments in your training. The race is not a place for testing new training techniques. Entry fees are high and it is a race you chose to perform in. The goal is to race well and test your grit. Race day is most definitely not the time to roll out a new method or gadget. The more you test and try out during training, the more you will feel comfortable before your race. Once you feel good about your setup and your workouts, there is no need to change anything, no matter what the people around you might suggest. Remember, every athlete is a little coach and thinks he knows the best way to do things. Be unwavering with your game plan and focus internally.

Please restrain yourself from doing any panic training. What this means is resisting the temptation of carrying out crazy speed sessions and repeatedly testing out your form, in the final few days before a race, just to prove you are race ready. This is absolute nonsense and actually achieves the total opposite of its intention. By focusing too hard on those pre-race tests, so close to the actual peak race, athletes tend to jeopardize mental focus for the race. If you spend too much time watching other competitors as they go through the motions of their pre-race training, you lose focus on your own race objective. If you find yourself straying, come back to your visualization practice or meditation. Protect yourself from creeping doubt. Stay true to your plan.

My mental coach from many years back explained it to me like this: your mental focus and energy is also like a tank of gas—don't empty it out two or three days before the race as you will need a full tank during your race. In addition, these types of "panic tests" are indications that you don't believe in your training and that you distrust your own abilities, setting you up for failure before you even get your number pinned on. Belief and trust in yourself are key components at each and every phase of your development as a triathlete. If you have struggled with this in the past, now is the time to rewrite your story. Respect the foundation you have built. Trust yourself. You are exactly where you need to be.

Considerations for Your Swim

In the last few weeks before the race, try adding a few race specific swims to your routine. Think outside the chlorine filled box. Evaluate the difference between your training conditions and the locale of your imminent race and make the proper shifts to your training environment. If the water will be warm down in Mexico, you should practice swimming in warm water and see how you react to it. You might sweat more so this might mean that you need more fluids beforehand.

The best way to know for sure is to test it out! It's always best to do a dry run in these environmental conditions yourself. Don't just take mental notes. Your body needs to experience the simulation for itself. There has to be a point of reference that you will be able to access come race day so you don't run into too many unpleasant surprises out there.

Use a similar approach when preparing for potential weather conditions. It is good to get the body ready for all eventualities. Be prepared for a wetsuit legal swim as well as the swim skin option. Add a few sessions with each suit in order to get familiarized with the slightly different buoyancy and water position. It's best to use this approach for hard workouts as this will simulate race conditions. It's not just effective for the swim itself, but it also gives you the opportunity to sharpen your skills on seamlessly getting in and out of your suit. Every second counts. Being confident and familiar with your suit material will go a long way in keeping your optimism high when the race is about to begin.

We don't take too much time to warm-up before the start of a race, as sometimes we aren't allowed too much time in the water beforehand. Because this differs from your average pool session, you can prep for this by trying out a hard set with a short 5 minute warm-up. Then you can relax before you jump in the water on the morning of the big dance, as you are prepared for any unexpected decision by the race referees.

In triathlon, we always start with a sprint at the beginning of the race and it's important to simulate this in your swim training the closer you get to the race. It is a must for the body to be familiar with the physiological effects you are experiencing when you push yourself to the limit in such a short period of time. Lactate builds up in your blood stream when you start exercising hard and you feel that burning sensation in your muscles. Building up your lactate threshold will make the fast pace at the beginning of the race feel easier on your body and less of a shock to the system.

To that point, in the last weeks before a race, we can talk specifically in terms of training sessions that includes fast 25 m sprints followed by an easier 75 m. The higher speed at the beginning of the set will mimic the sprint at the start of a race. Another application would include several sets of hard 100 m followed immediately by 200 m at a medium pace. By doing this you will prepare your body to deal with the high initial race pace and you will be ready to go, once the gun goes off.

These shifts to your training efforts, for each of your sessions, will have a transformational effect on your ability to get the engine revved up and ready to go beyond the first sprints of the race. Assuming you wouldn't prepare for the sprint start, you would experience an overwhelming sensation at the very beginning of the race that could negatively influence the next few hours of racing. Knowing what's to come and preparing your body is key here.

Bike Considerations

Leading up to the race, your bike training will change slightly, as your interval sessions will get longer and the breaks between them will get shorter. This will involve training at race speed but increasing the time for each interval, for example, starting from 30 minutes to 45 minutes and then even extend to 90 minutes nonstop. You may also add some shorter interval sessions where you go slightly over your race pace to prepare for those moments in the race where you must pass a competitor or push high watts up a hill. These shorter intervals might include, for instance, a set of 5x 8 min effort, or a high speed set of 8x 3 min hard efforts way over race pace. Imagine things developing as though you trained separate parts in the lead up and now you are starting to put them together, reducing the recovery time between. This will simulate the long bike section that you will face during a race and your legs will get stronger the closer you get to your race.

I usually train very hard and maintain a big volume and load until around 10-12 days before my peak race. That's the time when I am the most fatigued and I remind myself that it's normal to be tired at this point in the game. In the past I may have started to question everything, extreme fatigue taking a psychological foothold, but now I try to remember to be a friend to myself and not take things too seriously during this time. I try to get an extra hour of sleep each night, schedule extra massages, and be sure to eat very clean, and things start to work themselves out. Remember, you are testing the waters of extreme fatigue to prepare your body and mind for the race ahead.

It makes sense to use your race gear the week of the race and have all your material prepped early. Maybe you aren't yet sure which race wheel set up you will use because of potential weather changes. In this case, make sure both set ups are ready to roll so you can make a last minute call with complete confidence. Test your race shoes if they are different from your training shoes. If you need to change your bottle cages and nutrition setup, you might want to do that early to get used it (especially if you haven't raced in a while). Nothing should be left to chance by the time you toe the line. That means that you shouldn't try out new gear unless you absolutely have to.

What if it doesn't work out and you get totally thrown off your mission because of the change? It's simply not worth it.

Apart from your gear, it makes a lot of sense to begin using your race nutrition in the weeks leading up to the race, and test out your race dosages so you are used to the concentrations. Your body will then have time to adapt and you can pay attention to any stomach issues that may come up. It is ideal to test nutrition during interval training and when you are very fatigued to make sure you can digest and deal with your fuel under race conditions. Perform this test for both the bike and run training pre-race.

If you are using nutrition from the course, then I would highly recommend purchasing some bars, gels, and drink powder of that specific brand so you can be sure your body copes well with it during your race. Keep in mind that some products might contain fructose or glucose. Some athletes have a natural intolerance and can only absorb one of the two. Get familiar with the chemistry at work here so there are no surprises come race day.

Before my win at Asia-Pacific Champs in Melbourne in 2014, I wanted to get used to fructose and I trained with it for months. At some point the stomach issues stopped and my body adapted to it. I went on to win the race. It turns out that you can absorb quite a bit more energy through your liver with fructose than you can with glucose, so I thought it was worth testing out. In the race I chose a 2:1 ratio of glucose to fructose and had no stomach issues the entire day. This crucial decision gave me just enough energy, towards the end of the marathon, to chase down the leaders in the last 6 miles of the run. I excelled in my most difficult of all 3 race disciplines by changing up my fuel intake. At some point everyone has to make a gutsy move and go with it.

Considerations for Your Run

For running race prep I suggest adding a bit more asphalt running to your training regime as the race date approaches. The exception would be if you are preparing for a race on mostly soft trails such as at Challenge Roth, where most of the race course is on smooth gravel roads along the river. The longer the distance, the more important this adaptation phase is, as our muscles get tight due to the hard impact over longer periods of time.

Now is a good time to save some of your driving time to the trails and get used to the harder impact of running on asphalt surfaces right outside your front door. You might get a bit tight in your calves at first, but that will only last a short time. Stretching and massaging helps keep the tightness at bay. Another beneficial recovery method is the cold and hot shower during times that you feel especially sore or worn out. You can spray water right on the sore muscles for a few minutes alternating the temperature, which increases blood flow and therefore eases soreness.

This protocol will prepare you for the long, crucial run during the marathon. With a bit of premeditated concrete running, muscles will be better prepared for the stress and shock on race day and will perform better. It is also beneficial to use your lighter racing flats or race specific shoes on some of your shorter and faster runs to adapt your feet to them as well. This will also have an impact on your calves, so be prepared. Time this strategy properly. It's better to be sore 10 days out from a race than to suffer cramping on race day because your calves are overloaded.

Shifting Focus

Always focus on the things you can control and incorporate those things into your training and race prep. You will hopefully have a few test races before your big event of the season which should help you work out some of the kinks. But in every race, as in life, there are plenty of things that can go wrong and are just beyond our control. Maybe you'll get a flat tire, or even multiple flat tires. You don't want to end up freaking out, Normann Stadler style (just google "Normann Stadler meltdown" and you will see what I mean). You want to keep a cool head despite all the crazy things being thrown your way. Iron distance events are long and so much can happen to turn things around. Maybe your swim was a lot slower than expected due to a strong current, or you get an unfair drafting penalty on the bike. Maybe you are lead the wrong way on the run and end up doing some extra distance. The possibilities are endless. Your reaction should be consistent and measured.

All of these things have happened to me at some point. Although there are some things that are within our control (such as doing recon so you are familiar the course), there are plenty of things that are outside of our control. It can be very frustrating, but the best way forward in such a situation is to remain cool and roll with it. It's water off a duck's back. You can't risk spending time griping, complaining, and getting angry. It not only uses up time and energy that could otherwise propel you forward in your race, but it also puts you on your way to a negative spiral, that can put you off your mental game and ruin your race. Expect the unexpected. It's part of the game.

Adding in additional sleep and meditation practices in the

weeks leading up to the race is necessary to build up a great backlog of sleep and restoration to carry you through those last weeks before your race. Don't fret about the amount of sleep you get the night before the race. Everyone is going to be in the same boat here, so it should not impact you negatively if you are tossing and turning more than usual.

I have found that working on the mental side of race-prep has helped me out in big ways to keep my state of mind measured and focused. Meditation has helped me to remain cool at times when I might have freaked out earlier on in my career. It is definitely worth the time investment it takes to sit down and calm the mind every day. This calmness starts to permeate all areas of life. Once you make it a habit, you just start to notice that the things that used to bother you just don't concern you anymore.

It helps to give you some distance from the problem at hand, so that you are able to keep things in perspective and not react so strongly. The things you can't control during your race, fall into that nebulous chasm of gifts that you cannot anticipate. What is within your control is how you lead your body through the event with grace and ease. You are able to take a step back and realize that it's just a race, a very long race, with plenty of opportunities for things to turn around. Keep your composure in the face of calamity and you will be among the real champions to cross the finish line that day. Race week gets pretty crazy as there is a lot of things to organize. Time off from work, flights, and organizing the family are just a few things that you will have to consider. A well executed planning phase will reduce the hectic and unwanted added pressure. Of course a little bit of stress is acceptable and will always be there. In fact the ability to move through those elevated moments as gracefully as possible transitions nicely into that the race itself, full of its own uncertainty and stress.

You learn through experience. My first ever half distance race in Gerardmere, France back in 2000 was an exercise in poor preparation. It was a disaster. I arrived just a day before the race, with a long drive behind me. Not only did it downpour during my only chance for a course recognition, but I also realized that I left, not only my wetsuit, but also my racing flats and my race helmet at home. Where in the world was my head when I packed my race bag? I ended up using my training shoes, borrowing a friend's salad-bowl style training helmet, and renting a wetsuit that was too big. I was able to race, but had a pretty big disadvantage from the get go.

On race morning everything went smoothly and I was happy to be able to race despite my terrible pre-race organization. I started out well and took the lead in the swim, but halfway through my swim, the zipper on my borrowed wetsuit opened a bit and water streamed in. I felt like I was swimming with a balloon tied to my back. I still managed to make it out of the water in front. Despite the pitfalls and gaffes, I had a great overall day; riding with the big boys in my first half of the bike and even dropping them on the second big hill. I came into T2 first and ran out ahead of everyone. I never thought for a single second about how I was racing in my training shoes. Mind over matter.

I was flying on the course, eating my gels and drinking my coke like it was nobody's business when suddenly they stopped serving coke at the aid stations. I had the last of three loops to finish, about 8 km to the finish line. We all know you can't just go cold turkey with regard to specific sugars. That means if you start drinking fast sugary drinks—you need to drink them till the end, all the time, and frequently. I think the longer distance was getting to me as well, since this was double the distance I was used to racing. I was in pain and every little stretch of road became an endless highway to me.

Bevan Docherty was running well and was not too far behind me. I still had a comfortable lead but it wouldn't last. The last 200 m before the finish line (me totally delirious and Bev sprinting his ass off) he finally caught me and won by a few seconds. We were close friends back then as we raced for the same Bundesliga team and even lived together for a while. I was devastated but we hugged each other and he even apologized. I was such a mess and stuttered something like, F...you Bev - you won, congrats!!! I was in tears. We still talk about that day and have a good laugh remembering our first ever long distance event.

In retrospect I can see that I created a foundation for the disaster. Researching event conditions and focusing while packing are crucial and will help you avoid these types of fiascos. I was a bit lucky and had some help from friends to get organized with all my little issues before the race, but who knows what would have been possible if I would have been serious about my preparation. Understanding methods to navigate through your downfalls while also trying your damnedest to minimize them, is the key.

The Particulars

Let's get back to your own packing strategies. The weeks leading up to your race you should write yourself a checklist of whatever pops into your mind. Avoid last minute lists so you don't repeat the madness of my race in France. The organizational part, right before a race, is a bit stressful when you have not properly prepared. Planning ahead helps you to be organized, prepared and able to focus on the task of racing. I suggest laying out your race gear a week in advance. You'll still have the time to fill in any gaps and take care of any oversights. At bigger triathlon events the organizers usually have a triathlon expo where you could buy last minute items if needed. But, let's be smart and think ahead so you don't have to do the running around instead of relaxing and mentally preparing for your race.

Travel Specifics

When traveling by car, you have tons of space to pack any possible backups, additional wheels, tools, and your floor pump and so on. Space is not the issue. Those space wheels could come in handy, especially if the conditions are not clear pre-race day. You might want to opt for lower front rim (such as a 30-50 mm vs a deep front rim of 70-90 mm) due to the heavy side winds. Or you want to use a disc instead of you deep rim rear wheel. The car gives you the freedom to pack till under the roof. Most triathlete have bigger cars or even mini vans, as they come in handy-even for a spontaneous overnight stay sometimes.

When flying out, a few days to a week before a race, your strategy changes slightly. If it's a short 2-3 day trip, a bike bag and a backpack will usually suffice, but it all depends on your own personal needs. Travel easy and unencumbered. Nowadays most airlines charge a solid amount of money for a bike bag. Southwest, Jet Blue and Frontier are more affordable at $50-75 one way. American, Lufthansa and others can charge up to $150 one way. So be sure to check that prior to ticket booking as this will influence your overall cost.

I always suggest a cushioned soft case bag with wheels in the back so it's easy to carry along with another trolley/backpack on the other side. The bag also provides plenty of space for at least one additional separately cushioned wheel and plenty of space for pull buoy, paddles, shoes and helmet. Just make sure you watch the weight allowance and during your final check be tough and decide what you can't live without and what's easy to get from the expo or fellow athletes. You might just want to leave your pump at home and organize this upon arrival. Always keep in mind to travel light. Traveling is fun when you keep those basic rules in mind. I used to argue each time about the bike fees at the check in, but there is hardly ever a way around it. I find that it's better to save your nerves, focus on the job at hand and practice patience in the process. Keep in mind, there is always something that comes up when you travel. So roll with the punches. It's all part of the game.

Here is a list for you that will help you to double-check your race gear. This is my actual pre-race-packing list for an Ironman®. Use it as a jumping off point for creating your own packing list specific to your individual needs.

Pre-Race Tackle Box

- ID, money
- Tri membership card (for signing up)
- Pick up safety pins at race registration or have 10+ with you in your bag
- Possibly print out the layout of the transition from the race webpage
- Bring warm clothes for race morning after checking outside temperature/wind
- Additional transition bags (usually received at registration/with race package)

- Bike bottles
- Race number
- Timing chip (soft band!)
- Rubber bands (to prepare bike shoes for perfect slide in after transition)
- Towel
- Pre-race food (bars, prepared drink bottle, gel)

For Your Transitions:

- Pump
- Co2
- Spare tube
- Scissors
- Multi tool
- Tape
- Baby powder in shoes
- Personal items
- Ziploc bags

Swim Race-Checklist

- Sunscreen (waterproof, spray, alcohol base, anti-pore block)
- Vaseline for your wetsuit

- Chamois
- Swim gear
- Race kit (jersey and shorts)
- Number belts and timing chip around your ankle (number pinned on and maybe tape over the safety pins to make sure it doesn't come loose. Best is actually to squeeze the end together so the needle can't come out and potentially poke you).
- Race goggles as well as a spare pair (it's good to give your spare to your coach or your helper in case there is a last minute issue before the swim. Prearrange a meeting point).
- Wetsuit or swimsuit depending on the water temperature. I always bring both, just to be safe and assured.

Bike Race-Checklist

- Helmet (aero/road)
- Sunglasses
- Cycling shoes (add socks if needed)
- Rubber bands: Use thin ones to tie from the back of your bike shoes to the bike frame, in order to keep the shoes level so you are able to jump on the bike without the shoes flapping around. The rubber bands break once you get pedaling.
- Prepared race bottles

- Race nutrition that you will put on your bike (flasks, gels, bars, or salt tablets)
- Power meter — charged!
- Electronic Shifters (optional gear) - charged!
- Towel, which might be needed to wipe the dew off your bike if it is an early morning start. I like microfiber towels because they don't take up much space and dry quickly.
- Scissors, medical tape, and a mix of emergency tools. My coach usually keeps a little craft box with random items that might come in handy in a pinch.
- Headlamp: If it's early, you will need a light to see your bike to get it ready to go.
- Bike pump — if you already checked in your bike the day before, if not you could pump up at home and just throw it in the car?
- Spare tire and tube
- Race belt / number (if needed) / safety pins

Run Race-Checklist

- Race flats
- Thin race socks
- Extra gel and salt tablets
- Second race number, if applicable
- Sunglasses and potentially a hat (if it's very hot).

- Hat or visor
- Your charged GPS watch
- ziplock to run out of T2 (hat, GPS watch, gels, own drink, personal items)
- race belt with number (quick release system)
- Triathlon race shoes (Ironman®)

  Post Race

  - Wipes,
  - Towel
  - Shower gear
  - Clean set of clothes
  - Blister essential (bandages, disinfectant)
  - Food (get 20 gram of protein in <15 min, then individual food/drinks)

For the Pros:

- Sponsor gear
- Press conference particulars
- Country Flag
- Signature cards, pen, etc.

Now let's move on to a gear check. I believe it's crucial to have your race gear checked and tested before your race. Your bike is the most important piece, so make sure that everything is set up and tuned up correctly, way ahead of time. Make sure every little detail is considered, particularly in switching from training wheels to race wheels. Overlooking this element can cause issues with your gears. Some race wheels have different rim widths than normal training wheels. Therefore your brake pads and the distance to the rim need to be adjusted, if not even changed out. Remember the aluminum rims might have little particles stuck in the brake pads, which can mess up your carbon wheels. If you are not familiar with this, go to a bike shop to double check your adjustments.

Here is another trick to avoid puncture. Release air pressure of the race wheels after you check in your bike the day before. This will prevent them from sitting in the sun and potentially expanding or bursting. Because you released some tire pressure the day before to avoid puncture, remember to leave time to pump them up in the morning of the race. You could also tune up the race wheels with a dose of Pit Stop puncture spray. Release the air of both tires and put half of the spray in each tire (valve up, so it runs down each side nicely). Then pump up your tires to race pressure (8-8.5 bars = roughly 115 psi).

If you use extra clothes on the bike, make sure they are tight fitting on the body, so you don‘t add extra wind resistance to the bike, it will cost you unnecessary energy and time. If it's cold, keep your feet and hands warm before the race.

Race week can always get a bit busy. I've found an effective strategy for sketching out my week is to schedule my training sessions first and all other appointments after. Include everything here with a specific time, so you can plan your day-by-day operations precisely. My schedule before the Kona race often includes three to four appointments a day, plus my training. It gets incredibly stressful.

Unlike other events, Kona is a place for many networking opportunities and you should take advantage of this by being present at a few selected meetings with people who matter to you. It gets so busy that my partner has to be 100 % involved in planning food and drinks between training sessions as I am already halfway out the door to make an appearance at the expo or with TV obligations.

This system proved to be perfect in getting everything under control beforehand and creating a much more seamless transition into the accommodations of race day itself. Use your resources wisely. Utilize your team. Lean on your team and you can heap praise on them later. That is the balance of a true champion.

Race Week Schedule:

	Mon	Tues	Wed	Thur	Fri	Sat	Sun
TRAINING	2h bike easy, afternoon 3km swim (1000 base, 3x50 kick, 4x50 built, Main: 6x100 m race pace- 15" break-500 base, 500 paddles, cool down	45 min run (5' easy - 10min medium, 5' medium, 5 IM pace, 5' 70.3 pace, controlled. 15 min easy cool down (all non stop)	1.5 hr bike am, then drive to race race, check in hotel	Off day. Just 15 min easy swim (wetsuit/ open water/ test swim start/exit) easy, sleep in, get adjusted, gear check, bike built CALL COACH!	30-45 min easy spin, then check in. 15 min easy jog after-wards (use as recon, T1/T2, know the flow in T1/2)	RACE DAY 7:00am FULL GAS !!!	Off- lick your wounds
SCHEDULE		Packing bags	3h drive to race hotel-start 5pm	Race brief-ing at 12:00 at finish line	Bike check in 2-4pm		Awards 12:00 then drive back

Carbo Loading

Your diet is going to shift a bit, leading up to the race, where you will eat food that is easier to digest and high in carbohydrates. You are giving your body a rest from digestion. Make your food choices are good fuel. The last 48 hours before your race should always be gluten free which will help your body keep inflammation at bay. Your gastrointestinal system will be better prepared and working more efficiently during the race.

The last 48 hours before the race is the time you should load up on carbs. That doesn't mean you should eat more than usual or overeat. You should simply make sure that when you eat, carbohydrates are a priority. You want to carbo load—fueling up your body with energy. I am advocating for gluten-free carbs but at many races they offer pasta parties, which could be a good option for some people. Challenge Roth hosts a pasta party with an incredible buffet. Some other races offer very mushy and overcooked pasta. Talk to guys who have raced the event the year before to figure out if this will be according to your taste. Some might prefer a more quiet and private dinner with their race buddies or family and choose to go elsewhere, while others might be on specific diets that aren't catered to at these big events (i.e., gluten-free or vegan).

When you eat, avoid too much fiber such as vegetables and salads, or fiber-rich cereals. The tank needs to be full at the beginning of the race, so now is the time to fill up. With the big gluten-free and anti-inflammatory movement going on right now, some people are choosing not to eat gluten, meat, or diary for various reasons. In this case, the best you can do is simply to substitute pasta with rice, and stick to food that is easy to digest. I have been eating this way for years and I find it gives me the energy I need to excel in my race.

In case you are not familiar with the studies on inflammatory foods, this is definitely something to consider when picking out your body's fuel. Guess what, we have to heal our slightly inflamed muscles after each training session, so why should we add inflammation causing culprits like meat, gluten and dairy to the mix? While your body is working to heal the inflammation caused by foods, it can't recover.

I have tested this myself, and have had noticeable results with a whole food and mostly plant based diet. Even if the workload on your body is only increased by a small percentage, you must keep in mind that even a 1% increase in performance can have a huge impact on your results in an 8 hour race. It could make a difference between feeling fresh or feeling tired on race day, and it also keeps you reading labels (or better yet, eating foods without labels such as fruits and veggies) and becoming a knowledgeable consumer and healthier human. Think about it and maybe even test it out, you can only win.

Race Week Pearls of Wisdom:

- Avoid standing around in the sun while experiencing the excitement of the venue. The sun will drain your energy. Use a hat and try to be in the shade the last few days leading up to your race.

- Saving time and energy should be a priority, therefore try to combine a training session with picking up your race gear. Then you don't have to leave the house twice. I usually jog back after getting dropped off at the race briefing. Efficiency is the word of the week.

- Be nice to your support crew as they try to help you. It's a pretty intense time for partners when we start getting in the zone before a race.

- Try to get off your feet instead of walking around all day getting things done. If you're standing, you should sit, and if you're sitting, you should lie down. Instead of lying around you should sleep. Feet up is the motto here.
- Remember, first the work, then it's time to enjoy. I know how exciting it is to be at a big race wanting to soak in the atmosphere. When you are getting ready to race, it is mesmerizing, feeling that nervous energy from those around you. Stay focused, but don't overdo it. You also need the necessary ease in order to perform well. Finding the right balance is the goal here.
- Know the flow of transition: where the race starts; where the transition is and how the flow of the race goes. It's the athlete's responsibility to know the course. It helps to study it online before going to the race. It might be wise to take printouts of the transition with you and then go check out the swim start.
- Depending on the race, they might have open swim times for the days leading up to the race, when you can do your swim recon. It's a good practice to check the water temperature just to get a feeling for it. The decision about whether or not the wetsuit will be used will be announced in the briefing or one hour before the start. If you train on the course, go at the same time as the race to observe possible tide variations, light, visibility and possible orientation markers.
- Check out the start of the swim. See if there is a sandbar in the way (where you have to walk, or do dolphin jumps instead of swimming), so it won't catch

you by surprise. Identify whether the race will be a beach start, a pontoon start, or a deep-water start. You can find out from officials if you can't find anything in the race announcements or the briefing.

- Once you know the swim start, go to where you exit the water. Is there a ramp for the exit or stairs? How are you going to exit? Picture these scenarios for yourself and imagine carrying out the proper action in the race.
- How big is the surf? Of course this can change from day to day, but it helps you to mentally prepare if you see surf in real time.
- Look up the wind conditions and see how 15 mph feels. This will help you gain some relative clarity about what to expect if the forecast says 20 mph on race day vs. 5 mph. Numbers don't help much without experience to pair with the numbers.
- Walk from the swim exit to where your bike will be racked in T1. Your spot is usually labeled with your assigned race number, or a range of race numbers. Are there any visual aids close by? Pick out your landmarks. Don't forget that T1 will be filled with hundreds or thousands of bikes, so you need to nail this part. A picture or a short video might help you to review at home. Your T1 spot is where you will pick up your bike and proceed to the mount line, where you will be allowed to get on your bike. So make sure you know where it is. At most races T1 and T2 are the same and therefore the mount and dismount line might be close. Make sure you find both.

It is best to focus on your transition recognition pretty close to the race, so that everything is built up at the venue and you can find everything marked and laid out as it will be on race day.

Plenty of volunteers can also point you in the right direction. Picture yourself during the race at this point. You just got on your bike, now go through the beginning of the bike course in your head, and/or check your map. When you return from the bike leg, you need to dismount before the dismount line. You will come at full speed, so make sure you chart the exact point where you have to start slowing down and precisely where you'll be off the bike. Go through that in your head and picture yourself as you ride the last few meters on the bike.

Practice getting in and out of your cycling shoes before getting off your bike and discover the exact timing of this action. Many athletes look down while trying to open their shoes to get barefoot on top of the shoes so they can hop off the bike quicker. Due to the race speed and fatigue, they swerve all over the place and disturb others and often even touch the barriers. This is tricky but necessary to perfect so as to maintain your composure throughout the transition. The easiest way to transition is to stop at the dismount line, get off your bike and then get out of your shoes. It is much slower but even Thomas Hellriegel did that during the height of his career (he won the world champs in Kona). For me this is unbelievable and cost way too much time. Decide for yourself.

I would advise you to watch a few YouTube videos about the particular race you have chosen. This helps you to anticipate certain details of your surroundings during the upcoming race. You can pick up on the flow in and out of transitions, and become familiar with some aid station setups and so on. Some races have great videos that reveal helpful little details. I even do this to get to know various race courses I haven't raced yet. This will give you an indication of how the conditions were the past years. It will also create a familiarity with the setting so that you feel at ease and can focus on your mental game and the rest of your race preparations.

Once you get off your bike, you are back on your feet. You have to hand your bike to a volunteer or sometimes hang it back at the same location where you picked up your bike before. Which one will it be in your race? Run to your assigned spot where you find your clothes and running shoes. Many bigger races have a transition tent where you will have to run through to pick up your running bag. If this is the case then you have to change in the transition tent and put all your bike gear (helmet, possibly shoes and glasses) into the bag after you put on your running gear. With your socks and shoes on, you would be pretty much ready to get out onto the run course. Walk this path until you leave the transition area, so you know every step you will take and any possible spots that might cause hang-ups. From there you just need to know how many laps you have to run and where to turn into the finish chute.

If you can manage, go check out the finish line and visualize yourself running through. Now is the perfect time for that and it will help you to get that mental picture in your head for when you are really suffering on race day. For efficiency, I often combine this task with a short 20 min recovery jog the day before the race. It feels like I'm using my little jog as a reconnaissance mission. Combine the two and save some energy, but don't get crazy. There was a time in my career when I thought I had to save every little bit of energy and I hardly moved around at all. Come race day I felt too sluggish and couldn't race well. Be careful not to waste energy standing around, but train and keep the legs going. Don't overthink here.

Doing your homework could make a decisive difference on race day for you and it will definitely help to give you peace of mind. Just writing this brings my heartbeat up a bit. I still get excited after so many years in the sport I love and live for. Of course by now it's all routine for me and I am on autopilot before the race, just doing what I have to do. But this ritual of checking everything out is an absolute necessity and it will help you to focus and be confident for the race. You can go through it in your head several times before the actual race so you are able to do it blindfolded. The more familiar you are with the terrain, the more focused you can be with the actual race itself.

You know the course and the transition area, including the start and finish. Now think outside the box. Picture race morning where thousands of other athletes and spectators will be going to the same location at the same time. Where will you park? Early in the morning on race day there will be plenty of people roaming about, so you must plan ahead. Add some extra time to your planned departure from your home base. Sketch out a timeline from the time you wake up until the time you have to leave for the race. Plan 1-1.5 hrs at the race site before the race. Yep, there will be long lines in front of the Port-O-Potties and there might not be any paper left. Also remember: you might need extra time to get in your wetsuit without any stress. You also might have to run back to the car for your spare goggles, and so on.

Plan your day with backups. If you don't end up needing the additional time, enjoy the pre-race atmosphere, relax and warm-up properly. In a short quiet moment when you sit down, go through some visualizations. Focus on the beginning of the race, as later you will just move into autopilot and things will unfold. You have a lot more time to think during the last legs of the race, and the first part is usually the most face paced, so definitely want to use this time to get some clarity there.

Usually there is a race briefing the day before or the day of the event. Make sure you attend. There are likely some last minute changes and some important general information given. You will pick up your race packet at least a day before the race, so you can lay out all the stuff on your bed at home to get an overview. Then start setting up your bike with your number, the race belt, the timing chip, etc.

If you have all your gear laid out you can organize the bags in no time. It is good to have a final overview before packing the gear into each assigned bag. Every race is different. Your pre swim bag is for your warm-up clothes and everything you don't need for the race. The other bags are for pre-bike, pre-run and possibly the special needs bags for the bike and the run. Your pre-bike bag will be used in T1, after your swim, where you will take out your bike gear and put in your swim gear. In the pre-run bag, you will put in your bike gear and take out your run gear. As a piece of advice, place all your run gear in a smaller Ziploc bag and then into your pre-run bag, so it doesn't get lost in case it rains or if the wind picks up. Then you can run with the Ziploc in hand and fill your pockets when you are on the way out of T2—just be careful to tuck that bag into your pocket to avoid any littering penalties. You can drop it once you hit an aid station.

All additional items goes in your backpack. Prepare as much as you can, so at some point you can mentally set it all aside. All you need to do the morning of the race is to be race ready, and possibly fill up a few bottles. One more last minute check of your gear and then you are out the door, on the way to your race.

The Dos and Don'ts of Getting Race Ready

Dos

- Organize with your support crew. Where should they stand during your race and where do you need information called in for you? Where do you want to meet after the race? Do you need information during the race in addition to the "You look good baby" cheers from your partner.

- Train on your race bike and your race set up (including wheels, aero helmet) till you feel comfortable with it. Your race suit and race helmet need to be tested, but that's it. You can practice taking the aero helmet on and off in your garage 10 times, as well as getting onto your shoes right before the dismount line.

- Practice transitions. If you feel you need more transition practice, go to a quiet place and hop on and off your bike and get in and out of your shoes a few times. No need to accelerate like a sprinter, as you won't be doing that in your race either. The idea is to practice the technical side of the transition, and not to worry about getting a workout. This is all about developing your skills and not increasing your athletic endurance--it's not a brick workout. There is muscle memory on the one side and there is the neuroregulatory system on the other side. Simplified it means: The more you repeat any exercise the easier it is to retrieve, physically as well as mentally. Just do the transitions a few times before race week and then you will have this one covered.

- Charge your power meter and any other electronic equipment the night before the race.

Don'ts

- Don't panic train. Testing your abilities the days leading up to the race is counterproductive.

- Don't make changes to your bike position right before the race. Instead, test changes during various training rides. No “panic adjustments”.

- Don’t let your tri outfit do the talking—let your legs do it. You don‘t need to run around in a speedo with pink compression socks and your heart rate belt strap on all the time.

- Don’t overdo training in your race gear. No need to train several days in your race gear. Once you have tested it, you are good to go.

- Don’t over consume alcohol or caffeine. It is important to reduce alcohol and caffeine consumption the week before the race. Both are diuretics. You don‘t want to pee out your valuable electrolyte buffer before the race. Caffeine deprivation creates +/- 3 days of headaches. Factor this into your pre-race schedule if it applies to you and start weaning off the caffeine well in advance.

- Don’t drink the water! Depending on where you will go to race/train, be careful with water, ice and food (Montezuma’s revenge could be just around the corner). Plenty of pros seem to forget this basic law of the land when traveling abroad or just down to Mexico. The basics are the same everywhere: Be safe and use bottled water. Only eat peeled fruits & veggies like bananas. Otherwise vegetables and fruits need to be cooked to be 100% safe for you to eat. Be careful with local finger food and unfamiliar fare. Watch the dips, don’t use ice cubes and rinse your toothbrush and mouth with bottled water.

- Don’t experiment with new training techniques or diets. This is not the time to try out new tri gear from the expo or add new nutritional experiments.

- Don't change your gear around. Little tweaks won't make you faster. It just adds stress and potential risk.

Race Ready / Mind and Body

"I've been in a poor physical shape many times in my career and I've had some of my best results. My best performances happened because my mind was in the right place. The mind is definitely stronger than the body."

~ Kelly Slater

With all the organizational efforts leading up the race, athletes tend to forget about the actual race itself. Try not to lose focus on the main event. Make sure you take the time to set your mental clarity and your body awareness in order to prepare for what will happen when the gun goes off. Put your mind into racing mode and accept the fact that you will test yourself out there.

Plan accordingly and early for all the particulars around the race so that you will have enough time to deal with your mental state of mind on the morning of the race. This is what many athletes tend to forget. It takes a lot of energy to prepare each little detail before the race. Once everything is in order, take a deep breath and focus on your task: the actual race.

Remember that this is one of the most important times to focus on your mental game. You are getting closer to the big dance and you need to have a clear head to be able to tango successfully once the time comes. Your visualizations should take on more concrete meaning now that you have trained on the race course, and jogged down the finish line chute. Use these mental images to your advantage and find a quiet time to sit by yourself and run through these spaces in your mind. Imagine how it is going to feel to get to that finish line and remember everything you have done to prepare for this upcoming moment.

Don't forget to savor the whole process of registration, sorting out your battle gear, and getting everything just right. Walk tall when you check your bike in, and thank your ever ready steed in advance for seeing you through the longest leg of the race. Take a moment to go inside and remember why you decided to start this journey, and how incredibly far you have come. Now is the time to take a step back and be grateful, and get your mind ready for the fun part—doing what you love out there on race day. Approach the race with a grateful and positive mindset, and no matter what happens out there, you will have the best possible experience once the gun goes off.

Chapter 6:
Race Day

"What you get by achieving your goals is not as important as what you become by achieving your goals."

~Goethe

Here begins the climatic part of your journey. You'll be battling with the particulars of race day but most likely with a bit of self-doubt as well. "Did I train hard enough? Can I really do this? Am I the gladiator that is required to accomplish this feat?" Yes, you are. Believe me and begin there. Your belief and inner courage is the foundation for your epic day. Compose yourself. Focus your mind so your body will be allowed to excel today. This is the dance suited for a champion.

ON YOUR MARK:

The more you have mentally prepared for your race, the more you will feel at ease on race day. Visualization is a key factor in this preparation. You can use this tool at anytime during the lead up to your race and on race day. Have your specific mental game plan at your disposal on race day and lean on it when the nerves kick in. Your access to these tools should be as fluid as breathing and walking. If you are well prepared, your mind will be at ease, because you did your homework.

Remember, it is ok to be nervous as you get into race mode. I still get a bit nervous before a race. Your nerves just need to be within the healthy range. I have seen people throw up because they are overly nervous. Others don't seem to function at all, limiting themselves because they get too psyched up about every little detail. Others need to tell everyone how they are going to smash everyone in the race, like Schwarzenegger would. Best to keep your energy within a normal range and save it for the racecourse. You will need it.

The night before the event will rarely include the best sleep you ever had and it doesn't really matter. Adding in additional sleep and meditation practices in the two or three weeks leading up to the race will give your body more recovery time. As a result, you will be able to absorb those shorter nights of sleep, pre and post-race. A good cup of coffee will get you going in the morning and will contribute to getting your heartbeat going before the race. In case you decided to reduce your coffee intake during your taper, then the caffeine will do even more magic during the race, when you actually need it. Try waking up at least 2.5 to 3 hours prior to the race. Your body needs to properly wake up and get going before it goes all out.

Fuel

The first thing you should do once you wake up is have something to eat. Have your breakfast right away so you have plenty of time to digest and finalize your preparations before you leave your home base. In order to save valuable time in the morning, I usually prepare my spartan brekky the evening before. I put the plates on the table and coffee mug next to the machine (spoon and sugar already in it). When I get up on race morning I just walk by the kitchen, press start on the coffee machine and it is all ready in no time. It makes for a more hassle-free morning.

You might ask yourself what I consider to be "the breakfast of champions"? Here is what I eat and drink before each of my big races. Because the last three days before the race are gluten free, I have rice cooked in rice milk prepared the day before. This is easy on the stomach, but full of energy. Depending on my mood I mix it with honey and/or a touch of cinnamon and banana. Stay away from morning fruit with the exception of bananas.

I drink one to two medium cups of coffee and sip on some electrolyte enriched water to aid in mild salt loading prior to race. The amount of salt loading depends on the climate. If the race is in a humid locale I would add a bit more salt and/ or electrolytes to my diet. Conversely, if the race is in a cooler climate I would not have to worry about salt loading.

This is how I fuel in the morning before most races. If I can't have rice with rice milk, I choose four to five slices of toasted gluten free white bread with honey but the same drinks. The key is to eat food that is easily digestible. I know that not everyone is hungry at 4 am, but sometimes you gotta just shove in the food. All other tasks come after brekky as now you have time to digest and time to pack the final gear that you will need.

Now it's the time to prepare the "magic mix". You can fill up and mix your bottles according to your magic numbers (see table below). If you don't like that thicker consistency, you could add a bit extra neutral tasting energy (maltodextrin), or some extra electrolytes (complex salt) according to the weather. A quick check of the final weather predictions will tell you about the temperature, precipitation and the wind you can expect. From there you are now able to eyeball whether you will be preparing to drink less with a cooler forecast or more with a warmer forecast.

Some athletes like to prepare their drinks the night before but that doesn't leave much room for any necessary adjustments due to possible weather changes on race day. Many drink brands advise not to do this. My guidance is to keep it to race morning. Choose the size of bike bottles and mix the solution for your drinks between 6-8 %. If it's cold you will drink less but need a more concentrated solution than during a hot day. If it's hot, you'll be better off with a more diluted solution because you will be drinking more fluids that way. Either way, make sure you have your estimated fluid intake per hour, well calculated. Remember that your race bottles only have some of your energy in it and the food will provide the rest. The sum of both should add up to your estimated hourly carb / calorie intake. This part is crucial. Be sure you are familiar with these calculations well before race day. You have to nail this otherwise you might run out of energy in the race and then your race car is parked on the side of the road with an empty gas tank.

With all of the bottles that go on your bike, make sure you have also prepared one to sip on before the race. I usually use the same mix that I will use during my race. This helps you to get some extra salt in before the race and to maintain your energy and fluids. Be sure to start drinking your pre-race bottle as soon as you can. It's important not to just drink water at this point because this will just flush you out and not really hydrate you for the upcoming race. You want to start your race loaded with energy and electrolytes, as you will need them. Straight water will just run right through you. Your pre-race bottle may not the best tasting casual drink but it's the perfect mix to launch you into the start of the race.

Everybody is different, of course, but this is the overall fuel strategy that works best for me. I had a very trustworthy source, one of the world's best coaches, and he shared this formula with me. I never questioned it and it always worked. From the morning of the race till my reward food after I cross the finish line—here is what I do.

Fueling Your Bike

Be smart and place the bottles, gels and bars where you will experience the least amount of drag. Two bottles on the frame are always a safe option. Maybe one or two bottle cages behind the seat or one between your arms on the aero bars. Those options are clearly the best ones. Try out some aero bottles for your front end, they work great as well.

No need to start with five bottles, you will get drinks from the aid stations out there on the course. By doing that you just make your bike significantly heavier than it was before. It's sometimes pretty funny in transition to see how much money athletes spend on their bikes but then start gluing all kind of extras onto their bikes to have enough to eat and drink. You could have saved thousands of dollars by buying a less aerodynamic bike if you add all that additional drag to your bike. Having these specifics mapped out before race day is an intelligent strategy on your part.

We all face the same problems with aerodynamics out there, but always remember: we are triathletes and we are not racing the Tour de France prolog of just a few minutes at an incredibly high speed. We have to race several hours in our aero position and on our bikes and there are other factors just as important as the aerodynamics of our bike. This is our nutrition and refuel challenge during the bike section. Use some of the bento boxes or simply stuff your extra food in the back of your jersey instead. The fastest race car doesn't run without proper gas in the tank. So free yourself a bit from the illusion that you need to be the most aero guy out there by sacrificing your fuel. It surely is a balancing act. Pay attention and you will discover the most efficient equation for your convoy.

Drink your bottles according to your predetermined nutrition plan. Most people decide to go for at least 1 bottle per hour, with some sport drink powder, plus your add-on's (pure neutral energy in form of maltodextrin and electrolytes). Calculate your carb intake from each bottle and add your food from gels/bars to it to come up to the necessary amount you will need per hour. Take your body weight in kg and that will equal the amount of carbs you should be taking in per hour. Increase your carbs by 20 percent per hour when it is cold out. Just be sure to keep the weight of your bike in check with regard to the number of bottles you carry. If you are dealing with a race with significant uphill sections you don't want to carry extra weight. Pay attention to the locations of fuel stations for the race and plan to pick up extra race course nutrition along the way instead of adding extra weight to your bike.

Plan ahead for your own special needs if you require access to your own food during the race instead of the nutrition provided at aid stations. Find a good spot for your gels/flasks on your bike. Think aerodynamic when hiding nutrition behind your stem, or between your arms. Behind the saddle is also a good wind protected spot for storage or as suggested in your jersey pockets on your back if needed.

Fueling Your Run

Since it is difficult to digest solid foods on the run, you are all set and taking in concentrated forms of nutrition such as gels. They are easy to open and simple to use while you take on the marathon. A gel contains roughly 25 g of carbs (see the label), and you did all of your homework and know how many to take in per hour, combined with your on course drinks like coke. If you weren't sure about using a special needs bag for the run course, you may want to consider just adding it in "in case of emergencies". Then, you can just grab it if you need it and leave it if you don't.

During long distance events, I opt for a small bike bottle filled with coke at 1/2 full, with electrolytes mixed in. I just feel better, knowing I have it there just in case. I had times where I walk past it, like in Kona 2014 where I already threw in the towel due to the previously mentioned "rancid drinks" provided on the course, and had severe stomach cramps where I couldn't keep anything down. I ended the race driving home in the ambulance with Bevan Docherty. In my experience, Coke is best and above all other drinks during the run. So if you add extra salt then you have the winning formula unless you stop drinking it regularly till you finish the race. Remember the Gerardmere story: once you start drinking coke, you HAVE to continue drinking it frequently till you finish. Your sugar drops quickly, so at every aid station you have to add some of the liquid gold to your intake or you risk bonking towards the end.

Final Check

In your race package you received all your necessary items and have laid them out on top or next to each bag they provide. Make sure you save time for your final overview and for possible considerations due to mixed weather. Make sure you've included extra clothes such as arm warmers and leg warmers. Remember that when the race starts it will most likely be early and the sun won't be out but since you are racing you will be very warm. There are a lot of variables to consider and you must have options available to accommodate any potentiality. Double check and triple check all of your checklists. Take a deep breath and settle your nerves. Now give the green light for the entire entourage to roll out.

Once you get to T1, stay focused on your mission. Head to do your final preparation at your assigned transition spot. Place your race gear at your designated area in transition or at your bike. During the race briefing, the race organizers should have informed you about where to put what, and if you had to check in your bike the day before, it should already be in place and waiting for you to do race day setup. If there was a mandatory bike check in the day before the race, it is usually mandatory that you leave your bike, helmet (and possibly transition bags) at T1, and the rest can be added on race morning. Do not leave anything that is heat sensitive or perishable on the bike, or anything that you don't want to get wet (in case of rain). You should try to leave the minimum on the bike overnight and do most of the setup of these sensitive items on race morning.

Since you took the time to walk through the transition a few days beforehand, you should now know where everything is. It doesn't hurt to double check with officials if you are still unsure of anything. If you need body marking, this will happen on the way to T1, or at the start. Only competitors can go into T1/T2, so plan to be by yourself without any help. Don't put sunscreen on your arms and legs before getting your body marked as your number won't stick and this could cause potential timing issues. Once your gear is dropped off and in place at your transition spot, you are done with that part of the pre-race work. Keep checking the time so you stay on schedule.

Your support crew is not allowed to enter any of the transition areas. If you need to contact them after you leave T1, you should go to your prearranged meeting spot. I usually use Walkie Talkies, or my phone (depending on where I am) in order to find my team. That makes it very easy. Then I can meet up quickly and find a quieter spot to start my warm-up and pre-race stretch, outside of T1 but close to the start.

Do remember that a quick bathroom stop might be good to do earlier than later, as there will be plenty of people that feel the same urge just as the thought occurs to you. If I get stuck in the line, I use the time for stretching and visualization of the course. I usually bring my own toilet paper or tissues just in case there are any emergencies. You never know if the race organizers are prepared for the amount of people using the bathroom and it's normal to go a few times before the race.

Start warming up early and always be aware of the time so you keep on schedule (warm-up, check in, wave start). I suggest not using headphones so you can hear the announcers, but if music is what brings you in the zone, turn it up and have someone from your crew be on guard for announcements. Just pay attention and keep one eye on your watch.

For the actual warm-up, I suggest doing a short jog with a few easy strides towards the end. It's a good warm-up and will definitely wake you up. I used to ignore the warm-up as I thought sitting would save me more energy for later. I was mistaken. Prepare your body with mild stretches and a bit of activity, and in case there is not much time to warm-up in the water, use your standard training session warm-up to get ready. Using a swimming stretch cord to warm-up your arms is also very valuable to prepare for the sprint at the start of your race. Use the remaining time to go through a few key points in your head.

If you have enough time, use your warm-up jog for checking out the swim start. Spot the exit and the way through T1 and T2? This is all you need to focus on right now. Getting the start right is important, as there will be plenty of people around you. If you acclimate both visually and physically to the start and those transition areas, you will make room for the actions that follow. You'll be completely in your zone with no time wasted on logistics. Just swim, run and bike. The rest falls away into the background. This is the race.

Next, get suited up into your wetsuit or swim skin. Don't forget the Vaseline. You will need a friend to zip you up, so if you are outside of T1, then you should be able to get help with it. If you are in an area where none of your crew can enter, then just ask a friendly competitor to help. You still need to do a swim specific warm-up just before the start. This usually happens 15-30 minutes before the gun goes off. Use your standard pool warm-up for preparation.

Before you begin your swim, get into the water and allow water to flow inside the suit. It might be cold for a minute, but the layer of water inside your suit will help you to adjust the suit to fit your body and will allow you to get it into the perfect position. After that's done, get completely out of the water, hold your arms straight up and let the water run out of your suit. A thin layer of water will accumulate between your body and the suit, and the rest of the water will disappear.

Take note in your pre-race briefing whether there is a dedicated warm-up time and a dedicated warm-up zone in the water. If you aren't allowed to get in the water at all before the race, you can use a water bottle to prepare your wetsuit for your swim by squeezing water into your collar and down your arms. Hold your arms up to let most of the water run out of your suit. You are just creating a thin layer of water between you and your wetsuit, no bulges of water. Now you are ready to rumble.

Factor in the water temperature with your warm-up plans so

you are not freezing and standing around wet and cold before you start. Incorporate some accelerations and some kicking into your routine to warm-up the most important muscles you will need for a fast swim start. The accelerations promote the release of some pre-race lactate in your muscles which makes the hard sprint at the beginning easier for you. Prepare your mind and get your heart rate up. If you just focus on the first few seconds of the race, then the rest should follow on autopilot.

Make sure you know the conditions of the swim course on race day. For example, low tide means you have to run some distance until you begin your swim so a proper warm-up with a sprint and some jumps might be necessary. Keep in mind that if it's a deep-water start you still have to swim to the start line. For orientation reasons, check the position of the buoys and try to find the shortest passage for your swim. It's helpful to find a landmark within your line of sight of the buoys, such as a house, a tower or a tree line. This will help you to find the buoy more easily during your swim when you are surrounded by a few others and all you see is white splash from the guys in front of you. I do that at every race, because even the race organizers in the kayak or on the stand up paddle board might not be in line with the next buoy. So it's up to you to make the proper orientation. Trust yourself here. You have to know the course.

When it's time to stop going over the logistics of the race itself, you will know. Your work is done and now it's time to put yourself on autopilot. You've got this. Focus and relax before you are sent off to begin the race. During the next several hours, you will be forced to focus on the current moment. The real beauty in racing is that it forces us to pay attention to where we are, and not to think too far ahead or behind. There are no shopping lists going through our minds or thoughts about your last conference call, there is only this moment in time. A focused mind is always operating in the background during the race. It is present and yet invisible all at once. If we try to think about what will happen 100 miles down the road, we will falter. In the last few minutes before the race begins, simply be present.

After the Gun Goes Off

Just before the gun goes off, I am focused but completely relaxed. I'm like an empty vessel waiting to be filled by the experience of the race. If I am too uptight and anxious before the gun goes off I will have no room for the expedition before me. If I am not 100% in the moment, I might miss something important. I am neither in the past, nor in the future. I am only here and now.

The starting procedures usually consist of a countdown with a loud horn blast signaling the start. You are in position and then the gun goes off. It will always be a fast start as everybody is motivated and fired up. The defining moments will happen in the first few hundred meters, where the packs get separated out. Where do you want to position yourself?

If you don't like to be in the middle of huge mass of swimmers, try to find a less crowded spot around the edges in the water. The shortest way might not be the fastest way, as everybody wants to be on the perfect straight line and that crowded route might create more difficult obstacles. Be realistic but don't underestimate your abilities. If you are a good swimmer then go to the front. If swimming is not your strongest discipline, then don't push to the front of the pack, as people will swim all over you, literally.

Don't be intimidated by the symphony of swimmers. I find it

exhilarating to swim with so many competitors. It's an amazing feeling both creating the current and being carried away by the current of others. The water surrenders to the efforts of the competitors and yet presents one stream of movement like a single shape, cutting a path through the water.

Awareness of your surroundings is key to gaining full advantage of your position in the sea of swimmers. It's a good practice to frequently look up and spot a better position so you can swim more freely. You have prepared mentally for swimming next to people and will have the expectation of the influence of others on your stroke. This is triathlon, and that's part of it. You have practiced this scenario over and over again and aren't afraid.

Into the Fray

Now you are in the thick of it. You are engaged with the race. You are out there by yourself for the rest of the day. No outside assistance is allowed, no matter if you puncture a tire or if you cramp. That's good. It's a race. It's your race. I love to call it "man versus the elements". Control the controllable and let the rest be. Go with the flow and accept how things unfold during your day. There will be things you simply can't change and so why waste precious energy on it? As you navigate the unexpected, always be looking to get back on track. Finding that rhythm again is where your focus should be when things go south. There will be plenty of ups and downs and there will be unknown territories and challenges awaiting you. I think we forget that this is the experience we trained for. Move through it. Always bear in mind, it's just a swim, a bike ride and a run.

It's easy to let the race get complicated. For me it's a sport that means the world to me, but as a pro it sometimes feels like war. It is you or me. It's my job. I'm racing to bring home the proverbial bacon. There is no place for failure. Imagine if I would have had the proper hydration in Gerardmere? I could have won, but maybe I would have faded anyway. We will never know.

This is the moment I put away the job and disappear into the mystery. There are a thousand and one outcomes at any given moment during any race you take on. You will face many "ifs" yourself during your day. Be prepared for that. It's in the accepting of the unexpected where the resolution reveals itself.

What could go wrong? What should you do? How do you react with minimal disruption to your flow? Spoiler alert. These are just a few of the enchanting experiences that might come your way. During the swim, the waves might bother you or your goggles might fog up. There's not much you could do about that other than refocus and continue to swim. The goal is to focus every second on the fastest path from A to B. If an obstacle comes up, deal with it and then bring yourself back to your focus of a streamlined path to the finish line.

What happens if you puncture out there? You need to have a spare tire with you. Where can you place this extra equipment on your bike? If you chose to take it with you then you need to find a way to make it work. Some will sacrifice a bike bottle for it and cut a bottle open to hold all the puncture gear. It's also pretty easy to Velcro those things to a bottle cage behind your seat or even using a saddlebag.

If you want to go out on a limb, just take your concealing spray with you. In 99% of the cases you won't need it. On the other hand if you puncture you could be done with your race and DNF (did not finish: this is a terrible word. It happened to me before and it just doesn't look right next to your name when you look at the result lists later on). Weigh the risk and make your choice. Whatever it might be, deal with all those hurdles but never lose track of your mission on that day. You will find a way through it. Whatever you do, move forward.

Once you have ground under your feet again, you have accomplished your sea voyage and will look toward your transition spot in T1, the same one you jogged through just days before as you checked out the race course. As you are making your way, you can prepare for what comes next. Get your goggles and swim cap off and put them in your hand while you run. When you reach T1, put them down so you can focus on getting your wetsuit or swimskin off. Depending on the race, you will either have to put all of your swim gear in a bag, in the change tent, or leave it on the ground next to your bike. You will have practiced that in your mind, so there will be no surprises. Now is the time to execute.

Once you have dumped out you bike bag and reloaded it with your swim gear, you can start the next leg of your race. Put on your helmet, glasses and whatever else you might have selected for your ride and proceed to the exit. Recall those visual aids and landmarks that you locked in from the day before, and look for your bike. Stay focused through the transition and just take it one step at a time.

Your legs may feel like jelly since the blood is in your arms after your big swim effort. This is normal, and you shouldn't worry. Your body will soon adjust to the new muscle groups being tasked with the effort of a long bike ride. Log this fact into your mental game to avoid a panic reaction at the start of your ride.

At the end of the bike transition everything moves quite fast as there is nothing to be done other than taking your bike and running toward the exit of T1. Once you have your bike, proceed to the mount line and then jump on your bike. If you prefer doing the quick and speedy method, then you will jump barefoot on your already clicked in bike shoes, which will be held horizontal by the rubber bands. This is the method I recommend. You can opt to put your bike shoes on before you get on your bike but this can ruin your cleats and slow you down. Take this into account when you decide which option works best for your game.

When you take your first pedal stroke, the rubber bands will have broken and your shoes will be free. As you reach a good speed and find a good place to do so, you can slide one foot in and tighten the strap of your shoe. By doing this you will slightly decrease your speed, so before putting your other foot in the shoe, pedal a few more strokes. Then you are back up to speed and the next foot can go into the shoe. This is by far the fastest way but you will need to practice it a few times and focus on keeping a straight line with your bike and your speed, while getting your foot in the shoe. It's pretty simple after you have done it a few times. Practice makes perfect in this transition.

Once you are on your bike, settle in for the long ride. Find your pace and get on course. Now the longest part of the race is in front of you. A full distance event means a 112 mile (180 km) bike ride. There will be plenty of aid stations along the way, where you can refuel in case you drop a bottle or run out of fluids. Volunteers will hand out drinks and food, and all of this will be thoroughly described at the race briefing.

It is important to keep your intake of your predetermined nutritional formula going at all times. Since you did your homework, you know how many carbs per hour you have to eat for your size and you know how you will split it up between liquids and solids. Follow your plan throughout the day, regardless of pace, time and other outside factors. Consistency is the rule when it comes to your fuel. Steady as she goes. If you get off course here, it is bound to catch up with you at some point during the day.

Some athletes like to set an alarm every 10-15 minutes to be reminded to drink and eat on the bike. I usually go by this rule: 1 bottle per hour and ¾ bar per hour to eat. That is simple and gives me plenty of calories to burn. For me it doesn't matter how I split up the food and drink in that one hour, it just needs to go down the hatch. As we discussed previously, you should choose your nutrition according what works best for you. It could be gels, tabs, chomps or whatever you like the most. Although I like to eat "real" food during training, like homemade bars, I stay away from them during racing because it is just too much to digest. What is required is a lot of quick burning fuel, which is easy on the stomach when pushing hard.

The aid stations should be set up the same way throughout the race. They usually start with water and end with water. So if you have a very heavy load of carbs mixed into one bottle to last the entire race, you might only need to grab water bottles. I started doing that after ending up with severe stomach cramps in Kona 2013, where over 25 pro athletes threw up late into the bike section because of a potentially rancid batch of drinks provided on the course. If you keep a highly concentrated carb mix on your bike, then you can just drink water and the concentrate, and you will be set to go without having to haul around too much weight. It also works if you don't prefer the race sponsor's choice of sport drinks. In full distance events, some might want to use the special need bags we talked about earlier.

Just keep in mind that you are reliant on others to provide you with your special needs bag, and when you give up your self-reliance there is always opportunity for things to go wrong. One year, I got dropped by some of my competitors in Kona when I stopped for my special needs bag up in the little town of Hawi. It took so much effort to stay with the group and I just gave up all of that work so that I could stop and grab my bag. Braking takes time. Loading your gear onto your bike and getting back up to speed takes time. This little experience motivated me to think about adapting my strategy and relying less on special needs and more on my on-board nutrition and/or the nutrition provided on the course. Think about the pros and cons and do what works best with your overall strategy and at your particular level of competition.

Race Tempo

Pacing is key and will determine your race outcome. I understand how hard it is to keep your focus up all day and you will be tempted many times to go faster than you should. This is where the brain work comes in. Trust the math and execute your pace strategy no matter what outside influences may be taunting you to do otherwise.

Don't forget, the output (watts, power data) is as important as input (nutrition). Focus on your power output early on during the bike leg of your race. The more balanced and even your power data is, the more energy you will conserve and the faster your time will be at the end. Take a look at some of the SRM power meter files on the SRM blog and you will see that this is a major component to a fast bike time and to overall success.

You might ask yourself how to keep the numbers on your SRM low when there is rolling terrain involved. Our first goal is to have the highest average wattage for the duration of the bike leg, but that is hard to maintain when traveling uphill. You will put out significantly more power when going uphill. Even on a small incline of 3-5 % your watts will go way up compared to your normal average power. This is to be expected. Try not to go over 20-30 % of your average watts for long periods, as this will take a toll on your overall energy levels throughout the day, resulting in quicker calorie usage and dips in your energy later on in the race.

Picture your total energy level as a pie chart. You begin the race at 100% at the swim start and you should have an empty tank once you cross the finish line. Obviously you don‘t want to run on empty toward the very end. You might jeopardize your entire race by doing that. Be smart and pace properly throughout the day. Avoid the big spikes of wattage and keep the output as even as possible. In other words, make sure to burn all of your matches. You are going to want to cross that finish line with zero matches left in your book, just enough to get you through. Control yourself on the uphills and don’t stop pedaling on the downhills.

Think of your power as a line; the more horizontal the line is the better you will do. Too many up and downward spikes are not desirable. Rule of thumb: Balance your output during the race and save some energy on the uphills. Control the power on the flats and push the downhills in order to keep a steady output overall. That is the art of pacing. If you follow my suggestion, you cannot go wrong and you will set the foundation for success. The recipe is so elementary. Just stick to it and you will do great. Trust me.

Your heart rate is also a good indicator for pacing. Together with the wattage, it is the perfect one two punch for optimized performance. Many outside factors can influence your heart rate therefore it should be considered a more subtle indicator.

Use your heart rate data as an informational tool but don‘t let it limit you. Your heart rate can change based on how fatigued you are, and whether or not it’s hot or cold, or altitude is high or low. This parameter doesn't tell you why it drops, but it just does. In contrast to heart rate, the power meter will always be the same data regardless of weather conditions, fatigue or adrenaline spikes.

I'll say it again, pacing is key. It's the alchemy of your race. I know it gets hard sometimes. You might feel like everyone is passing you, which can be really discouraging sometimes. However, long distance triathlon really is a case of the turtle and the hare, and it take a strong mind to remain the steadfast turtle. Most people start the bike leg way too fast and then bonk towards the end due to over pacing. You have the tools you need and with practice you will have the mental strength to pace your way to the podium. Keep your long game solid.

If you plan and race your own race, you won't be giving in to the pace of your neighboring competitors. This is the number one potential threat to sabotaging your race and it’s all in your hands! Know what you have to do and don’t ditch your plan if you suddenly experience a high. During such a long and hard race, you will experience several highs and lows. Know that if you experience a high, the low will shortly follow. You won’t be lingering with either state of mind. Keep trucking as I would say, or keep chopping wood. You are on pace.

It might be interesting to note that professional racing has a slightly different strategy in terms of pacing. In most races I have to adapt to certain race tactics even when going way over my level, but these types of strategies could truly be race decisive. Pro racing tactics are totally different from amateur ones in that regard. But one thing holds true for both scenarios. During those moments where we are out there alone, suffering in the heat of the sun reflecting off the pavement, each athlete is for him or herself. During dark moments as well as light ones, when we are running through a huge crowd of spectators and getting so fired up, it is paramount for both pros and age-groupers to focus on their own state of the game. It is you versus the distance not you versus 2000 other competitors. Focusing solely on yourself and on your perfect pacing strategy will bring you much further than trying to focus on someone else's race, which sucks energy and gets you into a mentality of lack. Keep to your own race within the spectacle of the overarching race event.

Points to Consider

Comfort must always be addressed during the long 112 miles in the saddle. How you decide to manage your position on the bike during this voyage can make or break you both physically and mentally. You can be consistently aero and have less drag but if you can't hold your position for more than one hour you are screwed as well, because your super-aero position just ends up hurting you and all of those not-so-aero guys will be passing you. So everything has to make sense here. In triathlon you must always consider all of the pieces of the puzzle.

Please make sure you study the printouts and race info before the race to see where aid stations will be provided on the course. Usually they are placed every 10-15 miles (20 km) depending on the race and the heat conditions. Just make sure you orchestrate your ride so you can work them into your nutrition plan. I usually start paying attention when I have only one bottle left to drink. I know that will carry me roughly one more hour, so from then on I plan to grab another bottle just to be safe and stay hydrated at all times.

If it is bloody hot out make sure to grab a water bottle whenever you can to cool your head and body. I usually spray some water in my helmet from the backside, under my aero tail. That's really the only way you can cool your head during this section so be conscious not to get too much sweat in your eyes as you douse your head. Spray it on both arms and legs and also on your glutes. If you wear arm coolers, make sure they are wet so they can do their job. The dryer the heat the better they work.

A while ago, I was in Boulder to attend the pro panel of Boulder 70.3. I participated in a panel discussion where we all were asked about our race nutrition. I remember a female pro telling her interesting story about taking a minimum of 27 gels during her half distance race. I couldn't believe my ears. That's a lot! This is way too much nutrition for the distance. We are talking about a 4:30h half distance race. No wonder she had to drop out. I don't know many people whose stomach would handle that. I also know a fellow athlete from Florida who takes around 90 salt tablets per Half Ironman®. This is absurd and most likely not very healthy! Unless you have stock in the salt tablet company, this is bad for business. Overkill not only makes you sick, it makes your wallet a little lighter in the process.

Halfway through the bike course you will hit the special needs area. This area is well indicated and you should have no problem finding it. If you chose not to take part in the special needs idea, just continue on course. You could win valuable time in comparison to the people who stop. This decision should be a calculated one. Make sure you are on top of your race nutrition and not running low on intake. If you chose to take your special needs bag, finish off what you still have on board and then store the additional nutrition on your bike.

Be careful when handling this transition as it can be a juggling act to grab the bag, steer the bike, and empty out its contacts without spilling it. You need to decide if you will stop for 20 seconds or if you will keep riding while unloaded the loot. Be aware that the "waste drop" zone is usually pretty short. If you discard anything outside of these zones you will run the risk of receiving a red card, time penalties and even disqualification. Make your choice and focus on a flawless passage. From there on you are on your way back to T2.

Make sure you stay focused and pay attention to what's happening around you. When I raced IM Cozumel in 2012, I experienced discord from all directions during my last hard fight on two wheels. If I wasn't constantly checking my focus I could have easily lost my lead. I was all alone, in front, from mile 1 on the bike. I hammered along the course with a 7-minute gap. We had to ride 3 laps and, of course, on the 2nd and 3rd lap there were tons of age-groupers who had joined the course. They usually stick to the right side of the road, unless they are passing, but there were also the occasional set of three guys riding abreast, with me motoring past all of them. A few times I had to swing far over to the left side to pass safely. Other times there were long gaps before the next age grouper came along, which compelled me to move back to the right side of the road, head down, and holding 300 watts while maintaining my heart race at a nice 145-150 bpm.

I felt the same way you would feel: tired, exhausted and eager to get off my race machine. Before I could take another breath, I saw the back wheel of the person right in front of me and I could hardy swerve to the left to pass. This situation jolted me awake and spiked my adrenaline up for sure. Altered body chemistry was added to the mix of plates I was juggling at the time.

These little surprises usually come my way when I lose my focus. If you become complacent during your long ride you make room for these undesirable developments. Getting in that aero position can present some danger and create irksome scenarios. I should have known better and kept my head up with so many people on the course. Unfortunately I've had a few very close calls like this in my racing career. Each race presents potential disasters around every corner. You have to be prepared and focused. Awareness at every point in the race is key. Log and learn from these events and they will become fewer and far between.

Hopefully you will get through your bike sections without any issues, but when calamities do occur, there can be a silver lining. Perhaps you need to look for it but it's usually there. I competed in ST Croix 70.3 in 2012 and came away with a memorable "silver lining experience". I love the island of St Croix. The race, in contrast, is brutally hard and hot. The night before the race a big storm hit the area creating plenty of landslides. They told us they cleared the roads but that was not the case.

Traditionally I swim in the front group, so I usually get out of the water in front and ride with the main contenders on the bike. This day was no exception, and so I was on track. I felt great and so I stepped on the gas and found myself in 2nd place with a 1:15 min gap to the lead man at kilometer 12. This is the section of the race where you get back into town. Just 1k beforehand, we hit another dirt pile with solid rocks in the mix. I reduced the pace and got through it until I hit something. Of course I punctured and was rolling on empty in a matter of seconds.

I made it right into town, where T1/T2 and all the spectators were, and was able to stop and ask for assistance. There was no mechanic or wheel car provided and I had to accept the fact that I couldn't fix the big cut in my tire. I watched the chasing group go by, mad as hell. The organizers did not even make a one-foot path through the sand and the rocks, which would have been enough for us. Well, that wasn't the case for me that day, or for the 3 other top ranked guys that punctured.

Even writing this right now, I can feel myself getting upset. That is, until I recall the silver lining. I was walking home with my bike when I noticed an older guy who had punctured and was sadly dismounting his bike right in front of me. He told me that it was his birthday and so it wasn't long before I decided to give him my high tech front wheel so he could continue. He had the oldest bike imaginable. My front wheel looked so out of place on his ancient downtube shifter, but now he could finish his bike section. I was suddenly in a great mood again, and it sure made his day. A swift transition from pitfall to prosperity for both of us.

Isn't this part of the game? Surely I'll be on the other end of this exchange one day, rolling with the punches. I like to think that my misfortune was woven into resolving the snag in his game plan. Later I went to T2 and exchanged the two wheels as if nothing happened. I never saw the guy again but I'm sure he had as much fun as I did watching the show unfold. That was a lesson learned for me. Misfortunes are bound to come your way. Redefine them as opportunities for experiences on the periphery. They deepen your character and toughen your resolve. St. Croix turned into a memorable race for me despite the failure.

Toward the end of your bike section, you will most likely get tired and fed up with the bike riding. Anticipating this fact will remind you how timely an annoyance it is—a perfectly timed motivation for your run.

Approaching T2

Each race has two transitions, and with each of them comes a very specific point of focus. Visualize the upcoming tasks before you arrive. When approaching T2, unstrap your shoes and prepare to hop off your bike right before the dismount line. Never cross that line while still on your bike! Depending on the race, the bikes are taken from you and you can just run towards your assigned spot in T2 or through the changing tent where you will change from cycling gear into your running gear. If there is no tent, then it will be directly at your assigned T2 spot. In more low-key races, you have to run with your bike to your T2 spot and then rack your bike yourself. Both versions are pretty standard. You've already gone through this scenario in your head pre-race. Stay focused on recalling your study.

Regardless of whether you will be in a changing tent or have your running gear prepared at your bike, it's the same process. You are NOT allowed to take your helmet off until your bike is racked or taken from you at the dismount line. Your helmet strap must be closed from the time you take your bike after the swim, until your bike is securely racked. Only then are you allowed to unstrap your helmet. It could be grounds for a disqualification if you do otherwise. Once you know how it works, the proper instinct will be there forever.

Now that your bike is taken care of you can get rid of your helmet and glasses and start putting on your running socks and sliding into your racing flats, tightening them if necessary. Grab whatever you have prepared in your run bag and once you are all set, run towards the T2 exit and onto the running course. It is good to put a little bit of baby powder or some Vaseline in your running shoes, which helps to prevent chaffing.

Blisters hurt like crap, so taking a bit of time to prevent blisters before you get them is a worthy pursuit.

The better you prepare your T2 spot, the less time you will waste. Transition is the fourth discipline of triathlon. Many athletes tend to forget how easy it is to save 60 seconds in T1 or T2 versus running 60 seconds faster. You've already practiced your transitions pre-race. Focus and execute and you will save valuable time. Once you are out on the marathon course you will feel the effects of your swim and especially your bike effort. If you paced well, everything should be on track for the final leg of your journey.

Out of T2 and Onto the Run Course

Imagine yourself on the running course, high fiving your friends right after the transition. You are motivated, pumped up, and you can feel the goosebumps all over as you cut through the exhilarating cheers from the crowd. Everyone is calling your name and you feel like a million bucks. This is a good moment to check your pacing on your GPS watch which can show you the actually pace you are going at this point in time. You might be totally off pace but maybe you don't realize it because you so feel great. It is very important to run out of the transition area at a controlled speed. There is a lot of excitement generated with the crowd. Do not get carried away and forget your pacing plan. Come back to your focus and head out onto the course.

The first few minutes after the long, grueling bike leg of the race will feel pretty weird, regardless of how many bricks you did in training. It will take a few miles to loosen up your legs from the long bike ride and get comfortable with your normal stride. This feeling is normal. Have this in mind when starting out. Remember that you have been out on the course for quite some time now and you will feel the effects on your whole body system. You might think your legs are toast but they will shortly come good in 20-30 minutes.

Let your body adjust. The beauty of this sport is, that even when you think you are totally wasted and your legs hurt from riding all day, you can still perform on the run. The secret is in accessing new muscle groups that you did not utilize for the bike leg. No matter how tired you are, you can run, because your running muscles have been preserved for this leg of the journey. Trust your body.

Once you run out onto the course, don‘t get overwhelmed with the thought of how long the run will take and how tired you feel at the moment. Reigning in those undesirable thoughts begins with the mental preparation that you have designed for your race—you have done this a million times in your head. All of those steps in training have been leading to this, and you are ready. Do not project your thoughts to the end of the race. Stay here with each and every footfall, following through rotation to completion. Let the sound of your foot hitting the pavement keep you focused.

It is absolutely vital to run out at a controlled speed and within your range. Pacing, as on the bike, is the key factor to success or the reason for failure. I can't emphasize this enough. You know from training and testing what your realistic running goal time is. So when you break it down you know your average pace per mile or kilometer and where you should be, once you hit your checkpoints along the way. Have a few split times in your head, so you know what your goal time is for different mile markers. Your GPS watch will really come in handy at this point. This helpful tool that you have incorporated into your game will make all the difference for you.

I always set my watch settings to show the actual pace and average pace, so I see both at all times. It is good to know how your pace is in perspective to your planned average pace. In comparison to just using a normal watch, the GPS watch gives you one less thing to worry about, since you don't have to calculate anything. You might get tired later on in the marathon and you could lose track of the many mile markers and your checkpoint times. Also, you never know if the course is marked 100% correctly. You could be passing the marker for mile 5, but it is actually mile 5.1. Your time will be off by quite a bit. The GPS watch doesn't lie and keeps your information accurate. This is why I suggested this tool for you. It just might save your day.

Most running courses are designed to have multiple laps so it is more fun for the spectators to see the athletes more frequently. For athletes, the laps helps to break up the run into sections. Sometimes there are four laps in a race and sometimes there are only two. You will know this in advance and will be mentally prepared for it. This splits up the long marathon into smaller, more achievable goals. The horizon for each lap feels more attainable. It is a simple mind trick you should utilize instead of looking at the whole distance.

If you think about the entire marathon from the start, it's likely to overwhelm you. My sister, who is an experienced international mountain guide, confirms it for me. If you climb Mount Everest, you can't have the summit in your mind at all times. What you can do is focus on each step, from base camp to base camp, in order to get there safe. You first have to focus on the single steps, which bring you to the summit or the finish line. So be patient and set bite size goals. To keep that in mind, remember the "20 mile march" philosophy of Collins and Hansen, which was adopted from Roald Amundsen, the first explorer to reach the South Pole in 1911. Controlled pacing—step-by-step. No impulsive spikes in your effort. Stay with each footfall to stay with your pace.

Once you hit the halfway mark, there will be the option to, once again, take your special needs bag. You could have additional gels, salt and your own nutrition mix in it, but only food is allowed in those bags. If you are fine with what the organizations offers at their aid stations then there is no need for extras. Weigh the need for specialized nutrition against any time or momentum lost in pausing for your special needs bag.

The Home Stretch

The second half of the run will be the most challenging part of the entire race because of the accumulation of a very long and tough day. Your body is getting tired and you want to get it over with. It's that similar fatigue that you felt toward the end of each discipline but the run is the most grueling of the three. This is where your grit will come into play. Your will to keep moving forward is the most crucial part of your focus. Now is the time to access every inch of mental focus you have at your disposal. The mind always gives up before the body. You can never let your mind take over and accept defeat. The mind takes its cue from the body. Now it is time dig really deep and remember your purpose for scaling this mountain of a mission. This is your motivation, the fuel for your mind. This acts like a higher purpose in that moment and will keep you going.

Acclaimed exercise scientist, Dr. Timothy Noakes asserts that an athlete only uses approximately 80-82% of his physical capabilities. Your brain, the central governor, only allows you to operate within that range in your everyday life. It is a regulatory defense mechanism to protect the body, which can only be overpowered in life threatening situations. This is what the reserve is for. We hear stories about a super human mom lifting up the side of a car to free her child. These people are accessing the reserves of their body. These are the reserves you can call on anytime you feel your tank is on empty. This is where you must convince your mind that those reserves exist and that it's reasonable to access them.

Each race presents its own set of influences that affect your ability to both physically and mentally manage your race. If you race in Kona, the solitude is pronounced because there are hardly any spectators out on the course. The past two years I experienced a real shock out in the lava field. Roughly at the halfway point, on the run course out to the energy lab, they blocked spectators from going though. This is where you need the most outside support during the race. Compare that to Challenge Roth in Germany where they have a record breaking estimated 250,000 spectators along the course. You will be tasked with the effort of keeping self-doubt at bay whether you have mass crowds of support or empty lava fields before you.

Now that you have convinced your mind that you are able to push on to the finish line, you can definitely continue running at your pace. If you had to, you could even sprint. You may call upon some inner reserves as I did in 2012 at the Ironman® World Championships when the pain in my broken hand started to populate all of my thoughts. I had to stop running at some point because my mind was convincing me that I could not continue. My partner and my coach were trying to coax me on to the finish line but I could not find the strength to take another step.

It was only until I found that reason to continue, that my body was able to access those inner reserves. It was the moment I realized that I was losing my top ten finish option. That is when my exhausted mind persuaded my exhausted body to push harder than I have ever pushed before. The result was a top ten finish and a spot on the podium as well as a qualifying spot for the World Championships for the following year. Digging deep had its reward.

These are the extremes that we call upon to finish the race. Up to the halfway mark everybody can pretty much keep pace. After the halfway mark, this is where we see the true champions separating themselves from the pack. We are in Ironman® racing territory now. Moment to moment, corner to corner, your will carries you through and at some point you see the finish line and the big smile will return to your face.

It's a total mind circus towards the end. Prove to yourself that you are stronger than your limitations. This is your goal and it is in your power to make it happen. I have a huge amount of respect for everyone crossing that line, no matter what the clock says. Standing for hours at finish lines in world class triathlons, I get so inspired by what I experience and what I see. I want to share everything I've learned from the sport with you. It is just such a special sport. It connects us all on a higher level. It's profound living.

You will understand once you have successfully finished your race and it all sinks in. Those of you who have already experienced the gauntlet of a triathlon race, you know exactly what I'm referring to here. You will never forget this amazing day in your life. Plenty of stories will be told about your experience and you now deserve every right to brag about it. You are now, one of the few; a rare breed.

Post Apocalypse

Once the race is done and dusted, your emotions will be a bit mixed. Your body is totally crushed, but you are elated and delirious to have finally reached your goal. It's likely to have not gone down exactly how you had envisioned it so many times during your training, but give yourself some time to process the day's events as they did play out.

Long distance racing takes such a toll on you mentally and physically, that the few hours following the race are what I like to call the "shock phase". You are sticky, covered in gels, sugary drinks, saliva, blood, sweat, tears, and every imaginable body fluid your body has purged from the day's race. You sit in the finish area, unable to move. You don't really know how you are going to get back to your hotel. You don't even know if you can stand up, let alone find your crew members. Maybe they have finally caught up to you and you don't really know what to say to sum up the depth of your experience. You might be in the medical tent getting an IV drip to replace your fluids, passed out in the grass, or doubled over trying to catch your breath.

This is the quintessential moment where the champion lies gasping for air on the field of battle; physically and emotionally wounded but somehow purified and reborn. When I cross the finish line I am done with the world for a little while. This is normal for most people as you begin the process of mentally and physically absorbing the totality of what you have just experienced.

Restore and Refuel

Now that you've emptied your reservoirs and are reflecting on your achievement, you should start to think about refueling. To begin with, take whatever is served in the finish line area. Your tank will be running pretty low and anything will work fine immediately after the race. I usually crave carbonated drinks that are low in sugar, like soda water or beer. If you are planning to race soon after (not too likely for the lucky amateurs but likely for the pros), eat some protein as soon as you are able to get it down. I have to be honest, this is what you should be doing, but I can hardly down the protein myself sometimes.

It's good to keep your alcohol consumption to a minimum over the next few days in order to boost recovery, but who is going follow my advice on that one? I have a hard time sticking to it myself. And I agree, if you don't deserve a drink after your race, when else would you deserve a cold brew ? Just bear in mind, you are low on fluids and "feeling the buzz" goes VERY quickly in this condition. I am sure you won't be the one dancing around, but you might be the first person to fall asleep in the corner of the bar.

Everyone is different and every athlete craves different foods and drinks post-race. I suggest that you answer your craving. This is your reward after emerging from the fray. Cold beer and something fatty like french fries does the trick for me. There is the difference between what you crave and what you need. Consider a good balance but don't be afraid to honor what your body might be craving.

After your race you might not sleep too well despite being totally tired and very exhausted. A few things help, such as an ice bath shortly after the race and some compression or recovery boots. A flush-out massage is always the greatest in my point of view, but you might not have your personal massage therapist with you. Plan ahead and book early if you think you might need that. If the pain in your legs is too much you could use an anti-inflammatory to calm down the post-race inflammation. Elevate your legs and simply relax.

Some pros return to the finish area, after refueling, to hand out medals and let everything sink in. I've done that several times but I play it by ear. If I am too tired to get up then I simply stay in. There were days when I couldn't even make it to the awards ceremony.

Taking the time to reflect on the day's events will allow you to process each race as a unique chapter in the narrative of your life. Set yourself up for the evaluation process that will follow this day. You must give yourself some distance from the race in order to come to a place to analyze the specifics of your race. This is a huge transition. Try not to rush it. Each race presents its own set of choices as we make every effort to return to the ordinary world.

Chapter 7:
The Morning After...

> *"I firmly believe that any man's finest hour, the greatest fulfillment of all that he holds dear, is that moment when he has worked his heart out in a good cause and lies exhausted on the field of battle — victorious."*
>
> *~Vince Lombardi*

Imagine putting the brakes on a Ferrari going 110 miles per hour, and then sitting there watching the smoke blow past you. This is the morning after racing an iron distance triathlon. I have been there. I am with you there now. I tell you it is a process. Let yourself go through it. Rest and recover. This too shall pass.

REST AND REFLECTION:

You awaken with your eyes sore in their sockets, a bit disoriented. You look around, and you start to recognize the shadows on the walls of what is your hotel room. A tidal wave of memories start to flood in. Was all of that a dream? Did you really just manage to pull off completing a triathlon? You go to move your legs, to sit up and make yourself that beloved morning coffee, and that's when the tinge of soreness shoots up. Holy Schnitzel, that certainly wasn't a dream. You have the aftershock to prove it.

Chances are, you didn't sleep well the night before because you either went out to watch the last finishers come down through the chute at midnight, or you just couldn't calm down from your caffeine laden post-race-buzz. On the morning after, you might feel like you are straight out of a scene from

"The Hangover" complete with smelly race kits, bike bottles and half eaten gels, all in a heap on the floor; your tired, crusty bike leaning up against the hotel wall and random pieces of tape, zip ties, papers, plastic bags, and various MacGyver-esque items laid out on the table. Take it in. What a beautiful mess; a gorgeous disaster. It's like an art installation of your expedition, Jackson Pollock-style.

You have a headache, or more likely, a complete body ache that pulses with the beating of your heart. But, somehow through all of this, it makes it even more real—no need to pinch yourself—you did it. The feeling of accomplishment and the joy of achieving your goal are bigger than your pain. There is no such thing as a perfect race, but finishing the race is close enough to perfect for you. The feeling that you have can only be described as a satisfied soreness.

The first few days will undoubtedly be tough because your body will let you know that it took a serious beating and needless to say, it's pissed. It is best to just roll with it. The body is running the show. When it holds up the stop sign there's no way to resist. Wear those battle wounds like a badge of courage, and you will bounce back in no time.

I remember after my first Half Ironman® I couldn't walk properly for a while and after my first full distance race I was a total mess for days. I had blisters on my feet, chafe burns on my neck, and my legs just couldn't seem to remember how to walk. It was New Zealand in 2009 and while I was out there on the longest stint of asphalt I had ever raced, my partner was dealing with her own crisis. She had crashed her scooter and had taken refuge in a pie shop, where they bandaged her up and sent her off to search for her husband on the rainy battlefield. After the race, we were both in the medical tent, side by side.

We were suffering big time once the morning after came around. I was processing my recovery from a crazy Ironman® feat and she was healing from the whiplash, cuts, burns, and bruises of her accident. We must have looked like quite the pair as I tried to navigate the stairs by walking backwards and she shuffled around at a snail's pace. Sometimes my legs would work fine, and then all of the sudden they would give out, causing me to nearly collapse. Every race to follow built on that experience. You will begin to mine the benefits of the restoration process.

The advice here is to keep to your recovery schedule and let your body move through the restorative process. Don't even think about training! Just move yourself around a bit. A ten minute swim with some aqua jog movements will help to increase the blood flow and help to feel better. A super short and easy ride will accomplish the same. Absolutely lay off running for a few days to let your inflammation go down and heal your muscles. They have taken a beating and will have lots of tiny micro-wounds that will need some time to heal.

You are going to need a physical break from triathlon, and it is important that you allow yourself to take one. I have known many athletes that didn't take their physical recovery seriously enough and suffered in big ways because of it. You are no machine, and even if you were, you would still need to take a break! Make a conscious effort to take the time to recover. It's part of the equation of triathlon racing.

Fun Post Race Facts

- You might get "cankles". Bring compression gear for travel afterwards to handle potential post race swelling.
- You will feel the desire to brush your teeth after your

race. Too much sugar all day.

- You will most likely crave fatty foods.
- You won't poop for days if you went all out.
- You won't pee right away either. My personal record is 3.5 hours until I could provide a sample in the anti doping control tent.
- You will somehow feel sad even though you just turned over a crazy badass effort.

Post-Race Blues

The first few days after the race you might feel some emptiness inside where your iron heart used to be. Most triathletes experience this slump. We call it the post-race blues. It's a natural phenomenon in the sport of long distance racing. The expression Ironman® Blues is often used by athletes and appears to be even used as a medical term. It's pretty normal and is comparable to the aftermath of any huge emotional long-term investment. Looking at the arc of such an elevated experience, it feels like a completely natural occurrence. Before you go in and analyze all of the metrics of your race, the spirit must settle so it can eventually rise again, like a Phoenix from the ashes; the alchemy of the Ironman®.

You have been training and thinking about this race for days, weeks, months and in some cases even years to fulfill your dream of just finishing the Ironman® or achieving your personal goal. Whatever it might be, you worked towards your goal, sacrificed plenty of training hours, gave up family time and lived for a longer period of time on a strict regimen. The diet, the tough training plan, organizing the pool times, and now suddenly the race is completed. Now what comes next?

You might not have even thought about the aftermath. Now, you have all this time and no grand quest in front of you. It is a common phenomenon for anyone who has just surmounted an extraordinary goal. For me, as a professional, the emptiness can seem rather large, since I don't have as many other goals outside of the sport. You might have your job or family that helps you to readjust your goals post-race. Your blues might not be as bad. Good on you! Then just enjoy some downtime before storming into the next project.

When my partner was done writing her PhD, I noticed a serious drop in her mood the weeks following her dissertation. It was the culmination of nearly five years of focused effort. You would expect total joy and happiness after such a successful accomplishment. So many weeks, months and years went into that project and then it was finally done. She worked her butt off for many years to reach her dream goal, a huge milestone in her career, and once the task was completed and it sunk in, then everything started bubbling up. She started realizing how much effort it took to get the dissertation done and how glad she was that it was over. The biggest question after all this work was—what is next? What will happen now? The days changed drastically from typing several hours a day to simply resting and sleeping. There was an emptiness and an urge to simply do nothing. It was a mild depression-like feeling and it's hard to understand if you are not the person going through it.

Who you become after such an accomplishment stares back at you in the mirror. Am I the person who accomplished this? Am I different? Should I be feeling different? Is this what I expected? What is the reward for the accomplishment?

Ironman® racing is clearly different from completing a PhD, but the arc is similar. Once you cross that finish line and achieve your personal goal, you will be the proudest person in the world, especially if it is your first full Ironman® distance event. The minutes after the race are filled with joy and happiness. You will also feel the suffering you were going through those long, lonely hours out there on the race course. These seemingly opposing sets of emotions will fill you up in a surprising way. It will seem like a reinvention of your reality. All I can say is roll with it; do not deprive yourself of the experience. It is the sun, the soil, the water that produces the fruit.

What is your purpose in life after accomplishing such a feat? Is anything else in your life as meaningful as this accomplishment? After your first big race these sort of questions will hit you like everybody else. First you feel empty, tired, sore and simply more than just done with the chapter of triathlon and that's ok. It's completely natural.

The mind is equally exhausted. The mind begins its quest in understanding the monumental journey. You've pushed both mind and body beyond the scope of normal conditioning. The intel that you gather from the experience is actually valuable. Don't rush to the exit. Just linger for a moment in complete physical and mental exhaustion. That's the answer.

The "arrival fallacy" might creep into play during this time. This is the belief that once you achieve a desired goal, you will finally be happy. It is a fallacy because if we, as humans, achieve something so deeply desired, we may find that sustained happiness is elusive. What we hopefully come to understand is that it was in the doing that we were living our happiness. Achieving our goal is not the apex of our journey but rather the beginning of another. Rest for a moment and recall the entirety of your accomplishment. Enjoy the moment. What time is it? Where are you? The answer is here and now.

Enjoy and live in the present moment. This will bring you deep joy.

I realized my down point doesn't come right after the race. If time allows, I usually spend seven to ten days of vacation right after a big event, like the Olympics or Ironman® peak races. Perhaps there is a little distraction, sleight of hand going on there. During those short recovery trips, I still feel great and happy. I leave everything behind and travel to some remote place, such as Norway or the Provence to get away from the hype of the races. This seems to give me peace and time to reflect. It also helps me to have both feet on the ground. At the race I am always in the spotlight and have plenty of cameras in my face all the time. There is no downtime. And don't mistake me, that's a good thing, it is just very intense for me and I love keeping the balance of being the king for day and then finding myself in solitude on a fishing boat with my loved ones, sipping on a nice cold drink.

If your peak race is at the end of the season, then you are in luck. You won't have to worry about triathlon for a while. If you still have some races planned for the year, then just pretend that it is. You need to take a real mental hiatus as well as a physical one.

The beginning of the off season is always good fun. I usually have a little bucket list of things that I want to do and so I keep myself busy. Once it all slows down, there is time to relax and it's right then when it starts hitting me. I get more tired than usual. I sleep longer hours at night. I gain a bit of weight and add on those winter layers and allow myself to get a little bit lazier. The couch is my castle and I prefer to stay in instead of going out. This might be because I travel so much during the season and once the season is over, I am just happy to be home for once. Plus, my job is outside in the elements and once I don't have to train in rain, sleet, and snow, then I am very satisfied to just sit on the couch and veg out. Or if I get adventurous and it's nice out, I hop on my Harley or take out the boat for a day on the water.

The duration of the blues varies from year to year, but it can be anywhere from a few days to a few weeks time. It's not a clinical depression. It's more of a situational melancholy. You are no less of a warrior having just managed the whole Ironman® training and racing, but your body and your central governor is asking for a bit of added downtime now; a bit of yin to the yang—an opportunity to find a balance.

Your body will take what it needs, so go with the flow. Get rest, sleep a bit more and give in to some of the cravings you might have had the past weeks. Don‘t overdose on too much reward food and "off season drinks" though. It won‘t make you feel much better and has the potential to make things feel worse. This is not what you want. You got yourself in such good shape and you adapted to the perfect healthy lifestyle. The key word is balance. Reflect on what you did and think about the journey, both the good and the bad.

The blues will come and go. It is best to shift a gear or two down to recover. Your body will tell you when you are ok to restart and you will figure out what your plan for the future will bring. After experiencing this syndrome quite a few times, I advise you to not just rush into the next thing and occupy your thoughts with the another big task, but try to find the meaning in the blues. It is there for a reason. You might gain an interesting life lesson by trying to learn the lesson that the blues has to teach you.

Blues or not, one thing is certain. You gained bragging rights for the rest of your life and you are officially a total badass for following through. Deep respect from my side.

Living to Tell the Tale

During my day after, I usually take some time out and record a little video blog to get everything out of my head and into the world. I then post everything on my blog. I have videos there dating back to my first ever race in Kona, back in 2009. I allow myself to speak from my heart and take advantage of that raw emotion, which I know I won't be able to reproduce in even a few days down the road.

The experience that we have on the race-course, and the days leading up to and after the race, are ones that open up our ideas about what is possible. It is important that we take some time to reflect and document those moments. They can act as reminders down along the path when we might feel stuck and they can inspire others to contemplate taking a similar route to self-discovery.

I would definitely recommend that you start a blog to document your triathlon journey. Even if you think that nobody is going to visit your page, blogs can act as valuable tools. Journaling helps to dump your mind's wanderings out and somehow it helps to gain clarity. Sometimes we don't realize things until we say them out loud or type them up. Once you start your blog, you could even share it with others on Facebook if you like. Feel free to check out my blog at LiveAndLetTri.com and share your own blog with me on Facebook. I would love to see how you have used the methods in this book to reach your crazy triathlon goals!

Chapter 8:
The Analysis of Your Race

"Wisdom is always an overmatch for strength."

~Phil Jackson

"What we plant in the soil of contemplation, we shall reap in the harvest of action."

~Meister Eckhart

Take some advice from your seasoned coach. No matter how you position and reposition your analysis of your race, let the entirety of the experience wash over you first. Gather all of the elements and begin your investigation. I'm smiling ear to ear with pride.

Acknowledge, Celebrate, and Analyze

Many months of planning and hard work are behind such a big accomplishment. Racing triathlon is one thing but becoming an Ironman® is something special. Only a few people know what that really means. Count yourself among them. How much sweat and emotions went into your preparation — do you remember each part? It is a big achievement and you deserve to be very proud of it. You earned your bragging rights by going through all of this. Now it's the time to understand, accept and enjoy. You should relish in your achievements and give yourself a reward party. Don't forget the people that supported you on this mission from day one. It is a huge contribution. Acknowledge your team.

Reflection and analysis is rewarding and a very helpful tool for the future to come, not only for your sport related endeavors, but also for your everyday life. You learn from mistakes and you learn to understand the fine-tuning and the complexity of successfully managing a big project. It's not ideal to analyze the race too soon after it happened. You need a little bit of distance from it in order to look at it without emotions. Only then you will be able to be make the right, rational evaluation of your race. If you have one, involve your coach or a trusted guide in your post racing plans, as he or she might prove to be helpful in gaining perspective.

While you do your analysis, keep your active recovery going. Enjoy some relaxing massages once in awhile. You do deserve it! Do some light fun training without any time pressure or pace checking. Simply do it to keep fit, stay loose and feel good. This will be fun after all the structured training you had leading up to your race. It also gives you the opportunity to train with some other people and enjoy coffee rides and social jogs. Now is the perfect time to do that. Exhale and just enjoy the downtime.

Time and Space

After big and especially successful races, I always reward myself for a job well done. Fortunately some of the big races are somewhere exotic and are far from home. If you travel to New Zealand for the Ironman®, it would be a wasted opportunity to leave Monday morning to return back home, wouldn't it? I understand that you might have restrictions in terms of financials, family or from your profession that doesn't allow for an extended stay. That being said, I am a big promoter of enjoying some down time after the race if your schedule permits.

Of course the first few days after your race, you will feel the aftermath of the race in your body, so it might not be the best time to plan a sightseeing trip that involves a ton of walking. If you feel good, then more power to you. My own experience is that I am pretty useless the days after the race. I am still in my own world, a mix of stress, pain, glory, soreness and nothingness. Plan for this recovery if you are following my advice and extending your stay. Ease into your holiday

The first three days after an Ironman® I am still licking my wounds. Imagine your over-exhausted partner who was giving and giving and giving the past weeks to support your race. They feel some fatigue as well. And all the support and understanding gestures the past week are suddenly coming to a stop. They are decompressing in their own way. There is a need for recognition and for something more than just a thank you.

Trust me on this. I have been there several times and it doesn't get any better or easier. Your partner needs a break too. Since you had to stay off your feet the last days before the race, your support team was running around for you and you likely weren't the nicest person to be around (although you might not admit this now). They might be eager to experience something else than the ongoing sport conversations about triathlon. Keep that in mind. It is the right time for rewards. It's time to suck up the fatigue and emptiness and give back to the crew.

I tried several different scenarios and found out that the first three to four days are best not to make too many plans apart from relaxing, getting away from the triathlon craziness around the race area and simply letting your mind and body heal. Good food helps too. I'm always trying new ways to decompress after such a herculean event. Find ways to ease into restoring your mind, body and spirit as it serves your story.

A favorite post-race renewal for me would be following a very successful showing at _Ironman® Regensburg, Germany in 2012. I have very good memories of winning that race by setting a new course record. That was my first Ironman® title and for me a dream come true. That was one of my milestone races and Luxembourg's national TV channel RTL made a whole documentary out of it called "IM Kona" which later was sold to different countries and shown on TV. The documentary is available on Vimeo (https://vimeo.com/72841394).

After the race and all the necessary media stuff, I jumped in the car and drove three hours south, into the Austrian Mountains. I like to go there for spa vacations. It's the best you can possibly do when in Europe. You cannot compare it to any spa in USA, not even a 5 star spa resort. I lost all my prize money after that trip but it sure was worth it! I could even sneak in a relaxing swim at the pools there and grab a quick workout at the gym, in case you are a bit obsessed with triathlon like me. The perfect short vacation and best time to celebrate the glory of a successful race with loved ones.

My win at Challenge Roth in 2013 was a very special memory. I had the race of my life to celebrate after the excitement wound down. We had already planned a post-race trip as my partner had just finished her PhD in Economics / Business Ethics, the weeks before the event and presented her dissertation successfully. Months before she told me that one of her dreams was to get to know Norway. So that was our chosen location to decompress.

The end of July is the perfect time to spend time in Norway and experience the scenery around the fjords. So of course we had to celebrate one of her dreams. Needless to say when

I posted a winning performance of 7:52h, winning by over 12 minutes and achieving one of my lifetime goals, it was the perfect match for both of us. We left right after the race and flew out to see Norway.

We spent the first few days in a great spa close to Oslo, so we enjoyed some downtime to bounce back, enjoying some massages, good food and beautiful scenery. Then we drove around to see one of the nicest places that Norway has to offer — the city of Bergen. It was a 7hr drive through crazy scenic roads. We pulled off the road to witness the splendor of the Fjords and crashed at some nice hotels we found along the way. We swam in the ice-cold Fjords while taking in the beauty of the snow covered glaciers right next to us. We enjoyed the best, freshest fish we ever ate and later rented a boat to do our own fishing and sightseeing. It was just unreal. The funny thing is, it‘s just a very short flight from anywhere in Europe, and everything is so close. If you ever decide to go and you should, be aware that Norway is bloody expensive but so worth it. One of the best ever trips we ever took.

One year we were so exhausted that we flew home right away after my race. Home is like holiday for us anyway, as we live near the beach and have the most romantic city just three minutes away by bike. Unlike many other people, we don‘t get too much time at home, this could be the most precious thing for people that are on the road more than 220 days a year. It was a great experience to find this out and sometimes it is great just to be home. A good mix of post-race vacation, exploration and recouping from the comfort of home is the best advice I could give here. The formula is portable. Just listen to your body, calm the mind, and give yourself a break.

I need to race many more years to check off my bucket list. There are still a few big destinations marked out such as

Montana fly fishing, an Alaskan survival trip, a sailing trip in the Grenadines and many more. I need to win more races to afford those. I am well aware of that.

The rewards and punishment theme always works well in the world of triathlon. This flow of race and then recovery works well for me. It keeps me on my toes, balancing the mental and physical stress of triathlon with the rest and recovery of time off. This is where the slogan Live And Let Tri came from. Try it out yourself and you will not be disappointed.

Assembling the Pieces

Remember to sit with your accomplishment first, before you relax and reward yourself. Relive the moment of crossing the finish line a few times. Picture the emotions you have gone through. Remind yourself how many obstacles you had to overcome during that day in order to finish the race? How many up‘s and down‘s did you go through? You worked hard, so you deserve a little self-reflection and a treat afterwards.

This accomplishment is not only measured by the achievement itself. This can be an overall life changer for you. Imagine if you can come through the training, the sacrifices and the gauntlet of the race itself, what else can you put your mind to achieve? If you can put your mind into this project, you can put it into anything else your choose, using the same strategic approach you were taught in this book.

Realize where you have been in your life when you started out and where you are now after so many month of training and racing. Do you realize how much you have grown? I am sure you hear it plenty of times from your closest friends. Believe it. They noticed a change for sure. You are living the dream, doing what you like to do. You set the bar high and you followed it all the way though. Remember it‘s not really about your finish time or your how you placed in the race. It is so much more than that. Taking the time to discover what that means for you, in your journey, is part of the payoff post-race. The hills and mountains you have climbed, the problems and pitfalls you've overcome illustrate your true grit. That is something to celebrate and carve into your being.

Critically examine your race once you are ready for it. It should not be too close after the race as you will still have too many emotions and you might not look at it in a rational way. Your coach might tell you something you might not like, but it might be true. Best is to hear the perspective of someone that really knows you very well and has been with you throughout the journey.

Initially you process the little events that did not go your way. But upon further inspection you may start talking things through and find other aspects of the race to reflect on. Then after two or three weeks certain things fall away and you find that you analyze different aspects of your race in a new light. This is growth. This is what you carry on to the next race.

It's ok to have good and bad points filtered out after going through the race again. I hardly find any race 100% perfect, there is always something you can do better or more efficient. So grow with the evaluation and write down the points you need to work on. Evaluate what you have learned from the race. Every criticism should be welcomed, that's the only way to get better and learn from previous mistakes. Build on the good parts and improve the not so good parts, this will make for a well thought through decision about another race or another training block.

With a little distance from the race, you will be able to decode how to continue and how to plan the next few steps of your life. Take note of the weak spots of your race and then carry a few tweaks to your triathlon master plan. Small moves. There will likely be no major shifts in your planning for the next race. It's better to find where your pacing failed you and adjust your focus when you resume your training. How can you avoid the little trip ups that you experienced in the race? What will you do different? What will you maintain?

Remember to go back and look at your notes, the ones you made when you first set off on this journey. Recall how you felt when you were writing them, and how far off they seemed. In the post-race analysis it's best not to look too specifically at the metrics. It's better to measure the race against your pre-designed goals and use that to tweak your training plan in preparation for your next race. It's equally important to analyze how you managed each and every obstacle that came up during the race. This is what builds the foundation of strength to push you through your next race with greater ease. You made those crazy goals come to life and this is a tribute to your capabilities. This alone is worthy of celebration.

You are extraordinary, and you can create things in your life that may seem impossible—you have the power to turn your dreams into reality. This is something that is definitely worth reflecting on. You can go out there and use this as an example to help you become a better version of yourself, on and off the road. This is when triathlon become more of a lifestyle than a hobby.

Case in Point

In 2012 I was in the shape of my life before I raced Kona. Just 10 days before the race, I had an accident during my training and broke my right hand. My world suddenly had a dark cloud around me and I was in a bad spot so closely to my peak race. My dream and chance of winning that race was down to zero. A few days without training in the water and on the bike due to the high risk of escalating my injury left me doubting my chances of racing at all. Of course I wanted to try and so we taped my hand and secured a stabilizing splint.

It was tough to hold the handlebars at first but I wanted to try and give it a chance. I rode out on the highway and suffered along. At some point I was about to turn back home and wanted to U-turn when I saw an older lady with a prosthetic leg waving at me. I rode up to her and we chatted. She asked me for help to cross the road to ride back home on the other side and traffic was heavy. I wasn't really training and so I spent some time chatting with her and waited for a good time to help her cross the busy highway. She was mostly worried about clicking in the pedals with her prosthetic leg and then accelerating quickly to cross over in case of another car approaching.

I helped her out and we made it over to the other side. We shook hands and we were both happy. She rode back and I tried my best to figure out how to hold the handlebars and how to drink from a bottle using my injured right hand and how to shift gears. Then it suddenly hit me. My perfect world just got a hit when I crashed but I quickly put this into perspective because of my interlude with this fellow triathlete. She was struggling with her disability while fulfilling her goal of racing an Ironman®. I was so lucky to witness her effort being played out with pure dedication and joy. It was truly amazing.

So I realized I can suck it up and should still be able to make it through the race. I figured I might have lost the race before the gun goes off but I trained for it anyway, so let's try it, I might get lucky. So I got my crap together and prepared the best I could despite my little disaster. We figured out a way that was the least painful for me to function and so I raced. Obviously I lost valuable time on the swim, and the bike section caused major issues as well, but I finished the race.

Placing in the top ten at the world champs with a broken hand is very special accomplishment. I realized all of this a few days later. And I'm gathering intel even recalling this years later. Triathlon does make you a better person, as you will grow and learn to deal with much more than just sport. All those lessons I learned throughout my career contribute to the person I am today. It comes with better planning, readjusting as you evaluate race experiences and continuing to look for those pearls of wisdom that come from undertaking such an odyssey.

It might be nice to write your post-race analysis down, which I call the 'war stories' and share them with your closest people. Enjoy your pride, no matter if you set your goals too high or if you didn't hit the time you set out to achieve. You made it and that's what counts. You made it happen because of your drive to succeed. You had the courage to start and the courage to follow through. All those obstacles you overcame along the way, this speaks to the strength of your character and spirit. Sure, there is always room for improvement. Analyze and learn from it to create the framework for the future. Pay attention to the details and take some notes. You completed what you set out to do.

Maybe you saw your true potential when looking back and from that you will be fueled with motivation to move on to your next set of goals. When I look back to my best results, I can always find something that I could have done better. Maybe that's just the perfectionist in me. This is my drive and my daily fuel to explore how far I can push myself. Not just in sports but in any aspect of my life. The triathlon journey is very similar to any other journey or section in your life that you might come across. The lines are blurred when you break down the borders and let these lessons flow into every aspect of your life.

Picture yourself at your office desk, analyzing a potential investment. You would do it exactly the same as you would for your triathlon project. You would plan every single detail in order to make this project work with the maximum benefit. In order to accomplish that, every single detail is a part of the complex idea, and therefore it counts. Better planning, better the outcome.

Being prepared is key. Being prepared is power. But even if you do everything right in your preparation, there will still be some outside factors that you cannot influence. Be critical of yourself in your analysis but also accept that there are outside factors that you might need to finesse. Some of those could crush your dream. We are only human and we try to control every aspect in our life. Better to find your way through, no matter what life throws your way. This is what you learned when overcoming pitfalls in your racing and training.

Don't be too hard on yourself. There is always another time, another race and so many more opportunities. Trust me, this is easy to say with a bit of distance to some of my races, but if you would have asked me straight after a ‘not so good’ race what went wrong, it would have taken over my world and my emotions. This one race could mean the world to me, but the truth is, it is only important in that moment. It is in our nature to be critical of our path all the times. So a good lesson is to simply accept and to learn. Even if you achieved your biggest goal, and you are the hero for a few days, the glory slowly fades over time and you will find yourself back at the same point in your life. Sure, those credentials could open a lot of doors, but nothing lasts forever. Just be aware of this on your journey. The big question will always remain. In what direction is your compass pointing?

Chapter 9:
The Mindful Champion

"The future belongs to those who believe in the beauty of their dreams."

~Eleanor Roosevelt

We are taught that a life well lived requires us to follow our dreams. What becomes your passion tends to define your life and qualify your existence. With the ebb and flow of competition and the writing and rewriting of your triathlon resume, an understanding develops toward the wholeness of one's life story. Defining your life by punctuated moments of racing successes and failures can leave us still unfulfilled. Perhaps delving into the twilight of my career will impart some wisdom to carry you through your current station of training and competition. It's these moments of clarity that cause our dreams to stretch out and encompass a greater narrative.

Transitions

With space to live and breathe without the constraints of training, you might have asked yourself the question "what is next" after completing your extensive analysis of the big milestone race? Are you planning your next adventure, or do you find yourself content with making that one big bucket race and are now moving on to something else? Regardless of the path you choose, once the accomplishment sinks in, our brain often starts to bring up a variety of questions.

Suddenly there is a lot more time available during the day and that means there is more time to think instead of rushing from one thing to the next. With more time, there comes more questions floating around and some of them might bring you towards a "no outlet" zone. For most of us this is when the post-race blues set in. I like to call it a short term, post-race, depression period. Expect this transition and find your way through. Without the distractions of training and racing, pay attention to those points of reflection that may surface. This is the time where you practice mindfulness. This is the time where you absorb the physical and mental juggling act that you just performed. Without reflection there is no imprint to carry you through to the next stage, whatever that may be. Take the time. Trust me. It is a valuable pause.

I taught you how to become a master in planning and how you could rise through the ranks of triathlon by simply being smarter and more effective in your training. You have the toolbox to be a champion athlete. Now I am leading you through the downtime and what comes after the peak. This is about mastering your life and applying what you have learned in triathlon to your daily life. The lessons learned through training and competing, and overcoming obstacles is great grist for the mill of life, moving through many seasons.

What Comes Next

For me, it seems to be the same question that I ask myself after each season or after each big milestone race, particularly when I have succeeded in doing what I do best. I am a thinker and so I like to make sense out of everything. Since competing in triathlon occupies a rather large part of my day to day existence, my thinking can be isolated to that island of my being; my identity as a triathlete; my ego. In my downtime that leaves a large hole that I feel the need to fill. I could fill it with many things but what could equal the power and prominence of triathlon? Nothing is as extreme or challenging. Everything else seems average.

For many years this question of “what comes next" has been easy for me to answer. There was always another race and always another championship. Every Olympic cycle implied that there were at least two out of the four years of qualifying to keep me engaged. This always determined my overall goal, my racing plan and my training plan over the next season or two. So the road ahead always seemed pretty straightforward. It’s clocking in one season after another, driven by my own motivation and expectation of results and accomplishments.

At some point, however, with age and more racing experience, the world does not revolve around jumping to the next goal and checking off races from your list. We all get to that point where we ask ourselves a deeper question. Is life just about the next race, the next chapter or even the next step in life? After over 27 years of racing and chasing my dream, this question became a constant. Have you ever asked yourself what’s next after you’ve chased and maybe even fulfilled your dream of racing and achieving status, rewards and results? At any stage of the game, this could go pretty deep.

Let me tell you, no matter if you are a first time triathlon finisher or an experienced pro, we all get to the point where we stare at the wall to figure out the deeper meaning of it all. In an attempt to make sense of it all, more questions appear on the surface. This is what I want to share with you here, in this closing chapter.

On the surface I answered these fundamental questions quite easily. Triathlon is what I am good at and what my life's mission has been for so long. The added bonus was that I was able turn my hobby into a cool job. I was able to turn my passion into a money making dream. The joy of training outside, connecting with nature while racking up the training miles and then traveling across the globe competing with athletes all over the world, fulfilled me. I was always moving toward becoming the best version of myself. It was the inner drive that became a clear mission, year after year. What about thinking beyond that?

Throughout all of those years, I neglected a lot of other things in my life. My world had been my sport and everything that belonged to that lifestyle. But because I was getting older and adding in some injuries, I realized that I had been putting life on hold to chase one dream after the next. I prioritized the sport over everything else. I started to realize that maybe it was time to think more about stepping down and spending more time with my partner, exploring other things in life.

Injury as a Catalyst

2015 was that pivotal year for me. That's when I had the first glimpse of my life away from triathlon. Here I came to a deep pause and moved inward. I challenged everything I knew and loved to forge a new path.

In my lead up to the World Champs, which was my declared goal for the season, I raced the half distance event, Challenge Denmark, as a final tune up test. It went extremely well and I won, posting a course record in the cold and windy conditions in Denmark. I was on schedule to win that long expected gold medal at the Worlds just two weeks later.

I flew back to my base in Lucca, Tuscany to recover for a few days and then resume training till I was scheduled to fly out to Sweden for the Worlds Champs. During one of my last runs I felt a tremendous, sharp pain in my left forefoot, just as if I had stepped on a pointy nail. A sharp pain shot through my body and I felt immediately that this would be a bigger issue, knowing my body so well after many years of fine tuning it. I limped home and got it checked out right away at the local hospital, thanks to my good Italian friend Alberto's help and his home town connections.

The devastating news came the next morning. My season was declared over due to an accumulation of liquid near my metatarsal bone and surrounding areas. Any liquid inside a tendon or a bone is equal to inflammation and that means rest. There was no way around it. My foot urgently needed rest to recover. My world collapsed. All those months working for that one, specific goal just blew up in smoke.

I looked for a way out but the doctors gave me no other choice. I was forced to consider the possibility of sitting out for several weeks, watching my form disappear. My gold medal dream remained just out of my reach. The Tuscan tranquility that I chose for my race preparation suddenly became very heavy on my shoulders. The dolce vita flair no longer served me. I had no appetite and negativity ruled my daily thoughts and activities.

I started to think of what I could do to make the time go by quicker but nothing really interested me. I didn't even want to leave the house. Then, after a few days of devastation, I started to accept the situation a bit better while hobbling around with my new best friend, the walking boot. I was told I should wear this sweaty thing a minimum of six weeks in the midst of the long, hot, Tuscan summer. It was soaked in sweat after the first day. I wasn't too optimistic for the future.

A few days later, during breakfast on the terrace, my cell phone rang and the sport director of my racing team delivered some news. I remember each of his words clearly. He said, "Hey Dirk, we got the disc with the MRI pictures and we studied them and had it cross checked with a foot specialist as well. Here is the good news. It seems to only be a bursitis. We can fix it and get over this quickly. Get on a plane and come here ASAP. We will bring you back in no time." It all came down to a simple cortisone shot. The pendulum swung back in my favor.

"Whaaaat? No way! Are you serious?! How is that possible?" I replied not knowing if I was getting fooled. He was dead serious and I started to lighten up and reboot my motivation to put this behind me. I couldn't believe it. It's only an inflamed bursa instead of a bone issue. I thought, ok, if cortisone is the magic medicine for that, then let's do it. I had already looked into flights and found a perfect flight to Belgium and back in just one day. I would fly out early in the morning and return late that same night. My foot was getting fixed. I was excited and my mood turned for the better.

My emotions were going from super low to extreme high in a matter of seconds. This all sounded like Christmas and gold medals all together with just that one phone call. I had no time to let any of it sink in. I called my coach and told him to look into a new plan and shift focus to another big race. Then nothing would be lost and I could still take advantage of my optimum race-mode level of fitness. I was in triage mode. I needed to save my contract for the next few years. If I could race fairly soon, then all that hard work might still be put to good use at a different race.

I was still pissed as hell about missing my peak race at the World Champs. I had worked so hard. What if we would have known that before? I always want to grab that crystal ball so no matter what pitfalls come my way I can organize things to perfection. Why couldn't I just accept and move on just as I would do in a race? I couldn't shake this off.

Those extreme ups and downs sure showed some wear and tear on the both of us. How quickly our state of mind changes upon hearing the news we want to hear. Perception rules. I've revisited this moment recently, to see if I could draw on some insight. I've come to ask this question of myself. How can we streamline our consciousness to accommodate good and bad news with a measure of clarity, calm and complete presence in the moment? It's what I do in competition, navigating the pendulum swings that occur during a race. As in competition, so as in life.

But as it stood then, Team Bockel was in an emotional rollercoaster going 100+ miles an hour. There was only so much we could do. I had to accept the facts as they were and come up with a new plan. Planning has been my strength over all these years. I had always found a way to make things work. But during that time I never sat back and really let it all sink in to deal with the reality of it all. Events were happening way too fast for me and I had to act quick. I was jumping from one thing to the next. One minute I was in a depressed puddle on the couch and the next minute I was flying from one appointment to the next, trying to salvage my season and manage my pesky foot issue all the while.

The day I arrived in Belgium, I was convinced that this injection would take care of the issue and the team repeatedly reassured me that the procedure would work and I would be back up and running in no time. The injection was scheduled for mid afternoon, so I had some time to kill. Without even skipping a beat, I went swimming and aqua jogging in order not to lose any more valuable training time. I was already fighting against a 10 day lag in my training, but being in top shape, I knew I could be back in no time. My drive was propelling me through this bump in the road.

In the meantime, coach prepared the next schedule and soon I eased back into the training. My next goal was just six to seven week down the road at Ironman® Vichy in France. My fitness level improved quickly and I felt confident that I had a winning form for the next race. Hotels were booked and I was ready to jump in our van to drive west.

Just two days before our planned departure, disaster struck again and I experienced another sharp pain in my foot where I had to stop immediately doing my session. It came quick and severe. I knew exactly that this was the same pain. It's done. It's over, I thought. It was that familiar feeling of complete disbelief. I knew this was serious. What now? This could jeopardize everything I'd worked for.

I couldn't believe it. I was taking all the necessary precautions by running low mileage and by using an AlterG, low gravity treadmill, which is designed to absorb the shocks on the bone structure of your feet by supporting your body weight while running. None of this mattered because, as it turned out, my foot hadn't healed over the past few weeks. The cortisone shot must have just covered up the pain for a while. My world broke down once again. I sat down and cried. Then I reached for my phone to call the two people in the world that would know exactly what to do; my partner and my coach.

I know my body. I evaluate pain on a daily basis while training. I knew that this was not a good sign and I had to expect the worst. I went back through the same process of getting an MRI and waiting in lines on the hunt to finding a solution.

This time it was not only about my foot. As a professional athlete, you are the definition of your results. Everything is based on results. It was occurring to me that my season was going to end very badly. I knew that if I couldn't race I would lose my contract, which was up for renewal at the end of the season. Given this and my seasoned age of 39, it would be tough to find good sponsors for the years to come. A whole mix of negative emotions was competing for my attention.

When the results came out the next morning, I had my answer. My 3rd metatarsal bone looked white on the computer screen. White signifies fluid on an MRI, and in my case the metatarsal bone was absolutely white. I was told to be very careful and not to bear any weight on the foot. The bone was not in great condition and even looked porous. The bad news seemed to get worse.

It took some time to get the final word from my closest advisers on how to proceed. I was about to leave for my race and had no time to wait on the final word if I wanted to be on time for the race in Vichy. Decisions were made fast and furious. I opted for another cortisone shot just in case I was cleared to race. If it's not that bad, I thought I might be able to race and then deal with the aftermath of any additional damage to my already injured foot. This way I could possibly still win and secure my future.

Then the phone rang. The answer was clear and simple. It almost seemed anticlimactic. It was 100 % a no go for the race. Coach Michael put it in no uncertain terms. The foot might just hold 5 km during the final marathon or it might break more towards the end. It was doubtful that it would hold and so he strongly advised against racing. Even if my foot survived the run, it would probably cause permanent damage. He reminded me that I had a few more years left to race. I took his advice, like I always did.

My season was clearly done and this time for real. No more

quick fixes. No more ups and downs. Just one big down. My foot needed total rest. I had to minimize walking and was advised to wear the walking boot at all times. That was it. Done.

Like weeks before, I went from a very high to a very low within seconds. The pendulum swung back to its original position at the onset of the injury. Racing professionally bears a lot of extremes, but this time it was truly devastating. This touched my heart a different way than any other time before. This time I really hit rock bottom. I was totally, emotionally spent and didn't know how to process it all. I was left empty handed. All the effort I put in seemed wasted. There was no payoff for all of the hard work. The most difficult part was the roller coaster ride of emotions. Everything was off balance.

I made the news official and the only thing that I could do now was take a break. So that is what I did. Now that the final decision was made, everything seemed to move in slow motion. It seemed like there was nothing but time in front of us.

I needed a real break, not just from racing, but from everything.

The Shift

Our course was now changed. I turned to my happy place in order to get some peace, in the scenic surroundings of Hotel Mohrenwirt, in Austria. It's here that I realized, for the first time, that I needed to do some real soul searching. The stress of the ups and downs of my injury really took a toll on the both of us. The walks through nature and the gorgeous evening sunsets on the lake with my partner and our dog Peanut, helped me to process the situation I was in.

I realized that I had been rushing through season after season in an attempt to check off results and achievements but I didn't even know how to deal with any massive setbacks in my life. I thought maybe I didn't really know much else than sport in my life? I had so many unanswered questions floating around in my head. Who am I if I cannot call myself a triathlete? This is my identity. This is who others define me as; a professional triathlete. I had never hit such a crossroad in my life before.

It was around that time when the thought of a forced retirement first started to cross my mind. What if I had to stop racing? The more I thought about it, the more complex it got. I'd never had such a low point in my career. Being forced to sit out for such an extended period of time opened up a whole can of worms for me. I suddenly had to deal with just myself and all the unanswered questions of what I would do without the sport.

In racing and training I knew how to adapt to pitfalls. But this was different. My problem couldn't be solved by simply changing my racing shoe or figuring out a better pace for my run. This cut to the core of my identity. Who am I if I am not the Champion Triathlete. How do I fix this?

I could always hide out from life during a half day long bike ride followed by a grueling run along the river and then eat and then be content to fall asleep on the couch. It's easier to process life issues when you have a daily outlet; a place to channel your drive. Some people say you could just do sport for your sanity, almost a perfect, ongoing, physical and psychological therapy of sorts. But the transition out of that familiar grind proved very challenging for me. I was left with my own thoughts and bare nakedness of my inner self.

I downplayed the situation, thinking that at this moment I simply missed my job, my daily goal, my everyday mission of becoming better than the day before. There were endless hours of staring at the lake. Not exactly the endorphin high that I was used to when processing life's daily problems but I was trying to use this pause in my training to reevaluate my life. I didn't really want to stop racing just yet. I was clearly too good and too fit to call it a career at this point. The reality was that I was totally out of balance and felt lost in everyday life. Nothing really seemed to help me out of my misery.

Before long our situation became a point of transition. I am a planner. The conversation moved into a brainstorming phase. I set out to crack the code of this current setback. I obviously can't train, so I am free for two months while I recover. I could travel around in our van while my foot heals. Could I? Let's call it a rehabilitation camp in Norway. Things started to lighten up a bit.

I had good fun along the way but inside, it still felt as if my motor was running on idle, as if I had just stepped on the brakes until I could put my career back in gear. I still felt lost without my sport. Still restless with the craving for competition, I didn't know what to do with myself.

The Long Road Back

Back in the USA, in my usual winter base, I restarted with mild training, but the same issue came back pretty quickly again. The pain in my foot seemed chronic. I realized that there wouldn't be a quick solution to the problem. On top of that I found out that my contract would not be renewed by my sponsorship team that I had been racing for during the last two years. I was devastated even though I had expected the worst. Yep, when it rains it pours, I thought to myself. Bring it on.

Luckily the Luxembourg Olympic Committee and the Elite Sport Section of the army decided to support me and backed me up for another year. That made my winter time a bit easier. Clearly, there was no way I could continue training and racing without their support so that was a big relief and this laid the foundation for me to continue working my way back to competition form.

I was in the shape of my life in 2015. I was poised to win the World Championships in Sweden. All of the numbers in my training and racing were pointing to my biggest and most successful year. How quickly things can shift. I had successes in the first half of 2015 but I couldn't shake the feeling that my perfect year had turned into a train wreck. I had never been that close to having my dream season.

Sport is brutally honest at times, either there is a result or there is nothing. I had a some decent results in past years, but all I really wanted was the World Championships, the ones that never happened for me. I had to officially put that dream aside, at least for now, at least for this year.

After a few more weeks of rest I tested my foot again. Nothing changed during all these weeks of rest. I should have known. The foot was still inflamed and no improvement was in sight. That's when I really fell off the wagon. The doors were shutting to all of my dreams. I started drinking a bit more and felt nothing but sorry for myself. I started to get even a bit depressed and rarely moved off the couch.

This also affected my most treasured relationship with my partner. We had a crappy time over the next few weeks. This was the biggest struggle we ever had in our relationship. When a monumental shift happens in your life it affects every aspect of your being. The things that tended to take a backseat to my training and competing got pushed front and center. I couldn't hide it in my training. I couldn't train. I was off my game in my sport and in my life.

After the ups & downs during the summer, I actually thought the problem would just go away by itself. But it was still present. All of those familiar questions came back to haunt me. Would this mean that I really have to retire because of my injury? The Norway rehabilitation trip had been nice but reality was setting in once again. Was my career done for good? This kept crossing my mind.

A standard transition to the winter break had always included keeping my legs unshaven and that was always a sign of letting go of my racing season. During fall and winter and now even in spring I had mostly not shaved my legs and that itself seemed to be a sign. Was I drifting away from the sport? I didn't feel like myself anymore. Who am I? Where am I going?

I was in a panic about it. That's where my inner conflict really started to gain steam. I described my situation to some of my friends and family members as sitting between two chairs and feeling a bit lost. I didn't have enough confidence or piece of mind to choose one position over the other. So I sat firmly in limbo. To most people I put up a show and covered what was going on inside of me. I was embarrassed to show my struggle. As an athlete you always have to be an example that people can look up to. Showing weakness was simply not acceptable. That was not for me.

Growth usually comes from strife. In strife we sometimes reach for the easy way out. My easy way out was a bit of Jack or many beers while I couch surfed watching mindless movies. I felt I was losing my super fit body by sitting around, having hairy legs and waiting for my foot to heal. My short term solution seemed to be reaching for another drink and gaining another pound. After a few weeks that got a bit boring and I knew, deep down inside, that it wasn't moving me forward in any positive way. I was on the downward slope without a bottom in site.

During this lowest point in my life, my relationship with my partner suffered. So after a few long nights with many arguments, discussions and disagreements, we slowly managed to find a potential way out of my frustrating situation. Planning has always been one of our strong suits. To begin the process of digging ourselves out of this hole, we formulated a plan.

Let me explain what "slowly" for a pro athlete means. In my case it meant packing my bags and leaving the house not 12 hours after we had that long overdue talk. I was off to a ten day Vipassana, silent meditation, retreat.

My partner knows me. As in training and competing, she provided a pretty intense and immediate action plan. But this was not a spa retreat. This was going to be work. It wasn't work in the sense of an increased training schedule. This was way out of my comfort zone. When I left I was furious and maybe slightly confused. I felt pressured by her to go but I was determined to try this. For me it sounded more like torture. I am good at pushing myself to the limit, so I was up for the challenge. I can torture myself for endless hours in training and competition and I can still smile to the outside world. Torture is in the headline of my job description. Vipassana was my new mission. Even though I didn’t see the point of it, I still went.

A short flight to Texas and a quick shuttle bus ride later, I turned into a big, secluded property where I saw a tiny sign at the gate entrance that said, "Welcome to the Vipassana Retreat Center". I didn't feel too excited and after reading various articles about the center, I was not sure what to expect. There are varied opinions on the subject of Vipassana. Translated to English, Vipassana is "insight into the true nature of reality". This seemed like just the prescription I needed. But some claimed it was a sect. I was very cautious. I checked the surrounding area and noted the location of the fences so I could remember the area, just in case I opted for a hasty exit.

So what part of "being out of your comfort zone" is bad? I'm very familiar with navigating through uncomfortable situations. I'm a triathlete for crying out loud. I think we tend to put boundaries around methods of training or alternative methods of focus and philosophy. There are many times in my life where I have reached out for a new approach to my training. I started to realize that choosing to attend this retreat was no different. I was committed to the process. Shortly after signing in, my Vipassana journey began.

On my first day I was just miserable. My back hurt from doing the 10 hour mandatory meditation per day. The wake up gong was at 4 am, followed by mediation and breakfast at 6:30. My impatience ruled. I hate to wait for my food when I am hungry in the mornings. That's one of the reason I rarely trained before breakfast. No matter how effective that "training on empty" method is supposed to be for your metabolism, I couldn't swing it. No way. I am a coffee first kinda guy! So be it.

And yet, each day, at 4 am, I was up and meditating. I was taking it seriously. I was determined that I would win this race. Once I am in, I am committed to it 100 %, just like I did during my second military boot camp when I changed my nationality from Germany to Luxembourg. I had been here before. Once

I am in, I am dedicated. Here at the retreat, I had a mission: the 10 day meditation Ironman®. I am ready.

There were many internal fights, struggles and lots of self-therapy. I counted down the days. As you can imagine, some minutes in that isolated environment felt like days. I'm a social person. I missed the camaraderie of my fellow triathletes. I missed my partner. But if I'm to break free of this rut I was in, I knew I had to forge a new path. I felt it was like adding another tool to my growing toolbox. Half a lifetime later, on day 10, I walked out of the retreat pretty chilled and pretty content with myself. I made it. The past 10 days brought nothing but silence and peace for me. It was all about dealing with my own thoughts. There had been no internet, no talking, no phone; nothing but me and my own thoughts. Needless to say I had plenty of time to think.

During that time I learned a bit more about understanding my own ego and the fire that drives me and the things that do not. Just by observing and dealing with myself, without any distractions, the solitude seemed to unleash my soul. It was pretty intense in many ways, lots of challenging memories that seemed to be forgotten and stored somewhere in the very back of my brain came back up and had to be dealt with. Both good and bad memories were balancing themselves out, one on either side of the scale.

On my way back at the airport I immediately felt overwhelmed by the amount of noises and distractions that surrounded me. I felt totally overstimulated. Just sitting on an airplane was hard. It was eye opening. Now, this silent retreat was not my style. Normally I would not choose this path. What I learned is that if you limit yourself to the familiar, growth is unlikely to happen. Vipassana teaches you that we only react to outside stimuli, to noise, stress and things that might aggravate us.

We should learn to focus on what's inside, not what's coming from the outside.

All of this did make sense, but I wasn't too sure how to apply this in the real world. How could I adapt what I had learned to my current situation, dealing with my injury? That was the mission I carried away from the retreat. Could I quiet the pounding pressure from the familiar prompting of conventional culture and go deep inside to navigate through the path I was setting out before me?

Over the next months, I kept up a few practices from that retreat, which I thought were a good addition to my healthy lifestyle. That meant no drinking, no coffee and no meat. I found a rhythm with a meditation practice that I was comfortable with by adopting Transcendental Meditation. There is no right or wrong technique in meditation. I found my own way of incorporating meditation into my daily routine. It was just one more key to unlocking the mystery of my uncertain future by delving within.

For the following weeks my partner and I talked a lot about my experience. She had completed the same retreat a while ago so we could share a lot of deep thoughts and exchange a lot of ideas. I realized that life without triathlon would be possible and there wouldn't be too much to it. I had hit a pivotal point in my life. Slowly I started thinking of a life without being the superstar of the show. Deep inside my heart I accepted that if I couldn't come back, then it would be ok. I still wanted to at least try and heal my foot and then I would see if the fire was still in me. The trick for me was to move forward believing both realities would bring me peace.

After more than 27 years of racing and following my dream, quitting would feel as if I was losing my own identity. Who would I be without triathlon? Realizing that there is more to my life started to be a recurring thought. Sure I have other goals in life apart from racing and training all day. But would that be enough?

The Champion, Redefined

I started ticking off a list of things that were prominent in my life and that I found success with. One of the things I found out over the past ten years was that flipping a house potentially brings way more money than racing triathlon. In fact, my partner and I thrived at the task. This affirmed the fact that I didn't have to race for dough anymore. This was one option that took the monkey off my back. If I would come back from my injury and race again, it would be out of pure passion, and not just to bring home the bacon. I kept crossing off the list of my reservations to retiring from professional competition. In the end it would come down to my internal motivating factors. How hungry am I to comeback and compete?

If I would step away from triathlon, my previous life's mission, then I wouldn't lose the greatness and experience that I had accumulated over the past years. I would still be the same guy. I could still stay closely involved in the sport, even without actively racing. I could make leaps in life through what I had learned through the sport I loved for so many years. I would be able to master the challenges of life, just like I had done in racing.

In order to let go of all possible outcomes I had to imagine both possibilities. I could come back from this injury or I will retire and move on with my life. I started to accept a possible defeat deep down inside of me. What if I can't race again? When that question surfaced, I started to panic again. I talked to my partner and my coach, Michael, but nobody else. It was difficult not knowing the outcome. I knew I needed time to heal. Now if I could just wrap my head around coasting through the darkness of the unknown, I knew I'd be ok.

My life has always been filled with extremes. My emotions were swinging back and forth from recovery to retirement. The silent retreat gave me a certain peace in accepting any outcome that might play itself out. What would be the extreme opposite of a chill silent retreat? Tony Robbins: full on, full of energy, motivational speaker and master strategist.

I had planned to see Tony Robbins and thought it would be a good time for me to get a motivational kick in my ass to channel my uncertainty. I signed up for his 4-day seminar in West Palm Beach. It was crazy, but in a very positive, transformational way. He is the definition of a superhuman, no doubt about it. We jumped from our seats all day and night and yelled 'YES'! It was absolutely insane. I felt like I could conquer the world, injury or no injury.

After the four day, super intense seminar, it became crystal clear to me that the drive that I have in me doesn't need to be isolated only to triathlon. It could thrive anywhere. My self-worth is not just tied to the world of sport and my reputation. It took some real soul searching but I was making progress in figuring out what I could do to broaden my identity and be at peace with myself.

In order to achieve this clarity, I started again with figuring out what made me really happy and content in life. I listed a few things and prioritized them in order of importance. It turned out that working out and being fit was a key point for me. Go figure. But could I be content with working out when there was not a championship to motivate me?

The next item on my “happy life list” was a healthy diet. But if I'm not required to eat healthy to compete in triathlon, will that motivation still be there? I like to feel good. Eat a healthy diet and you'll feel good. I reasoned my way around that point. Next.

The last critical element that rose to the surface was my drive for achievement. I truly enjoy putting my inner drive to work. I am a driven person. I thrive off of accomplishments. As much as I like the journey of life, my inner drive needs to be fed. It makes me feel complete.

Now I had something to work with. Three pillars to support the foundation of my life and guarantee personal fulfillment. I was in a transition phase, so I started putting it to work. It was as if Tony Robbins was in the room commanding, "NOW is a good time for that!”

Pillar One: Happy fitness

How does fitness differentiate from high level training? My buddy, Sully, always wanted me to run some trails with him, but I never took him up on his offer. I was too focused on my training. I just ran in order to get faster and trail running never really fit into my training schedule. There was always the looming risk of twisting my foot. Too much risk; not enough reward.

Each training session needed to fit an exact purpose. I only run with my GPS watch on a road where I can hold my designed pace, safely and according to my training plan. Fun is no consideration when following a carefully and detailed plan from coach. That was then, this is now. I think I'll be running some trails with Sully. I just love to run on trails, regardless of any pace and time, just for the pure joy of running.

I guess our ego always wants the stuff it can’t have. We think that it's all or nothing. I trained my heart like a super V12 engine while I was in competition mode. So I may have to adapt my "happy fitness" to a normal V6 motor. Compromise. I can see myself overdoing my fitness activities, having this “full gas” mentality. I simply can’t unlearn what I taught myself over the past years, in a few weeks or months. It'll take some time. That is absolutely clear. But that is also very doable.

The shift came gradually. As I worked through finding the Dirk that could exist and thrive outside of the drive to compete, a whole world opened up for me. I found that the equation for my personal happiness was to maintain a workout routine balanced with maintaining healthy food habits. I was on target with the fitness part of the equation, so I shifted my attention toward a new relationship to a healthy lifestyle regarding my diet.

Pillar Two: Happiness Through Healthy Food

There is a cycle to the diet of a professional triathlete. Generally, during the racing cycle, we pay great attention to our diets. Good fuel input = optimum output. But this cycle wanes during the offseason. I've always noticed this swing in my commitment to healthy eating. In retrospect, this demonstrates an imbalance. It took a serious injury to make me realize that paying real attention to my diet benefits me as a whole, no matter where I am in my training cycle.

This opened up a brand new commitment to healthy eating, one that I eagerly shared with my partner. We each pursued our own avenues of commitment to quality food. I actually came to a better place with my diet than I ever had been in training. There were no more grand swings away from this new approach, only the occasional splurge that was enjoyed without guilt. There was more time to devote to choosing good food and enjoying the clean, clear feeling it gave me.

My internal drive propelled me into trying juice cleanses, colonics and liver cleanses. I researched some dietary methods that focused on alkalizing the body. You think that's a bit extreme? I recognized that this method of operating suited me at the time. The key is to find your own path to healthy food choices. There is always going to be an ever changing field of exploration into optimal body function. It's a brave new world out there. There's room for all of us.

It extends beyond the simple chemistry of it all. I found that when I searched for high quality food I wanted to share it with my community. Buying locally, I started to see my city alive and conscious of providing generous, healthy options for food choices. I found local farm resources for cage free eggs. I was proud to support this vibrant, clean and clear direction that my city was choosing as well as cities I was visiting in my travels. It makes me feel good. It makes me happy.

I want to look fit and feel fit. I found that I could do that outside of the intense training of triathlon. Using the catalyst of the Vipassana retreat and the Tony Robbins seminar, I was in the right state of mind to push forward with this second pillar of my renovated lifestyle. It's the right thing for my body and my soul. The foundation I was building made room for me to include the final pillar: my powerful, Duracell capacity — my inner drive.

Pillar Three: My Inner Drive & Motivation

If I didn't have my race goals to fuel my drive and motivation, where would I channel my unstoppable hunger to achieve and perform.

It sure isn't easy having two over achievers in one family, trying to live the semi-retired life. How could two "type A" personalities follow their own personal legends while supporting each other in a healthy relationship? This wasn't going to work. Or was it?

To my surprise, indeed it did work, at least for a while. If you follow your passion and your heart, effort is required. No one is going to just knock on your door and say, "Hey, you wanna live a healthy, fulfilled life? Here's a pill to make all of your dreams come true." Not only would that be a pointless pursuit, it just doesn't work that way. It's personal and unique to each individual. It's a mystery that we all have to work out on the path to self-fulfillment. Once we decided the effort was worth it, we made the move together.

After some consideration I recalled what brought me to where I was in terms of life achievements and accomplishments. Triathlon achievements aside, I pretty much succeeded in every real estate project that I ever started. Why? I am meticulous with details and planning. So why not use my proven skill and knowledge for some new projects? I would apply those qualities of skilled project management to a developing master plan.

The life I shared with my partner had a history of spontaneous, gut instinct, decision making, executed with a fairly calculated, analytical eye. We sat down and started planning our next adventure and potential future projects. Presto! We came up with a master plan for our current life situation. It was a plan that allowed us to live a healthy lifestyle and quench our inner drive. We asked ourselves: What if we would sell our house and travel in a van for a while where we could both write our books on the road? We would be free, and could travel and work from wherever the wind takes us. This is where I wanted to shift my drive. So with a mission and a goal, I could thrive while my foot heals.

After a bit of research the decision was made. Our house was on the market in no time and the van was bought just a couple of weeks later. Was that the right thing to do? I was still debating the decision even though it clearly made sense. That was the best and nicest house we had ever built. Giving that up in such a special location would be tough to top, but it seemed well worth it for the profit to fuel the adventure.

At times, my old self came back and I thought that I couldn't just turn my back on my career. I felt that I had more in me. I knew it. I had proven it over and over to the world. What more was there to prove? Would more victories make me happier? Would a comeback from my injury make me happier? Or was there a deep desire to continue racing regardless of all the fame, the money and the results? There were times when I still felt a bit lost, but I kept moving right along and managed to keep busy with selling all of our belongings and designing the new sprinter van.

It became clearer over time. There was no proper training possible until my foot would heal substantially. Once the foot heals then I would think about the next step. For now I live my life. After the foot heals, I will test the jogging and then I would start running. But for now I live my life. And if the easy running goes well and it is fun and I am fast and enjoying the training, then I might even race again. But for now I live my life. And if I race again, I will find out if I race for fun or full tilt and full of gas in competition. But for now, I live my life, traveling in our van across Europe and back home in the good old US. No matter where we decided to go, Van-life was the way I was choosing to propel my life forward.

The new life plan was to travel the country in our van and simply be free and enjoy life without thinking of my pro career. I would make the proper call regarding my injury in due time. I could train and recover while pursuing other passions and adventures with my partner in life, moving in the direction of an inner peace. Life doesn't need to be put on hold because of a snag in your life plan. I decided to go ahead even though I knew that this was a bit crazy and extreme. I just followed my heart, regardless of what conventional wisdom might dictate.

Sometimes life just tests us to see how brave we can be. Whether you are in the grips of training for your next race or peeling yourself away from the sport in some way. Take the time to preserve everything you learned from triathlon to set yourself on a new path. There is no separation. The transition can be seamless if you take the time to look within and trust yourself.

Pillars in Motion

Towards the end of April I was in a much better state of mind. Things with my partner were going great. The only lingering issue was the status of my injury. I flew back to Luxembourg and faced a tough decision at the doctor's office. I knew that I had an obligation to heal my foot so that I could do my job. I felt like I couldn't decide whether to keep racing unless I got to the bottom of my injury. The only way to know what caused my foot to act up was to undergo surgery, but this would put another season in jeopardy. Although this was not an ideal scenario, I had no other choice after so many months of struggling with my injury. I committed to get to the bottom of it and opted for the knife.

Just two days later, I checked into the hospital and was scheduled for surgery first thing in the morning. Once Dr. Griffen opened up my foot, she saw plenty of inflammation in the metatarsal area and went to work. They had to shorten some of the metatarsal bones, using a procedure called 'Weil Osteotomy'. They cut tendons, shortened bones and even put two permanent screws into my metatarsal heads.

After checking out the procedure on YouTube, it was clear that this would be a tough recovery. It was pretty intense watching the graphic surgery and imagining that had been done to my foot. There would be no weight bearing on my foot for weeks. I'd be on crutches, wearing another walking boot and plenty of rehab sessions on the road to recovery. I felt pretty defeated. I guess deep down I had hoped for a quicker recovery so that I could train sooner. Now, given what the Dr. had found, I wasn't sure if I would even be able to run again. I was ready for a long road of recovery.

Idle Time

While I was lying in hospital and during my time off at home, I had plenty of time to think. There were times when I got really frustrated and angry. Not the federation nor the Olympic committee had a plan in place for when an athlete is at their lowest point, maybe even facing a forced retirement due to injury. Most of the athletes are let alone to figure out the next step by themselves. There is no safety net in place for support. This had been my job. This was my profession. Nearly 30 years of life dedicated to the sport and successful at my profession and there is no support when my body breaks? There is nothing put in place to smoothly transition out of the sport when faced with the possibility of forced retirement?

That should not be the case, not in any country. I made a commitment to myself to address this to the ministry of sports. It might have been a natural reaction; my drive kicking in. If I was going to be laid up, recovering from surgery, I was going to put my time to good use. I already had several pages outlined over the past weeks. This is not just about me. I felt a kinship to all the other athletes in my position, past, present or future. It was good to feel a purpose in my life as I began my recovery.

I am not made to lay around and stare at the ceiling. I am a freaking work horse with plenty of horse power that needs to be put into action. The uncertainty of my career continued to weigh on me. I started to doubt my future as a top notch triathlete. This might be it. In one moment, I was ok with it but the next moment brought anxiety over my future as a professional athlete. What would I do instead of racing? I prefer certainty in life. Uncertainty is not really my strength, neither is patience. But with the boot on my foot I had no choice. I had to face this uncertainty head on.

Once I returned from the hospital, I stayed with my best friend Chris and his lovely family on the Mosel. We had just sold our place in Luxembourg and so could use a nice, familiar place to begin my recovery. I had postponed the European van trip, because of the logistics of life, post-surgery. Plus I needed some hands on work to be done after the initial post-surgery recovery. They took us in for the next weeks, helped us and cared for us along the way. My planned van life could wait a few more weeks. No big deal. Time was on my side this time.

It only took a few days for me to turn walking with my crutches into a workout. Just days after the surgery I figured out how to lay on the ground with my foot elevated on the couch and work out with dumbbells to improve my upper body strength. I slowly I added some core exercises. That helped quench my sport addiction and made me feel better about my injured self. Glimpses of hope were ignited once again.

To some degree I still didn't really see a way through but over time I could slowly picture a way back to my normal life. That normal life was starting to include both potential outcomes. In my head I painted pictures of a typical comeback. I embraced the moments where I saw the potential still in me. That's when my mind pushed away the facts and I was imagining being back in training mode. Then there were moments I completely let go of controlling the situation and just lived my life. It was something that developed deep inside my heart. It was a bit of a battle in my mind between two potential outcomes. One minute I was excited about the van adventure and the next minute I was writing the screenplay of my comeback victory.

I already knew that it would take months for the foot to heal fully. During that readjustment period, I reaffirmed my love of working out just for fitness sake. It took some time for this over motivated, thoroughbred athlete to adapt to the new pace when there is no lofty goal or grand mission in mind. It's simply doing exercise with the purpose of staying fit. I did it in order to have a reason to shower or to simply to satisfy my need to move around. In my off time I listened to the audio book "Born to Run". The book talks about how humans are made to run and to move and that was always in the back of my mind when I worked out. Moving around is part of who I am. I love working out, even if it is at an adjusted pace or with a different motivation, just for the sake of fitness.

The waiting and standby situation continued and I kept thinking and evaluating my handicapped situation and my future. The longer I waited, the more my mind started to drift away from triathlon in an attempt to understand what was happening to me and what was actually developing deep inside my heart. In the past I only had a few rare moments when I thought of giving up or retiring but the more I thought about it the more I accepted it as an option for me.

No matter how I turned it, I still had a difficult time imagining giving up my pro status, the glory and all the cool little things that come with the success I worked for. On the other hand, I started to be unsure if I really wanted to put in the 5-8 hours of hard training each day to come back to competition shape. The more I had to put my training on hold, the further I drifted away from the sport and the more comfortable I became not punishing myself day in and day out. I was back to square one. The final answer seemed unreachable for me.

Despite missing my training, I also started to adapt to life with my priorities rearranged. Although I was forced to experience it at first, over time I got more and more used to the fact that my foot might not recover fast enough in order to continue with my career. Did the universe give me a sign to give up and move on or was this just a test to figure out how passionate I am to continue and fight for medals again? I was clear on what I had to apply in my life in order not to drift off again to a negative space. But even if I would come back and race again, at the age of 39 I didn't have many years left to compete at a high level. Then I would be facing the same crossroad once again. So would it really make a difference? It would just postpone dealing with the same issue just a few years later. So I had to go through it now with all the uncertainties in tow.

After endless hours of thinking about it, I wasn't sure how I could even figure out the difference anymore. How could I get a clear answer to this question. I was confused. The drive to find out was so strong that I couldn't stop thinking about it. As an athlete, I make things work and if not I can still somehow find a solution. I am made for the extreme. You name the task and I will manage and exceed it, just like I always did. So I came back to my daily meditation. Even if the issue keeps coming up daily I take time to sit and reflect. Dramatic comeback or retirement? I was back and forth all the time.

> *"Finally, I am coming to the conclusion that my highest ambition is to be what I already am."*
>
> *~Thomas Merton*

Sometimes my path seemed clear as if somebody had written the play for me. Deep inside I knew that I just had to let go and follow my heart. Just follow the flow of life. Just be Dirk. I didn't have to the be that successful action figure in sport. I could just be me. Even though it sounded so simple I had to wrestle with it daily.

At times, it felt like having two voices in my ear, one on each side. One constantly said, "Stay where you are and make it work. The foot will heal and then you are back at it and you will come out of this even stronger". Then the other voice countered and said, "Just be brave and move on with your life. There is so much more out there for you in this beautiful world. Follow your heart. You had a great career. This might be a sign to move on with your life. Take the advice and move on. Lock in your decision and rededicate your life to your new priorities."

Well, I didn't even know what it means to follow my heart. Does that mean continuing with triathlon or quitting? Was racing a habit or a passionate job I had chosen? My partner tried to help me figure it all out and at some point asked me what I really loved in life? Is it the sport, the training, the racing or is it the stuff that comes with it? I couldn't even properly answer that question. At the same time she was in the middle of her own journey. A restless quest to heal her body and mind in order to overcome the disappointment of her infertility and her own struggle to find her place in the world. We both had unanswered questions and tried to understand the life lessons that had been given to us.

According to the Myers Briggs test, I knew that I am ESTJ personality type and that is how I analyze things. I am a "type A" personality. I always know what to do and I helped plenty of people along the way. Only this time I seemed to be stuck in the mud, big time. I was still living halfway in denial. Somehow I already knew deep down in my heart that it was time to move on. I just had to figure out how to set aside my ego and move forward. The answers will come.

Weeks after the surgery I got the triathlon comeback itch so I cross trained for several months to keep my body on standby. This proved to be very frustrating. Instead of running I always hopped on the elliptical machine to mimic the running movement. It sure works well but this restricted training is very annoying. I dragged myself through a few sessions just to keep my options open and to simply stay fit. I didn't have a clear goal in mind. I found a way to train purely for my health and well-being.

It had been such a long time since I'd been in competition, the road back seemed so far away. Even the strongest mind would break sooner or later. Imagine you could swim and ride but you simply could never run? Training without running started to make me feel off balance, like I'd lost one of my triathlon senses. Imagine your form is great but you know it will take at least half a year till you could properly run again. Nothing but frustration occupied my mind. I was strong mentally, so the cross training worked for quite a while. But at some point, you've got to ask yourself the recurring question. WHY am I doing this again and does this really make sense?

I am either a full-on guy or nothing at all. Like most athletes, I struggle with moderation, not just in sport but in my daily life. I am not happy with just a few red hot chilly flakes on my plate, I need A LOT. It's not enough to burn just a little, it needs to burn like a mother! On a long haul driving trip I power through at all costs. Why? Because I think I can do it. It's that addiction to the feeling of accomplishment. It's as simple as that. Everything needs to be completed 100 % or the mission has failed. It may be a bit of the soldier in me talking. For me it is simple and always has been that way. All or nothing. Full gas or go home.

I didn't really want to let my frustration take over my social media platforms, as I had an obligation with my sponsors both present and future. So I reduced my sport tweets and shared more out of my private life. Surprisingly the interest in my persona was still the same as before. That was somewhat satisfying and so I thought I could buy myself some more time to figure out if my foot was going to cooperate with me at some point. Most of my loyal, long term partners backed me for the coming year and committed to continue their support, although I was not lucky enough to find a main sponsor. I could live with that.

The struggle of letting go was a constant in my life. Picture a pro athlete who raced most of his life, defining himself as an uber athlete for many years on an international stage. How do you make the decision to pull out like this? No last hurrah. Just put out to pasture because of an injury. An anticlimactic end to the career I'd worked so hard to build.

There is an internal motivation and an external motivation to competing as a professional athlete. I would have to address both to accept my potential career ending injury. First was my inner ego, struggling to deal with giving up my superhuman status. Secondarily was the gear swag from sponsors. Every year I got a crap load of stuff, enough to share with family and friends. All that cool, free stuff and top of the line gear which filled my garages was a bonus to the satisfaction I got from competing well.

Looking back to the Vipassana retreat and the Tony Robbins seminar, I leaned on my alone time to continue to gain some clarity on what makes me truly happy in life. This really helped me to deal with my situation. I used to postpone life when I was in the heat of competition. I never had time to think. Then I was injured. That break sort of forced me into self-reflection mode. By challenging my comfort zone with the silent retreat, I was able to hit the reset button. The silence allowed me to go inside where I could allow these thoughts to come and go. As I started to regain my balance I was able to capitalize on the techniques from the Tony Robbins seminar which gave me clarity in terms of my goals outside of triathlon. This seemed like movement in the right direction.

Fact is, we all struggle at times, climbing the mountain of triathlon. Sooner or later we all get to that point where we will hit a crossroad. When you get there, take some time to reflect in order to properly deal with just yourself. Solitude will help to bring clarity. Don't wait until you are injured to take the time. On your off day take time to just reflect on where you are, not where you are going and not where you have been.

When fear or uncertainty creep in, let them come and go as

effortlessly as a cool breeze. Facing your fears during times of transition is often helpful as a catalyst for a call to action. It just helps you to experience life on a deeper level. Settle within. Let all of the details fall away. It will give you inner strength when you get back to the mission of triathlon. This is precisely what I was constantly tapping into on my road to recovery.

On the Road Again

It was time to start the European van voyage. Even though the progress with my foot was constantly in flux, I was eager to put that plan into action. A few minor builds for the van and we were off in no time. I was so excited that I forgot about all those problems and just enjoyed the days the way they came. Having no plan and no agenda was my plan. Pure excitement in my eyes, I put the van in gear and another journey was in front of me.

I knew I could easily finance the newly adapted travel plans for the next few years and during that time I would have all the time in the world to figure out what the next step in life could be. The foot might heal and then I would know more. There were so many options that I thought it would become clearer once I had time to think and was not occupied by the day to day in my life. Competing or not competing, I could pivot easily, as I always had, from a home on wheels. Said and done. No distractions paved the way for the road in front of me.

After traveling the world for the past twenty plus years, I thought living in a van would be the best way to be free and see the world while healing body and soul. We could go wherever we wanted and we would always have everything we needed. It seemed to be the perfect formula to find my footing. Since we were saving on monthly rent, we could always rent a place short term if we felt the urge to have a roof over our heads. We simply did what we really wanted to do, regardless of any other constraints in life. Various swimming pools around Europe gave me a place to shower and day spas were the perfect hideout on crappy days. Could life get any better?

I was picking up hints from inspirational teachers and writers like breadcrumbs along the way. After reading 'The Alchemist' again, it became so obvious to me that all you have to do in life is follow your personal legend. Resting your personal legend exclusively on the shoulders of triathlon victories would seem to leave a life lived with just one note to be sung. Simply listening to your heart and following that path of joy reveals to the champion that the journey is the destination. At some point I could see this injury as an opportunity to channel my drive in other arenas of my life.

I was so psyched about the van excursion that a concrete plan was made to adapt the lifestyle when returning back to the US; same concept, different locale. For the US, everything has to bigger and better so we chose a slightly bigger van and started with our build up plan for the conversion. Hudson, a good friend who also built our house in St. Augustine, was the right man for the job. He is a master at paying attention to every little detail and is very resourceful. We ordered a carload of parts and left him with a long list of plans to figure out while we were on the road, touring Europe.

It was the perfect plan. Everything else would unfold along the way. I truly believed that even though it was against my typical high octane approach to problem solving, this approach would suit my recovery. I really started to love my new life. I was keeping fit, caring for my foot and I was happy, seeing the world through the windows of the van.

At the same time, my foot slowly improved and I was able to do a few easy runs. I really enjoyed being able to bike and run again. All of my triathlete senses were coming back online. Sometimes I joined my partner's daily yoga session. Although yoga didn't really fuel my full tilt operating mechanism, I was truly finding a balance that found the value in these more subtle moments. I really didn't miss the sport as my profession and through time I started feeling content with the mild fitness workouts and simply living the way we decided to live. The typical flashback and minor regrets are common and I let them come and then let them go. It is all part of it. We cannot script the end of this part of my life. I have to live for today. The foot will take care of itself. I support the healing by living in this present moment, without agendas. This feels right. I'm finding the pace of my life as each day comes.

This is how I discovered what I truly wanted deep inside and the process to find out what really brings me forward in life in terms of happiness and personal satisfaction. For me the van life was a boost. It sure took some time, but the journey to experience it was worth the ride. I felt high on life in natural way. The key was to be flexible and to keep trying out new things with this new perspective on my life.

These opportunities were literally forced on me due to my injury. Or was this part of some master plan that was unfolding and all I had to do was to let go and embrace all of it? It is not easy to consider saying goodbye to a lifelong career, especially when it's forced on you due to a sidelining injury. A little distance from competition made these leaps easier to navigate.

Sometimes it could just take that one single race that could make a triathlete decide to quit the sport. You could be one of those bucket list guys who just wanted to finish one Ironman®

distance race in order to earn your lifelong bragging rights. Once the mission is accomplished, a deep feeling of pride and sense of accomplishment follows and then you move on with your life.

For the majority, though, triathlon training and racing becomes a lifestyle that could last for a long time. It will become a part of your identity and give you a feeling of belonging. This kinship develops, whether you race just once or race hardcore, as a professional for many years. No matter which group you belong to, remember to revisit your internal and external motivations for continuing your training and racing. A full life requires vigilance at every turn. Keep your mind and your options open.

Whatever you do to extreme, over an extended period of time, will someday get old and the passion will fade. As triathletes, we all are running from session to session, clocking in the workouts between work and family life and making lots of sacrifices along the way to reach our goal. Some might feel that there is not time for anything else in life and then at some point your mission starts falling apart.

I know from some of my training buddies that once you get to that point, usually it goes quickly and people often turn away from the sport completely, even changing their lifestyle. Sometimes people get totally fed up for an underlying reason. These are the pivotal moments that we must take the time and space to work through. This is the time to reflect. Lean on your team, your family, your coach. The answers will come.

Nobody really prepares you for your life after sport. There is simply no singular plan for the post competition lifestyle out there. When working through these possible low frequency phases, our life's mission usually becomes clearer. You finally have time to answer all those questions instead of running from one appointment to the next.

Pretty much everyone who has moved on from triathlon has stayed true to the culture of their beloved sport. The drive gets funneled into something new, even if it takes years to figure this out. The healthy eating, the body aware culture and the look never lets you escape after years of being in the triathlon community. Those countless hours of bike riding and connecting with nature won't simply be gone. The drive to compete and to strive for excellence could very well be channeled into other areas of your life.

In my case, after more than 27 years of racing, I also have this huge inner drive that needs to find satisfaction in something else; something bigger than me. For me to decide to sell everything and downsize to a van was a long time coming. This might not be your ideal scenario but if you look at it with an open mind and listen to that voice deep inside, you might find what works for you. I took my own drastic measures in order to stimulate my mind. In the words of Tony Robbins I executed a "massive action plan". I had to, I was clearly on the edge. There are plenty of ways to find out what works for you. The only requirements are effort and an open mind. This is the journey everyone must experience.

Seeing the World Through a New Set of Eyes

I was reading an article from The Guardian referencing a book, "The Top Five Regrets of the Dying" written by Bronnie Ware, a palliative care nurse. It seems that she discovered what people regret the most in life, lying on their deathbed, is that they wished they had the courage to live a life true to themselves, not the life that others expected of them. They wished they wouldn't have worked so hard and had stayed in touch with friends, and having it to do all over again, would live a life full of feeling and meaning. This revelation crossed all boundaries of age, heritage, geographical location and status in life.

Here is some deep wisdom for all of us. In the depths of the intensity of training and racing in triathlon one must stop to realize that there are equally profound moments that don't measure great feats. They rely on quiet moments of reflection where we are granted the time and space to witness the wonder of the grand cosmic pause. We disappear in these moments almost as a context to the brash and bold gauntlet we run in competition of Triathlon.

> *"In every life there are events that reshape one's sense of existence. Afterward, all is different and the past is dimmed."*
>
> *~Annie Proulx, Barkskins*

Don't live in fear and later have all those regrets about your life. Now is the time to make the first step. You must have had fear starting your first race in triathlon but you still did it. You must have had doubts but you knew it was the right decision. It is always the battle between the rational mind and the emotional mind. Your rational mind tells you that this is what I want but then the emotional mind creeps in with fear and doubt. The emotional mind coaxes us do something closer to our comfort zone.

I want to motivate you to think and evaluate your life outside the box. Ignore the constraints of modern society. Don't just try to fit in. Live your own version of life. Think outside the box even if it seems hard at first. Remind yourself of what you have learned through the sport during the endless hours of training. Just as you planned your season and your training, you can also plan your family life, career or business. Don't change it from one day to the next, pace yourself just like you learned during your triathlon racing. It is the same system, applied in real life.

Nobody will come knocking on your door to deliver all of the goals and aspirations you dream of in your life. You need to work for it. Life is always going to give us challenges. It's really in the first step, moving toward transformation, that the fear is overcome. Action is required and it always starts with the first step, no matter how big or small that step might be. Acting is the key. Don't start measuring it yet. That will automatically happen over time.

You will pass milestones on the way to the big goal. There will be ups and down included, and the road ahead might be bumpy (it usually is, sorry). Preparing for that and accepting this fact will make it all much easier.

Through your triathlon training you have learned discipline and perseverance. Use this very valuable tool as you move in the direction of your life's purpose. You didn't stop in the middle of your workout, did you? Having a clear defined goal in mind taught you to follow your dream and never to give up. Some triathletes say: Death before DNF (Did Not Finish [the race]) that may sound a bit extreme but it shows the dedication of the breed of super athletes that we belong to. We want to achieve it and so we will work for it

Above all, we set out to achieve something crazy and superhuman. Finishing and succeeding at such a grueling event should give you the necessary confidence to tackle every area of your life that you can imagine now. We taught ourselves how to become a champion and this is where we allow that to follow us into every aspect of our lives. The journey never ends. The thread is never broken.

As I sit here watching the sunset on the horizon of a warm, sultry St Augustine evening, I have such a feeling of gratitude. I'm so glad I took the time to follow my heart, to be free, with no constraints, like this simple sunset of my chosen city of St Augustine.

The uncertainty of what tomorrow will bring is a gift.

Life is perfect just the way it is.

All of my thoughts are where they should be.

Everything in its right place.

Life doesn’t begin with Triathlon and it doesn’t end with Triathlon. What you learn having trained and competed in Triathlon will flow into the rest of your life. There is no curtain pulled after you stop the big race. The scenery is different. **The champion remains.**